BURNOUT ACROSS THIRTEEN CULTURES

BURNOUT ACROSS THIRTEEN CULTURES

Stress and Coping in Child and Youth Care Workers

Victor Savicki

Westport, Connecticut
London

Library of Congress Cataloging-in-Publication Data

Savicki, Victor.
    Burnout across thirteen cultures : stress and coping in child and youth care workers /
Victor Savicki.
        p.   cm.
    Includes bibliographical references and index.
    ISBN 0–275–97453–7 (alk. paper)
    1. Social work with children—Cross-cultural studies.   2. Social work with
youth—Cross-cultural studies.   3. Burn out (Psychology)—Cross-cultural studies.
4. Youth workers—Job stress—Cross-cultural studies.   5. Social workers—Job stress—
Cross-cultural studies.   6. Human services personnel—Job stress—Cross-cultural studies.
I. Title: Burn out across thirteen cultures.   II. Title.
HV713.S32   2002
362.7—dc21   2001036707

British Library Cataloguing in Publication Data is available.

Library of Congress Catalog Card Number: 2001036707
ISBN: 0–275–97453–7

First published in 2002

Praeger Publishers, 88 Post Road West, Westport, CT 06881
An imprint of Greenwood Publishing Group, Inc.
www.praeger.com

Printed in the United States of America

The paper used in this book complies with the
Permanent Paper Standard issued by the National
Information Standards Organization (Z39.48–1984).

10 9 8 7 6 5 4 3 2 1

Copyright Acknowledgments

The author and publisher gratefully acknowledge permission for use of the following material:

Savicki, V. (2001, April). A configural analysis of burnout in child and youth care workers in thirteen countries. *Journal of Child and Youth Care Work, 15*, 185–206. ©2001. Reprinted by permission.

Savicki, V. (2000). Comparison of culture and burnout in English and Scottish child and youth
care workers. *Children International, 8* [On-line]. Available at: <http://www.childrenuk.co.uk/
chaug/aug2000/vsavicki.htm>.

Savicki, V. (1999). Stress, Burnout und Bewältigungsstrategien in der Jugendhilfe-Ein interkultureller Vergleich [Stress, burnout and coping strategies in youth work: An intercultural compari-
son]. *Forum Erziehungshilfen, 5*, 232–238.

To Kathy,
my fellow traveler

Contents

Figures and Tables

FIGURES

TABLES

Preface

This book has evolved over several years. In the beginning, a cross-cultural study of burnout in child and youth care workers took form as a simple two-country comparison between the United States and Germany. As part of a teaching exchange to Universität Kassel in Kassel, Germany in 1996, I proposed such a study to take advantage of the opportunity of living in a different culture. I had been writing and researching burnout for twenty-five years, so a simplistic, clean, two-country comparison seemed like an uncomplicated approach to advance my interests. This state of affairs, however, rapidly changed.

In a serendipitous circumstance, a past exchange student from the former East Germany, Astrid Illner, suddenly needed a research project to finish her degree program at Friedrich von Schiller Universität in Jena, Germany. She distributed my questionnaire in the former East Germany while I arranged for data collection in the former West Germany. Now it was a three-culture comparison.

Both the Association of Child and Youth Care Practice in North America (ACYCP), through its research committee headed by Peter Gabor and Varda Mann-Feder, and the International Federation of Child Educative Communities (FICE), through the persuasion of Carol Kelly, agreed to support my research project. Immediately Poland and the Slovak Republic from FICE agreed to participate; as did Canada-French and Canada-English from ACYCP.

Then, at the FICE Congress in Copenhagen in 1996, Denmark, Scotland, and England came aboard. At subsequent ACYCP and FICE conferences, Israel and Australia agreed to participate. Finally, Austria joined the research while I was on a teaching exchange to Vienna in the fall of 1998.

At that point, I decided that the information gathered was too large for a journal article. It deserved a book. However, I perceive this book as only a brief pause in the data collection. Other cultures have already expressed interest in participating, and are expected to be included in the next edition. Let me know if you are interested.

RELATIVE EMPHASIS OF THE BOOK

People have asked me, "Is this a book about cross-cultural burnout with child and youth care workers as the sample? Or is this a book about child and care work with cross-cultural burnout as an interesting feature?" The answer is the former. I believe that in this research, child and youth care work, as a field of practice in its own right, serves as a surrogate for all human service professions. As I explain in Chapter 1, child and youth care work has substantial overlap with the fields of psychiatry, psychology, social work, nursing, education, and occupational therapy. Many of the same issues arise in all of the fields. There are unique aspects to child and youth care work, which I will take some pains to describe. However, I believe that the processes of burnout and cultural influence are active in much the same way for helping professions generally, and that child and youth care work provides a representative instance of a helping profession for the purposes of exploring these processes. I hope that this book will be useful to practitioners in any of the helping professions.

PLAN OF THE BOOK

The book is separated into five parts. Each part builds on and is related to all other parts, but the parts and the chapters within them can be understood separately.

Part I: Basic Concepts covers the conceptual bases for the field of child and youth care work, burnout, and culture. The overall objective of the book is to weave these three themes together, as the title suggests. Basic background on theory and research for each of these topics will aid the reader in understanding subsequent sections.

Part II: Process, Practice and Culture Comparisons sets forth the structure of the research and some of the descriptive results with regard to cultural variability and characteristics of the research sample. This section will help the reader understand the processes behind the description of later findings, and it will sketch the range of differences between the thirteen cultures in the study. Both broad cultural dimensions and descriptions of demographic characteristics and working conditions will be examined.

Part III: Culture and the Determinants of Burnout is the heart of the research. This part includes a pan-cultural analysis of aspects of burnout and also a configural analysis that attempts to consolidate findings about burnout. Both the pan-cultural and configural analyses will relate aspects of burnout to the work environment, working conditions, demographic characteristics, and personal styles of coping with stress. Some effort will be made to draw conclusions about burnout that spans cultural differences.

Part IV: Cross-Cultural Comparisons is a series of comparisons between cultures. It follows a more classic cross-cultural research format. The span of participating cultures allows for interesting comparisons—both similarities and differences. For example, several one-country, two-culture comparisons are described (e.g., Germany-East and Germany-West). Former East Bloc and West Bloc European cultures are compared. And even cultures that intuitively seem to have a similar historical base and language base will be contrasted (e.g., English-speaking cultures such as Canada-English, England, Scotland, United States, and Australia). Finer cultural distinctions can be drawn from this level of analysis.

Finally, Part V: Themes and Recommendations draws together the findings from previous sections to identify themes relating to burnout, and makes specific recommendations for burnout prevention, treatment, and recovery. This section attempts to pull together findings in the three conceptual areas of child and youth care, burnout, and culture which were described in Part I.

ACKNOWLEDGMENTS

No project of this size can be accomplished by one individual. I would like to express my gratitude to many people who helped in the research. First and foremost, I wish to thank all those child and youth care practitioners who took time away from their jobs and many times devoted their free time to answer my research questionnaire. Without them there would be no study.

Special thanks goes to people in the specific cultures who toiled to make sure the questionnaire was culturally and linguistically appropriate for their culture. They distributed the questionnaires, ensured they were completed, and sent the completed answer sheets on to me. Their efforts have come to fruition. They are listed here alphabetically by culture.

Australia: Vaughan Bowie, Margot Gook, Michael Kennedy

Austria: Eva Reznicek, Sascha Bartel, Frauke Binder

Canada-French and Canada-English. Varda Mann-Feder

Denmark: Margot Liberkind, Frank Mulhern, Solveig Jakobsen, Søren Hegstrup

England: Margaret Ward, Stephen Lloyd

Germany-East: Astrid Illner

Germany-West: Dieter Goeschel, Wolfgang Trede

Israel: Immanuel Grupper

Poland: Jolanta Marszychka-Suchecka, Jaroslaw Utrat-Milecki

Scotland: Margaret Lindsay, Graham Bell, Frank Mulhern

Slovak Republic: Jana Svetlikova

United States: Bill Wellard, Christopher White

Finally, thanks to colleagues and other special people who helped make the final product better: Merle Kelley and Maxine Warnath for encouragement and careful reading and comment and Traci Grugett for formatting and proofing.

BASIC CONCEPTS

One goal of this book is to integrate three conceptual areas: child and youth care work, burnout, and culture. Prior to integration, however, comes the requirement to understand the concepts separately. Each of the concepts has a substantial corpus of literature. Part I will review the existing literature in each of the three areas. The reviews presented are not exhaustive. Rather they highlight ideas, research, and theory that will reappear later as an attempt is made to understand the results and to place them in context.

In Chapter 1, "Child and Youth Care Work: Past, Present, and Future," this unique field of human service practice is both related to other human service professions and separated from them. Child and youth care work shares many assumptions and techniques with other human service professions, yet it has evolved into a distinct practice field by virtue of its historical location of practice (day and residential facilities) and its clientele (children and adolescents who are troubled or troubling). Several topics are reviewed: work activities, work settings, contemporary and future trends, and the struggle for professionalization.

In Chapter 2, "Burnout: Its Impact and Precursors," the research and theory regarding burnout is reviewed. Burnout has received much attention since its appearance in the literature in 1974. Substantial agreement exists concerning the impact of burnout on human service workers on both physical and psychological levels. There has also emerged modest agreement concerning the precursors to burnout. However, much of the burnout research has taken place in the United States and Canada. Little cross-cultural perspective exists in this literature. Also, several theoretical approaches have been advanced to account for burnout. The focus of this chapter rests on an integration of literature on chronic stress, cognitive-mediational stress theory, worker development, situational stressors, and organizational impact. This literature and theory will be reviewed with the goal of setting the stage for evaluating the results of this research study in later chapters.

Finally, Chapter 3, "Culture as a Lens to Examine Burnout," defines culture as the term is used in this study and examines critical dimensions of culture that have been identified. The current research uses the dimensions of culture identified by Geert Hofstede (1980) to explain important features of culture. The general thesis of the book is that culture affects the relationships between burnout and its precursors. In order to test this thesis, quantitative measures of cultural dimensions need to be ascertained. Also, the impact of culture can be felt at both the environmental and personal level. The distinctions and relationships of culture as context and culture as cognition will be elaborated. Methodological groundwork will be prepared for subsequent data analyses using both pan-cultural and cross-cultural approaches. The chapter cleans the lens of culture in preparation for examination of burnout.

The overall goal of Part I is to present basic background on theory and research for child and youth care work, burnout, and culture in order to aid the reader in understanding subsequent sections of the book.

CHAPTER 1

Child and Youth Care Work: Past, Present, and Future

Child and youth care work has a long and valuable history in all of the cultures represented in this study. This chapter will discuss its history, primary practice modalities, venues of practice, and several other important issues relevant to its development as a distinct field of human service. However, prior to describing its unique characteristics, I would like to elaborate the relatedness of the field of child and youth care work to other human service professions. Although this book will focus on the child and youth care field, the book's message is addressed to all human service professions.

CHILD AND YOUTH CARE WORK AS A
REPRESENTATIVE HUMAN SERVICE FIELD

Child and youth care work maintains historical linkages with many human service disciplines. For example, connections with social work occur through child welfare practice and with psychology through child development and treatment approaches. Connections are evident with education both through special education and through the use of teaching and instruction practices. Commonalties exist with psychiatry through attention to severe mental, emotional, and behavioral disorders. Also, similarities exist with nursing through an emphasis on daily care and physical nurture; with day care through the practice of organizing safe and caring structures; and with occupational and recreational therapy through an emphasis on play and the medium of action as well as verbal interchange (Barnes & Bourdon, 1990; Savicki & Brown, 1981). All these professions share an aspect of human service practice that makes their practitioners vulnerable to burnout; that is, effective practice requires emotional contact between the professional and their client–patient–

✓ student. The emotional availability of practitioners opens them to potential harm or injury at the affective level of human functioning. Burnout is a measure of how much difficulty a practitioner experiences at the emotional level as a result of their work. Much of what we know about burnout today derives from an accumulation of research findings covering many different subcategories of the helping professions. The focus of the current study on child and youth care work as a helping profession attempts to contribute further knowledge to this accumulation.

HISTORICAL ROOTS OF CHILD AND YOUTH CARE WORK

Child and youth care work is as old as the human race, yet it has only separated itself from related professions more distinctly in recent decades. For the most part, child and youth care workers take care of children and adolescents who for one reason or another cannot live with their families. In the past, children who had been orphaned, abandoned, or otherwise disconnected from their families were often taken in either by extended family or by extended community. Charitable and religious groups often accepted those children who could not be otherwise placed. However, with the dawn of the Industrial Revolution and the social and geographical displacements spawned by the move away from rural, agrarian economies, publicly funded and operated facilities grew to fill the need for care of children left without family. In addition they accepted children and youth who had special needs, for example, mental retardation, physical disabilities, or emotional disturbance. Within these institutions professional child and youth care workers were conceived and nurtured. These people cared for children and youth who were not related to them by blood, extended family, or community. In the 1800s and early 1900s, much of this care took place in large facilities, often protected from or distant from large towns or cities. Some of these institutions acted as warehouses for children and youth who could not be accepted or cared for elsewhere. They often followed an "out-of-sight, out-of-mind" philosophy. The quality of care was quite uneven, ranging from Oliver Twist-like, austere, and punitive facilities to those with a reputation for high quality care such as Boys Town in the United States. Workers in such facilities were often hired without attention to skills or commitment; any warm body would do. Often the assumption was that anyone could instinctually assume the parent role without difficulty. The child and youth care field still struggles with this assumption.

A different approach to child and youth care work began to develop in post–World War II North America and Europe. In Europe the sheer number of orphans and children and youth traumatized by the war demanded a concerted effort to respond to their needs. In North America, key individuals shaped the field with new ideas and advocacy. Fritz Redl (Redl & Wineman, 1951), Bruno Bettelheim (1967), Al Treischman (Trieschman, Whittaker, & Brendtro, 1969), Henry Maier (1969), Harry Vorrath (Vorrath & Brendtro, 1974), and others provided models and theoretical support for the notion that child and youth care work is a distinct field. This field began to specify requirements not only for workers with compassionate and nurturing personality characteristics but also for personnel demonstrating explicit sets of knowledge and skills. A person who was "big hearted" and humane was not necessarily sufficiently qualified. In Europe the social educator model gained prominence. Workers following this model include Educateurs in France and Sozial Pädegogen in Germany, Switzerland, and the Nordic countries. This model focused the treatment of troubled children on the goal of reentry into regular society. Many European countries now have college programs and degrees in child and youth care work. This type of degree enjoys a status similar to that of education and social work. Unfortunately, there is dramatic variation between countries in the levels of education available, the status of child and youth care workers, the laws governing child and youth care, the salary and benefits available, and the requirements for employment. This variation is, to some degree, at the core of the movement to professionalize child and youth care work.

WORK ACTIVITIES

A major feature of child and youth care work is the emphasis on treatment within the daily living milieu of the child. Most frequently this milieu is contained within the walls of either residential or day treatment facilities. Access to moment-to-moment opportunities for social education and treatment marks the life of the child and youth care worker. In the course of daily events, there occur "teaching moments" in which the psychologically relevant concerns of the child are not recalled from a distant past, nor imagined at a deep psychic level, but rather are actually erupting in the present. Issues are enacted in the present; treatment occurs in the present. Issues are hot and malleable, not repressed or deeply covered. Child and youth care workers become behaviorally and emotionally involved with the child during these moments. They provide a protected environment in which such issues can emerge and be addressed. Beyond providing a caring, nurturing, and safe living environment, child and youth care workers also may engage in group work and individual treatment. Their contact with clients typically follows a continuous contact format rather than the serial contact format dominant in the "50-minute hour" treatment structure. That is, child and youth care workers spend their work days with the same small group of children and youth all day rather than seeing different clients sequentially throughout the day and week for short, prescribed time periods (Savicki, 1993). The continuous contact model typically calls for teamwork. Several child and youth care workers are responsible for their charges throughout the day across a wide array of activities. The workers need to coordinate among themselves to assure that various assignments are accomplished. They also must adapt to the unique needs and crises of the children as they arise. Child and youth care workers may also be part of a multidisciplinary team with other professionals to assess, diagnose, educate, treat, and care for their clients. The intense focus on child development and the care and treatment of children and adolescents differentiates the child and youth care worker from other professionals who may serve on multidisciplinary teams. The role of child and youth care workers continues to evolve (Vander Ven, 1990).

WORK SETTINGS

Child and youth care workers perform their duties in a variety of work settings. Arieli, Beker, and Kashti (1990) categorize residential care settings as incidental, remedial, and socializing. Incidental settings are those in which the goal is physical care with no structured efforts to change the children or youth residing in them, such as orphanages. Remedial settings assume that residents suffer from "a specific weakness, deficiency, or deviance" (Arieli, Beker, & Kashti, 1990, p. 47). Residents are separated from the outside environment and exposed to curative or adaptive experiences and treatment to overcome the specific "deficiencies" that have been identified. Often the medical model forms the foundation for such treatment. Socializing settings employ educational or developmental models seeking to use the interactions of the residents as a laboratory for corrective behavioral and emotional experiences, such as the Israeli kibbutz.

In a more simplistic way, child and youth care work facilities may be characterized by the time in which residents stay in them and the access allowed to outside influences. Residential facilities provide overnight accommodations. Residents live permanently in seven-day residential sites, whereas in five-day residential sites, they go home on weekends. Some of these homes are large, distant institutions while others are small group homes within the community of a town or city. In day treatment facilities, the children or youth attend during the day, much as they would a regular school, and return to their homes in the evening. Finally, child and youth care workers have also become more prevalent in outpatient facilities in which the children and youth attend individual or group meetings at specific times during the week while maintaining a regular home and school or work presence in the community. An acceptance of the expertise of child and youth care workers has led to a broader range of job venues (Savicki, 1990).

CONTEMPORARY AND FUTURE TRENDS

An analysis of child and youth care work's goals, tasks, and work environments indicates that the role of the worker can be characterized as complex, segmented, and dynamic (Duncan, 1979; Savicki, 1990). That is, the goals and tasks of service and the environment in which they are accomplished are multifaceted, able to be divided into meaningful subunits, and changeable. For example, a child and youth care worker deals with multiple facets of the child (e.g., physical, psychological, nutritional) over several possible segments of expertise (e.g., caregiver, therapist, teacher) or location (e.g., residential facility, family, school, community), while dealing with ever-changing or dynamic situations (e.g., the child grows, the living situation changes, treatment priorities shift). If this analysis is accurate, then Duncan (1979) suggests that specific organizational structures will yield optimum results with regard to quality of service. He proposed that a match between job characteristics and the organizational structure that would best support them would expedite productivity. Following his conceptualization in the field of child and youth work, organizational structures would need to provide for flat hierarchy, decentralized service delivery, an emphasis on teamwork, and a high value placed on communication (Savicki, 1990). Many of the current and future trends in child and youth care reflect these structural suggestions.

Job descriptions and positions for child and youth care workers have expanded dramatically beyond the basic requirements of physical care that characterized these positions in the first half of the 1900s. Specialization of service has become common. Child and youth care workers now may focus on drug and alcohol treatment, play therapy techniques, group therapy, family therapy, school consultation, community transition, vocational training, street work, gang task forces, and many other specialized areas. More difficult and complicated clients have demanded more sophisticated and specialized service. Likewise, positions in management are more often filled with child and youth care workers. Clinical supervisors and various levels of administrators benefit from actual experience with children and youth (Denholm, 1990; Vander Ven, 1981). Embedded in the increase of specialized roles is the demand for teamwork and communication.

There is some debate about how specialization should take place. Some promote the notion that child and youth care work is characterized by general knowledge and skills across a wide range of areas, thus meeting the need for specialization within a single practitioner (Shealy, 1996). Others see generalist practitioners as limited and not necessarily accruing status equal to other specialists (Savicki, 1990). Some view the possibility of independent practice for child and youth care workers (Vander Ven, 1990), while others promote the concept of a generalist team (Krueger & Drees, 1995). Nevertheless, in many cultures, child and youth care has shown a shift away from the medical model to more developmental models based on education and socialization (Barnes & Bourdon, 1990; Brendtro & Ness, 1983).

PROFESSIONALIZATION

A major concern of the field of child and youth care work in many cultures focuses on the desire for child and youth care work to be viewed as a profession (Kelly, 1990; Lindsay, 2000; Powell, 1990). Although child and youth care workers in some countries enjoy a status akin to professions such as psychology, social work, or education, in other countries the child and youth care worker is viewed as a semiskilled, entry level worker performing duties that require no special training, under the direction of true professionals who assume all of the responsibilities and claim all of the credit. Child and youth care workers have labored heroically to define themselves as distinct from other human service professions. They seek recognition for their efforts. In cultures where service to children and youth is valued, such status has been awarded. In other cultures, including the United States, values of service and actual support of children and youth are lacking. Other professions have gained dominance and see no reason to acknowledge child and youth care work as separate from aspects of their own domains of practice. Separate training and education are only rarely available. Laws and regulations do not usually require education and training as a prerequisite for employment. It is interesting to note the wide gaps between countries with regard to the "professionalization" of child and youth work.

TURNOVER

Finally, in many countries the rate of turnover of child and youth care workers poses a major impediment to high quality of service. Child and youth care work, as an entry level position, is often populated by young, idealistic workers who want to try their hand at helping children and youth. With little or no training, low salaries, and insufficient supervision and support, these workers are soon overwhelmed by the intensity of the work. They find it difficult to separate themselves from the pain, anger, and anxiety of their charges. They expect to make major improvements in the lives of their clients, but find themselves frustrated not only by the severity of the disturbance they are exposed to, but also by their lack of skill and knowledge in fashioning a positive outcome. Commonly, child and youth care workers stay only two to five years in the field and then move either to a new position or a new field entirely (Krueger et. al., 1987; Vander Ven, 1990). Burnout is a major factor in the revolving door phenomenon of worker turnover. Agencies are always recruiting and training new workers. They regularly lose workers who are just beginning to provide high quality service. The research in this book is aimed at to slowing the turnover cycle.

CONCLUSIONS

Child and youth care work has distinct characteristics as well as meaningful overlap with other human service professions. The focus on the care and treatment of children and youth living away from home (residential treatment) has defined the field in the past. However, trends indicate an expansion of duties and venues of service. Although unique in some ways, child and youth care work is at its core similar to other helping professions with regard to the centrality of emotional contact as a medium of effective performance. It is this mode of work activity that sets the stage for burnout in all human service professions.

CHAPTER 2

Burnout: Its Impact and Precursors

Have you ever felt burned out? When I ask this question in workshops and presentations, roughly 75 to 80 percent of people report that they have suffered from this phenomenon. But what do they mean when they answer in the affirmative? Both anecdotal and scholarly evidence shows that different people mean different things, sometimes substantially different things, by the term "burnout" (Maslach & Schaufeli, 1993). This chapter will discuss the definition of the term, explore its development and end point, and offer some theoretical background for why burnout develops. Key research findings will be identified that will be relevant to the cross-cultural study reported in this book. Finally, an integrative model will be presented that attempts to capture both theory and research results.

SETTING THE STAGE FOR BURNOUT

Since its appearance in the literature (Freudenberger, 1974), the concept of burnout has drawn intense interest. To some extent this interest derives from its focus on the psychological reactions of workers in the helping professions. Such workers had become more aware that through the very process of delivering care and treatment to others, they were becoming cognitively and emotionally injured in ways that ultimately would interfere not only with their own physical and mental health, but also with their ability to deliver the quality of service that they desired. Although the phenomenon of burnout had probably always existed in human service situations, it rose to larger consciousness with several trends in the helping professions and in Western society in general (Maslach & Schaufeli, 1993). Specialization, bureaucratization, and individualization were all post–World War II trends in the United States and some other cultures that left workers feeling less grounded in the values and skills of caring, more subject to rationalized, emotionally unresponsive organizational structures, more pressured to perform, and more alienated from both their clients and coworkers. As Shirom (1989) said, the concept of burnout "apparently filled a void in labeling a hitherto unnamed, but prevalent, phenomenon" (p. 25).

At the same time, work values in the United States shifted to emphasize work as self-fulfillment rather than merely exchange of work for pay (Katzell, Yankelovich, Fein, Ornati, & Nash, 1975). Workers generally expanded their expectations concerning what they wanted from a career and from a specific job. Thus, under today's expectations of work, merely presenting one's body at work for the duration of the work day is no longer sufficient. Human service workers especially seek to express a "calling" to help others and expect their work organizations to help them fulfill this goal. Everyday "tools of the trade" for such workers rely on dedication, compassion, and emotional contact with their clients. The desire for fulfillment at work demands working conditions and personal resources that can support emotional contact in the face of difficult conditions. Helping others can be marked by repeated interactions with difficult, upset, and sometimes uncooperative people whose life circumstances or tragedies often lead them to be less than responsive to the good intentions of the worker (Savicki & Cooley, 1983). The agonies and ecstasies of such work can develop an intensity that may energize workers when at an optimum level. However, the work can also easily overwhelm workers who do not possess the requisite personal or environmental resources and even eventually overburden many of those who do. The stage was set both for a broader experience of burnout by human service workers and for a more profound value or concern over its effects.

DEFINITION

From the beginning, the concept of burnout has been both graphic and elusive. Because of the metaphorical nature of the word, early writers talked about burnout as "smoldering," "flaming," or "blazing" and workers experiencing burnout as "going down in flames," "burnt to a crisp," or "crispy critters." Such language is entertaining but gets us no nearer a workable definition of the concept.

In a more serious vein, researchers have attempted to capture the essence of the burnout phenomenon. Many authors have proposed definitions (Cherniss, 1980; Edelwich & Brodsky, 1980; Freudenberger & Richelson, 1980; Maslach & Jackson, 1981; Pines, Aronson, & Kafry, 1981). Across all definitions, certain commonalties appeared.

First, there is a predominance of dysphoric symptoms. . . . Second, the accent is on mental and behavioral symptoms rather than physical symptoms. . . . Third, burnout symptoms are work-related. . . . Fourth, the symptoms manifest themselves in "normal" persons who did not suffer from psychopathology before. Fifth, decreased effectiveness and work performance occur because of negative attitudes and behaviors. (Maslach & Schaufeli, 1993, p. 15)

Very early in the research efforts surrounding burnout, a questionnaire was developed that has become the de facto measure of burnout: the Maslach Burnout Inventory (MBI) (Maslach & Jackson, 1981). The MBI embodied the definition of its authors: "Burnout is a syndrome of emotional exhaustion, depersonalization, and reduced personal accomplishment that can occur among individuals who work with people in some capacity" (Maslach, Jackson, & Leiter, 1996, p. 4).

For good or ill, the three-dimensional definition of burnout proposed by the Maslach Burnout Inventory has guided the majority of research in the field. Studies have examined whether the three factors (emotional exhaustion, depersonalization, and personal accomplishment) could be replicated with various types of workers (Bartz & Maloney, 1986; Belcastro, Gold, & Hays, 1983; Dolan, 1987; Gold, 1984; Golembiewski & Munzenrider, 1983; Iwanicki & Schwab, 1981). The three dimensions were replicated with teachers, nurses, and managers. The original validation sample used by Maslach and Jackson (1981) included police officers, nurses, agency administrators, teachers, counselors, social workers, probation officers, mental health workers, physicians, psychologists, psychiatrists, and attorneys. The three-factor structure of burnout seems robust and applicable to many "people-oriented" occupations.

However, the three-factor definition of burnout has caused some consternation among researchers, since there is no single score that specifies burnout level (Leiter, 1993). Several studies have examined whether all three factors are useful or if a one- or two-factor description of burnout might be more efficient (Lee & Ashforth, 1990; Wright & Bonett, 1997). Cordes and Dougherty (1993) argue that it is premature to drop dimensions from the burnout conceptualization since there are "differential patterns of correlations between each component and other study variables" (p. 628). Accepting this conclusions while recognizing its imperfections, the current study retains the three-dimensional definition of burnout for the research reported in this book.

Finally, burnout has been compared to several other measures of psychological adjustment and work satisfaction. The issue was the conceptual independence of burnout in relation to other potentially identical or substantially overlapping constructs. The MBI subscales were only moderately related to various measures of job satisfaction. They were not at all related to social desirability; that is, the desire to respond what was perceived as socially acceptable ways. The relationship of burnout to depression, though somewhat complex, seemed to reflect the MBI's specificity in relation to dysphoria located at work as distinct from a more general depressive mood (Maslach,

Jackson, & Leiter, 1996). In general, the three-dimensional description of burnout captures unique characteristics of reactions to working with people.

In summary, burnout is a complex, affective response to work. The three-dimensional approach has been both fruitful in so far as differentiating aspects of a complex phenomenon, but confusing regarding the search for a single-scale definition. Accordingly, future chapters in this book will deal with burnout both in a multidimensional (three scores) and a unidimensional (one score) manner in order to examine the phenomenon of burnout from multiple aspects.

SYMPTOMS

What are the indicators of burnout? Unfortunately, there is no set of indisputable signs that apply to all people under all circumstances. Humans, being the diverse species that we are, defy exact categorization. However, researchers have reported a list of symptoms that may accompany burnout. Such signs and signals may be useful both in exploring what it means to be burned out and in raising the vigilance of workers who may be entering the initial stages of its development.

Kahill (1988) reviewed early burnout research and categorized burnout symptoms into five different clusters: physical, emotional, behavioral, interpersonal, and attitudinal. None of the following lists are exhaustive, nor is the presence of any one of these symptoms an indisputable indicator of burnout. However, the lists do impart a sense of the range of responses to the burnout phenomenon. Physical symptoms may include tension, irritability, low energy, fatigue, insomnia, headaches, gastrointestinal disturbances, chest pains, and poor appetite. Emotional symptoms may include disillusionment, depression, feelings of helplessness, anxiety, hostility, alienation, apathy, and boredom. Behavioral symptoms may include absenteeism, turnover, decreased job performance, increased tobacco, alcohol and drug use, and talk of leaving one's job. Interpersonal symptoms may include less socializing, withdrawal from clients and coworkers, role rigidity, impatience, moodiness, and less tolerance toward others. Attitudinal symptoms may include cynicism, rigidity of thinking, loss of self-esteem, and negative attitudes toward clients, coworkers, the job, and the work organization (Cordes & Dougherty, 1993; Kahill, 1988; Maslach, 1993). The pattern of symptoms is different for each individual depending on the work context and his or her own psychological vulnerabilities and resources. The threshold for perceived burnout also varies for different people, so that the level of objectively verified stressors is not a perfect indicator of the probability of burnout. Thus, neither objective measures of stress nor type of symptoms can be seen as absolutely indicative of burnout. When a cluster of symptoms reaches a level of intensity which cannot be ignored, the burnout process has probably been advancing for some time, although mostly unnoticed. Looking at the end point of burnout has been instructive, but options for recovery in such extreme cases are few and difficult. In terms of human costs, it is more effective to take a preventative approach.

DEVELOPMENTAL PROCESS

Early writings about burnout focused on its end point. Recently, much more emphasis has been placed on identifying the developmental process of burnout itself. What are its precursors? Can we predict onset and duration? How does the process advance? What speeds it up or slows it down? Can we interrupt, reverse, or inoculate against it? Can we learn to identify and recognize it in early stages? A focus on the developmental process of burnout is useful in addressing these and many other questions.

Theoretical Explanations

Several theoretical explanations have been advanced to account for the development of burnout. Some of the theories and perspectives called upon include social psychology (Maslach, 1993), existentialism (Pines, 1993), social comparison (Buunk & Schaufeli, 1993) and self-efficacy (Cherniss, 1993). A cluster of theories more frequently used with stress and burnout can be characterized as gauging the relative weights of stressors in comparison to situational and personal resources of the individual experiencing those stressors (Scheck, Kinicki, & Day, 1995). These theories draw upon early conceptualizations by Kurt Lewin (1935) regarding the relationships between the person and his or her environment. The cognitive mediational approach (Lazarus, 1999), the person–environment fit model (Caplan, Cobb, French, Harrison, & Pineau, 1975) and the conservation of resources model (Hobfoll, 1989) all indicate that a level of stress that overwhelms or threatens to overwhelm the individual will tax the individual's resources and coping abilities, thus leading to arousal and perceived strain. The advantage of these models is that they may also predict an individual response that is energized and accompanied by a strong sense of well-being. When stressors that are challenging but not overwhelming are conquered, a sense of mastery ensues. In other words, stressors can be seen as both problematic when resources are not sufficient, and yet fulfilling when individual and environmental resources permit successful resolution. From the point of view of the three dimensional description of burnout, both the negative affects of emotional exhaustion and depersonalization and the positive reaction of personal accomplishment can be predicted by such models. Such a multiple perspective is consistent with the growing emphasis on positive psychology generally (Seligman & Csikszentmihalyi, 2000) and positive views of stress specifically (Folkman & Moskowitz, 2000).

Socialization, Encounter, and Metamorphosis

Burnout is more common with younger workers (Maslach & Schaufeli, 1993) and has been linked to entrance into the helping professions (Cherniss, 1995; Edelwich & Brodsky, 1980). The concept of socialization to work (Feldman, 1976) provides a framework for how precursors for burnout may exert their effect. Socialization has been described as consisting of three parts: anticipatory socialization, encounter, and metamorphosis. These three sequential aspects of the worker and the organization adjusting to each other contain the seeds of burnout.

Anticipatory Socialization

In anticipatory socialization, workers begin to discover what is involved in the specific job that they are considering. Anticipation precedes actual day-to-day exposure to the job that occurs when workers actually begin their jobs in a specific organization. Workers compare their values, skills, knowledge, and abilities to those they believe are demanded from the job. The organization enlightens the worker concerning job responsibilities and organizational values. Much of anticipatory socialization takes place during the application, screening, and selection process as the worker and organization decide whether they are compatible with one another.

In the helping professions, another aspect of anticipatory socialization derives from preservice training. That is, professional education classes and degree programs socialize students into the profession while they are completing the requirements for a degree or certification. Preservice training can amplify a general impression of the helping professions which has been called the "professional mystique" (Cherniss, 1980). This set of beliefs implies that professionals will generally have high autonomy and job satisfaction, work with responsive and grateful clients, and show undiluted compassion and caring. Such beliefs can set the stage for disillusionment when workers are exposed to the metaphorical bumps and bruises of actual work with clients which never quite matches the ideals endorsed by the mystique (Edelwich & Brodsky, 1980).

Encounter

Encounter begins as the worker enters into the organization as an employee. Some aspects of socialization during the encounter can begin with training and orientation prior to the worker assuming actual job duties. However, the most substantial part of socialization takes place during the day-to-day interaction with coworkers, supervisors, and clients. Unless the organization has just been founded, the new worker enters already established structures, both formal and informal. Theoretically, socialization is a process of mutual influence, but practically, it is the new worker who does most of the accommodating.

Accommodations to many aspects of work must be made: values, work and family, interpersonal relationships, group relationships, and skill development, to name a few. Seen from afar, organizational values may have looked different than they do from within the melee of moment-to-moment choices. The worker has to choose whether value disagreements between personal and organizational beliefs are serious enough to leave the job or moderate enough to suspend the differences while on the job. Conflicts in expectation between home and family emerge early with issues of working hours, salary, the prospect of overtime, and the expectation of task completion on nonpaid time. Role demands may conflict. On the job, dyadic interpersonal relationships of worker to supervisor and worker to coworker may test the worker's ability to cooperate or conform. Likewise, relationships with groups may conflict with the worker's expectations of how he or she typically behaves in groups and how groups ought to function. Early in the job, much of the above adjustment is overlaid on the compelling task of learning the basics of doing the job the worker was hired for. Even for the most well-educated and trained worker, the transition to job duties in a specific organization requires adjustment. Each workplace has evolved a unique manner of transition with different personalities and different clients. Both supervisors and coworkers may communicate both formal and informal expectations for how a job is to be done, or these expectations may remain a mystery to new workers in the face of a noncommunicative job setting. These multilevel expectations set the stage for role ambiguity and role conflict regarding the actual job task. Socialization requires substantial energy during the first few months on the job and may last beyond a year.

Metamorphosis

After repeated interactions and with some good will on all sides, metamorphosis occurs. The potential conflicts and ambiguities are resolved well enough for the worker to feel a sense of belonging and loyalty to the organization, to feel competent in job performance, and to be prepared to contribute ideas and innovations to the organization. However, the resolution of issues may only "satisfice" (Simon, 1957); that is, they may be sufficient but not completely satisfactory. In this case the worker continues to carry some level of conflict and ambiguity. Likewise, when new coworkers or supervisors arrive or when the job changes in some fashion, these same issues can be revisited. The same issues that appear early in the job in the process of socialization also appear later in the job with burnout. The seeds of burnout from socialization sprout and mature beyond the metamorphic stage.

Phases and Sequences of Burnout

By definition, burnout develops over time. It is an accumulation of strains in response to chronic job stressors. Several approaches have been suggested concerning a sequence of development in the burnout process (Leiter, 1993). Leiter and Maslach (1988) proposed that the three dimensions of burnout were ordered in a sequence beginning with emotional exhaustion followed by depersonalization and finishing with diminished personal accomplishment. The rationale for this sequence was that increased emotional exhaustion led workers to defend themselves from work strains by emotionally detaching from work, which eventually led them to become less effective. In contrast, Golembiewski and his associates (Golembiewski & Munzenrider, 1988) proposed a phase model of burnout in which depersonalization leads to diminished personal accomplishment which is then followed by emotional exhaustion. In this model, initial attempts to protect one's self from work stressors interfere with job performance and thus lead to a higher sense of fatigue derived from working harder but becoming less effective. In fact, there may be no unvarying sequence of the three dimensions of burnout (Schwab & Iwanicki, 1982); rather, the strength of the individual dimensions of burnout may be related to other factors.

Another approach to conceptualizing reactions to job stress embodies a cycle of high and low strains in response to longevity in a job position. Shirom and Mazeh (1988) proposed that job satisfaction for teachers followed a five-year cycle. Initially (over the first two years) job satisfaction was high; but it dropped steadily until the five-year mark, when, on average, it went up again. This pattern was repeated over the length of the teaching career. Shirom and Mazeh speculate that workers took time out (e.g., via maternity leave) or changed the character of their jobs (e.g., promotion or new job responsibilities) at the five-year mark. These changes "reset the clock" on the cycle. It is quite possible that such a cycle is relevant for burnout as well. Although some longitudinal studies have found that on average burnout remains relatively steady over time (e.g., Wade, Cooley, & Savicki, 1986), others have found that burnout rises steadily (Savicki & Cooley, 1994). A key methodological difference may account for these disparate results. When workers were followed up regarding their burnout level and whether they had changed jobs or taken time out, average burnout stayed stable. Possibly, scores from workers at different places in the burnout cycle cancelled each other out. However, a study of workers who had remained in their current position without change showed that all three dimensions of burnout indicated increasing strains (Savicki & Cooley, 1994). These workers had not had the opportunity to find relief from the accumulation of stressors in their current job position. Periodicity or cycling of burnout may be predictable in relation to longevity in a job position.

The cycle notion of burnout development fits both with the concept of socialization to work and with the notion of overwhelmed personal and environmental resources. After the initial period of adjustment to a new position, workers settle into their jobs. It takes a few years of exposure to low-level chronic job stressors for the accumulation of strains to begin to have their impact. It is not one large devastating stressful episode that is crucial for burnout, but rather the aggregation or build-up of low- or moderate-level stressors that wears down the worker's coping resources.

BURNOUT AND CHRONIC STRESS

Burnout, in its purist form, develops in the context of chronic stress. In contrast to acute stress, which has definable beginnings and ends, chronic stress persists over long periods of time and can be recognized by "circumstances of continuing hardship" and "unremitting demands" (Gottlieb, 1997). Likewise, "multiple and interacting stressful experiences tend to be the rule rather than the exception in many circumstances of chronic hardship" (Gottlieb, 1997, p. 7). There is evidence that both psychological and physiological responses to chronic stress are significantly different from those to acute stress in the workplace (Fujigaki & Mori, 1997).

Gottlieb (1997) proposes that chronic stress may be more difficult for individuals to cope with than acute stress. "If the source of chronic stress resides in the relatively enduring circumstances of life . . . then it may not be possible for the respondent to identify a specific stressful transaction" (p. 11). Thus "unacknowledged stressors" (Lazarus, 1999) may wreak their damage outside the awareness of the individual, and it may be difficult to specify their exact time of onset because of their repetitive and enduring nature (Hepburn, Loughlin, & Barling, 1997). Hassles (Kanner, Coyne, Schaefer, & Lazarus, 1981) come the closest to fitting the enduring chronic stress definition. Hassles are low-level stressors such as "excessive paper work" or "too many interruptions" that provide background stress intense enough to notice but not usually severe enough to provoke active attempts to reduce or eliminate. The accumulation of such stressors has been correlated with burnout (Savicki, Cooley, & Gjesvold, in press). Beyond stressors that may be acknowledged upon reflection, there are those that may be responded to automatically prior to coming into the individual's awareness (Cramer, 2000). Previously successful coping devices may become habitually invoked in response to identical or similar stressors, so that the individual is unaware that the stressor exists. Chronic stress may set the stage for an accumulation of strains that grows ever more toxic without the individual being consciously aware of them. Burnout as a psychological phenomenon may be metaphorically similar to repetitive strain injury as a physical phenomenon. Continued low-level responses in the context of poor work conditions eventually produce deleterious effects.

When Carver (1998) discussed thriving in the face of stress, he proposed that an opportunity to consolidate one's resources, skills, and abilities is necessary to increase one's performance under future stressors. Unremitting, chronic stress deprives individuals of consolidation opportunities. In the absence of such opportunities, even successful coping with challenging stressors may lead to a depletion of personal resources for future coping. Beyond the depletion of personal resources, chronic stress in concert with depressive affect "can undermine people's social resources and amplify their distress just when they most need the support and help of others" (Gottlieb, 1997, p. 8). In summary, chronic work stress provides the context for a wearing down of workers which may become exacerbated and lead to burnout.

RESEARCH FINDINGS

Over the years, much has been written about burnout. Early articles were in the "Woe is me" pattern of decrying the effects of burnout and proposing solutions based on intuition and anecdotal experience. Hard research followed.

Meta-Analysis

Lee and Ashforth's (1996) meta-analysis of correlates to the emotional exhaustion, depersonalization, and personal accomplishment summarizes results from 61 of 77 research-based studies done with the Maslach Burnout Inventory from 1982 to 1994. In general, these studies considered various helping professions, but did not isolate child and youth care work specifically. Lee and Ashforth categorized variables that correlated with burnout into the broad categories of demands and resources. Demands included job stressors such as workload and role conflict. Resources included a variety of environmental features such as social support, job enhancement opportunities, and reinforcement contingencies. Several job stressors were related to both emotional exhaustion and depersonalization: higher role ambiguity, role conflict, role stress, number of stressful events, workload, work pressure, and lower role clarity. For resources, strong relationships with emotional exhaustion and depersonalization were found with lower number of work friends, skill utilization, and higher unmet expectations. The authors speculated that in relation to emotional exhaustion and depersonalization, workers were especially sensitive to work demands and might perceive that more energy should be expended to reduce stress demands than to enhance resources. For personal accomplishment there was a weaker relationship with both demand and resource variables. On the demand side higher stressful events was most strongly related to higher personal accomplishment. On the resource side, more work friends, and greater participation related strongest to personal accomplishment. The pattern of correlations indicate that personal accomplishment is a qualitatively different job-related affective response than the other two burnout dimensions.

Personal coping styles were differentially related to burnout. Lower preventive coping was related to depersonalization; while higher control coping was related to personal accomplishment. Related research indicates that escape coping is also related to higher levels of emotional exhaustion and depersonalization (Koeske, Kirk, & Koeske, 1993; Riolli-Saltzman & Savicki, 2001a).

Burnout in Child and Youth Care Workers

Finally, although child and youth care workers are exposed to many of the burnout producing conditions specified, few studies have focused on burnout in child and youth care work specifically. Typically, child and youth care workers are aggregated with other human service professionals, even though clear task and work structure differences exist (Savicki, 1993). As in other professions, child and youth care work produced both writings of opinion and theory and empirical research studies. Opinion and theory articles focused on the unique nature of child and youth care work, the impact of burnout on workers and agencies, linkages of individual history and personality to susceptibility to burnout, theoretical explanations for burnout, and recommendation for prevention and further research (Curbow, 1990; Freudenberger, 1977; Mattingly, 1977; Raider, 1989).

Several empirical studies focused on relations of burnout to personal characteristics of the child and youth care workers. Fuqua and Couture (1986) found internal locus of control positively related to personal accomplishment. McMullen and Krantz (1988) found that higher learned helplessness and lower self-esteem were related to higher levels of emotional exhaustion and depersonalization. Environmentally oriented research articles found that burnout in child and youth care workers was related to staff relations, job ambiguity, role conflict, and overload (Boyd & Pasley, 1989; Kingsley & Cook-Hatala, 1988). In a more qualitative study, child and youth care worker turnover was linked to workload, lack of clear performance feedback, and lack of supervisor support (Fleischer, 1985). In general, many of the findings that applied to the helping professions generally seem to apply to child and youth care workers.

Savicki (1993) differentiated the unique job structure of the milieu in child and youth care service delivery from other human service task structures such as the "50-minute hour" and the supervisory role. High levels of continuous contact with the same group of clients within their daily living space clearly marked child and youth care practice as unique from other helping professions. Examples of empirical differences in work environment included child and youth care workers reporting a relatively loosely structured workplace more prevalent than did other human service workers and describing a work situation in which they experienced high levels of autonomy to make moment-to-moment decisions about their work, while at the same time feeling constrained by regulations and procedures imposed from management. There was no difference in perceived pressure to work between different task structures.

These differentiated working conditions were associated with different patterns of burnout. Child and youth care workers indicated that emotional exhaustion was related to work pressure and chaotic work structures. Personal accomplishment was related to higher levels of coworker support. Burnout in child and youth care workers seemed to be influenced by the constantly changing events of the milieu and by the team-oriented nature of the work.

On the other hand, workers engaged in the "50-minute hour" work structure who saw different clients, one after the other, in series of individual meetings indicated that lack of supervisor support was related to emotional exhaustion and higher levels of innovation were related to personal accomplishment. These "serial-contact" workers relied on their supervisors for social support, since they were not involved in team-oriented treatment, and their sense of achievement at work was linked to how much the workplace encouraged workers trying new approaches as individuals within the structured series of meetings that marked their work day. For both milieu and "50-minute hour" workers, the structure of work seemed to influence the environmental factors that were linked to burnout. Such a result is consistent with the notion of differential exposure to chronic stressors based on the differential importance of environmental factors that have been dictated by task structures.

In summary, these findings highlight the interaction between demands (stressors) and resources, both personal and environmental. The significant relationships between environment and personal variables suggest a pattern of response that may be linked to the various dimensions of burnout. Research focus must now turn to revealing which patterns of variables create the most toxic chronic stress contexts and which variables may be able to counteract such persistent stressors.

MASLACH AND LEITER'S INTEGRATION

Maslach and Leiter (1997) made several integrative comments concerning burnout and its precursors. First, they promoted the idea that burnout dimensions should be viewed as potentially bipolar. Opposite ends of the bipolar continua could be described as not merely the absence of burnout, but rather the presence of psychological well-being at work. Emotional exhaustion was contrasted with higher levels of physical and psychological energy. Depersonalization or cynicism was contrasted with involvement and commitment to one's job. Diminished personal accomplishment in the form of perceived and actual ineffectiveness on the job was contrasted with a heightened sense of job self-efficacy. As they advocated, "burnout is not just about the presence of negative emotions. It is also about the absence of positive ones" (p. 28).

Emphasis on organizational or situational precursors to burnout focused on mismatches between individual worker capacities and needs in comparison to organizational structures and demands. Maslach and Leiter (1997) espoused the position that organizations, not individual workers, are most responsible for chronic situations that foment burnout, and that emphasis on individual worker responses can undermine real solutions to burnout. "As far as the organization is concerned, when burnout is seen to be a personal experience . . . it becomes a personnel problem rather than a strategic management problem" (pp. 33–34). Thus they discuss six areas of organizational structure and design that can create mismatches between the individual workers and their work situation: work overload, lack of control, insufficient reward, unfairness, breakdown of community, and value conflicts. Once again the emphasis is on diminished resources rather than work demands (work overload) when this is placed within the framework of the demands versus resources categorization of Lee and Ashforth (1996).

A MODEL OF BURNOUT, RESILIENCE, AND EXPOSURE TO STRESS

Figure 2.1 attempts to integrate the ideas presented in this chapter. It combines issues of burnout and its opposites, as well as chronic stress, and resilience. In Figure 2.1, the initial level of personal resources of the individual worker is used as a starting point. Clearly, this level will be different for different individuals. As the individual is exposed both to chronic situational and organizational demands and the everyday ups and downs of client contact, the worker's resources are tested and expended. The question of whether the individual's resources are continually depleted, are restored to beginning levels, or are actually increased over time depends on the ability of the organization to provide conditions that nurture resilience. *Thriving* occurs when the organizational and situational factors support, or at least do not interfere with, gains in the sense of efficacy, energy, and involvement. Stressors in this situation are perceived as challenges to be conquered, with subsequent celebration and increase in professional growth. Restoration of momentary depletions of resources may help the individual recover their initial resource level (*resilience*). The worker in this situation does not advance in professional growth, nor do they decline. But situational and organizational factors that do not aid in recovery or that actually create environments that also deplete resources lead to an inevitable decline in the worker's ability to rebound from the effects of stress. In such cases of *impaired survival*, the worker continues to work but with declining energy, efficacy, and involvement. Stressors that may have seemed manageable in the early stages become threats as resources to deal with them wane. With no respite, the first stages of burnout begin; negative emotions are added to the mix of chronic stressors. "Basically, emotions are not just private and personal but rather social experiences. . . . When we express our negative feelings it affects the world around us, making it a more unpleasant place, and this in turn fuels our negative feelings—and the downward spiral continues" (Maslach & Leiter, 1997, p. 30). The end point, succumbing to burnout, may be tragic; but allowing the decline illustrated in Figure 2.1 to persist is even more tragic since it is theoretically possible to reverse the trend.

Of course, there can be tremendous individual variation in these proposed patterns. The initial level of resources will be different for each individual. In addition, some demographic and work-related characteristics may mediate

Figure 2.1
Model of Burnout, Resilience, and Exposure to Stress

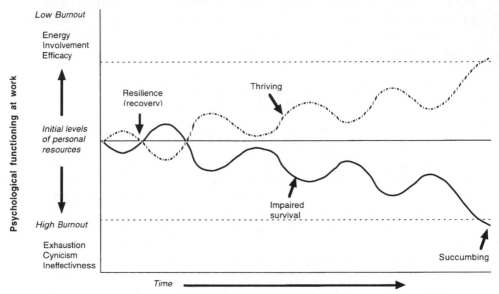

Contact with chronic situational and organizational stressors and
with episodic client stressors

stressors, such as age and periodicity in one's professional career (Shirom &
Mazeh, 1988). However, the model does seem to capture key features of the
burnout development process as well as the potential for positive outcome
from exposure to stressors (Folkman & Moskowitz, 2000). We will refer to
this model in later chapters as issues of prevention, remediation, and recovery are discussed.

CHAPTER 3

Culture as a Lens to Examine Burnout

Many research studies have investigated the impact of the immediate work environment on burnout (Lee & Ashforth, 1996). But there is another level of environment that has powerful effects which have not been well researched in relationship to burnout, namely culture (Golembiewski, Scherb, & Boudreau, 1993). This broader level of environment, and variations of individuals within it, has been seen as somewhat difficult to operationalize (Triandis, 1996; Van de Vijver & Leung, 1997). The omnipresent and somewhat ambiguous nature of the concept of culture has made it more the province of anecdotal reports than of systematic scientific investigation with regard to the phenomenon of burnout. Researchers acknowledge that cultures differ on important issues, but how these differences may affect burnout has not been well described.

In order to use culture as a lens through which to examine burnout, several areas of knowledge must be employed to set the framework for that examination. First, a reasonable definition of culture must be established. Second, a useful method of measuring culture must be articulated. Third, theoretical and methodological issues need to be clarified. Finally, initial connections between culture and burnout should be reviewed. This chapter will attempt to explore these areas in order to clean and focus the lens of culture and aim it toward the phenomenon of burnout.

DEFINITION OF CULTURE

Adler (1997) defines culture as "that complex whole which includes knowledge, belief, art, law, morals, customs and any capabilities acquired by a person as a member of society. It is a way of life of a group of people, the configuration of all the more or less stereotyped patterns of learned behavior, which are handed down from one generation to the next through the means of language and imitation" (p. 14). In general, culture is the emergent property of the structure and interaction of people living together. It is an abstract social construct that gains value through its ability to help its members negotiate daily tasks and challenges. Older members of a culture attempt to pass it along to younger members. It gains its influence not only as a set of general environmental constraints, but also through its ability to shape members' behavior and perceptions.

Many factors may influence the development of different cultures (Triandis, 1996). Language, geography, history, and political systems all may shape culture as its members live together. Although exposure to mass media and modern technology may be seen as having some homogenizing effect across cultures, differences will probably remain. For example, even though Italians and Americans both have been exposed to mobile phones, they interpret this technology through their unique cultures. For Americans, a cell phone is a way to get away from the office or other constraining environment so that he or she can have more individual free time. On the other hand, Italians perceive the mobile phone as an effective way to always be in contact with the important people in their lives in order to maintain those crucial relationships.

As we talk in more detail about cultures, and especially cultural differences, a clear distinction needs to be made between cultural descriptions and cultural stereotypes. Not everyone in the same culture is exactly the same. Therefore, we use cultural descriptions as a shorthand notation for large, overall differences between cultures. At the same time, we need to allow room for recognition of individual differences within a culture. Judging people solely on the basis of their group membership is a stereotype. It may be a reasonable first approximation, but it needs to be tempered with additional information. As we move through this book, the aim is to use descriptive language and avoid evaluative or judgmental jargon—to be ever open to additional input.

CULTURE AS CONTEXT—CULTURE AS COGNITION

In theory, culture provides another classification of environmental influence at a more general level. Work environment is clearly the proximal environmental condition for burnout, while culture or the cultural environment is more distal. Figure 3.1 illustrates that two cultures, in this case Denmark and the Slovak Republic, differ significantly on the cultural value of individualism, that is, the emphasis on individual action. The average measured scores of this value for the two cultures qualify as statistically different. Following this example, for the purposes of analysis, the effects of culture as an environmental variable can be construed to impact all members of the culture relatively equally. Therefore, the best representative indicator of overall cultural influence can be seen as the average level of the people comprising the culture. In the current analysis, the overall environmental influence of a cultural environment will be operationalized as the mean score on cultural work values for each culture; thus, each member of a culture has an identical score.

Figure 3.1
Cultural Differences and Cultural Conformity Variations: Distribution
Comparison between Denmark and the Slovak Republic on Individualism

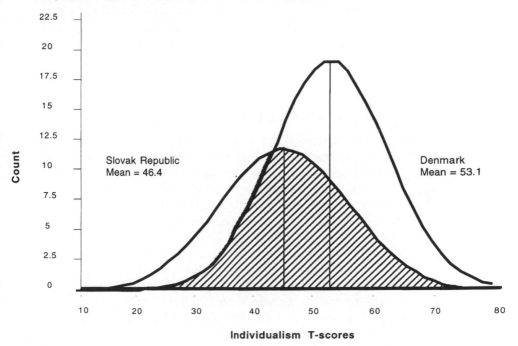

Even though cultural influence may be general, theorists have also suggested that individuals internalize cultural influence as a "structure of habits" (Triandis, 1995) and as mental programs or "software of the mind" (Hofstede, 1997). Thus, culture may be carried as a personal variable (Trompenaars & Hampden-Turner, 1998), used in the cognitive appraisal and coping processes under stressful conditions, as articulated by Lazarus (1999). Figure 3.1 indicates substantial variation in individualism for each culture. Within each culture, large individual differences occur in the degree to which individuals subscribe to the overall average score of the culture. Also, as illustrated by the shaded area of Figure 3.1, some individuals from significantly different cultures will actually share identical scores due to their deviation from the norms of their own culture. For the purposes of analysis, the effects of culture as a personal mental program will be different for each individual depending on his or her level of conformity to or deviance from the overall cultural norm. In current analysis, the influence of individual conformity to cultural norms will be operationalized as the deviation from the cultural norm of the culture of which the individual is a member. Therefore, individuals within a single culture will have different cultural conformity scores.

Thus, both the general and the individual influence of culture will be included as we consider how culture impacts burnout. The aim of this research is to focus on what has been called "subjective culture" (Triandis, Bontempo, Leung, & Hui, 1990). The research in this book conceptualizes the child and youth care worker as "an enculturated being whose subjectivity and motivation is, in part, culturally constituted, yet also as an agent who is capable of resisting, modifying, and reflecting on cultural meanings and practices" (Miller, 1997, p. 112).

MEASUREMENT OF CULTURE

A crucial step in describing the impact of culture is to develop a common language to define its impact. Because it is an abstract concept, clear measurement of culture has been fraught with difficulty. A Dutch scholar, Geert Hofstede (1980), has elaborated a simple yet powerful set of dimensions of culture based on values encompassing work. Hofstede's landmark study of cultural work values synthesizes information for 40 different countries from over 60,000 individuals. Through factor analysis and other statistical methods he formulated four dimensions of cultural work values: (1) power distance, (2) uncertainty avoidance, (3) individualism–collectivism, and (4) masculinity–femininity. By looking at all four dimensions together, it is possible to gain an insight into the character of a culture.

For an extended treatment of these dimensions, please refer to Hofstede's work (1980). Only brief descriptions of these dimensions are given here. The hope is that the reader will have enough knowledge to understand the constructs without feeling overburdened with too much detail.

Individualism versus Collectivism

Individualistic cultures emphasize personal action and responsibility. The social framework is only loosely knit. Members view themselves as autonomous individuals. The needs and desires of the individual take precedence over the needs of the group. In contrast, collectivist cultures emphasize interpersonal relatedness and group action. The social framework is tightly knit. The distinction between in-groups and out-groups has immense meaning. Individual needs are often sacrificed to satisfy the needs of the group, and in return individuals can expect to be cared for by their group (Luthans, Marsnik, & Luthans, 1997; Matsumoto, 1996).

Masculinity (Career Success) versus Femininity (Quality of Life)

Masculine cultures emphasize characteristics that have sometimes been associated with the male gender: autonomy, assertiveness, work, and the importance of possessions. In contrast, feminine cultures emphasize social-consciousness, nurturance, the centrality of social connectedness, and the importance of people (Hofstede 1998). Because this dimension is an indicator of a cultural value, Adler (1997) prefers to use the terms career success versus quality of life for this scale because these terms are less likely to be mistaken as indicators of gender. The "career success versus quality of life" labeling will be used in the current study.

Power Distance

Power distance indicates the value in the culture for hierarchy and differences in status. In high power-distance cultures, managers believe that they can dictate the behavior of the subordinate, and subordinates believe that they have little recourse but to follow. In exchange, leaders show benevolence and paternalism. On the other hand, in low power-distance cultures, managers and workers assume more equitable status, and leaders must consult and collaborate with subordinates. Often there are fewer levels of hierarchy of status distinctions within the organization.

Uncertainty Avoidance

Uncertainty avoidance indicates the degree to which cultures feel threatened by uncertain or ambiguous situations. Rules, procedures, and rituals may be established to buffer uncertainties of individual judgment. High uncertainty-avoidance cultures develop rules and procedures to cover a broad range of possibilities. They are more likely to be formal and constrained. Low uncertainty-avoidance cultures let individuals react more spontaneously and "go with the flow."

In addition to the clarity and research base offered by the Hofstede cultural work values scale, this set of dimensions offers the additional advantage of providing a point of comparison in both time and industry. The results of the current study with child and youth care workers in the late 1990s can be compared to data collected with computer industry employees in the late 1970s. There is evidence of both consistency and drift in the Hofstede measurement of culture over time (Fernandez, Carlson, Stepina, & Nicholson, 1997).

METHODOLOGY AND THEORY

In the current research there are several types of data representing several levels of analysis: individual–psychological, individual–demographic, organizational, and cultural. Clearly burnout is an individual–psychological response, as are styles of coping with stress. Demographic factors such as age and gender form a second type of individual variable. Work environment, work-related factors, and organizational factors form a third level. General culture comprises a fourth level. Individual conformity to cultural norms, although technically an individual response, is couched in the language of culture. The mixture of levels of analysis poses potential complications for hypothesis testing and interpretation.

In order to simplify such analysis and interpretation, a modified model of stress and coping originally proposed by Lazarus (1999) will be used. As Figure 3.2 indicates, environmental and personal factors combine to form a person–environment relationship. Environmental conditions such as the daily stressors of child and youth care practice, work-related factors such as hours per week worked, and work environment factors such as social support all describe the specific stress and situational factors that impinge on a worker. The personal factors such as demographic characteristics and personal styles of coping provide a filter through which the environmental factors are perceived. Environmental events by themselves do not necessarily result in burnout; rather, it is the events in combination with personal characteristics that set the stage for appraisal and interpretation of those events that are related to burnout.

As mentioned earlier, culture provides a layer of analysis different from all of the others mentioned. On the one hand, it can be construed as an environmental influence, since the norms of a culture pressure its members to think, feel, and behave in specific ways. On the other hand, members of a culture do not forgo their individual psychological differences. Some are more intelligent, more anxious, or more extroverted than are others. These individual differences provide the mechanisms to interpret the demands of culture differently. Such differences account for the range of conformity to cultural norms as illustrated in Figure 3.1. Therefore, in Figure 3.2 cultural conformity appears on the personal factors side of the model, while the more general cultural work values appears on the environmental factors side.

Given that multiple layers of analysis must be considered, there can be several methods of sorting and combining these layers (Leung & Bond, 1989). In a typical cross-cultural analysis, individuals in two or more cultures are compared on some variables of interest. If differences in those variables are found, they are thought to be influenced by culture. In this case, having a measure of cultural dimensions is clearly an advantage in interpreting how culture may have contributed to the differences found.

In a pan-cultural analysis, data are pooled from individuals from two or more cultures without regard for their culture of origin. In this case, patterns may be found between variables of interest spanning all cultures. Again, having a measure of cultural dimensions may be helpful to determine if cultural patterns may have contributed to the results over and above the impact of variables at a different level.

Finally, within-culture analyses may be conducted. The overall environmental conceptualization of culture is removed from this analysis, since all members are exposed to the identical cultural factors. However, cultural conformity might provide useful information, since it is based on individual differences within a single culture.

Figure 3.2
Stress, Coping, and Culture

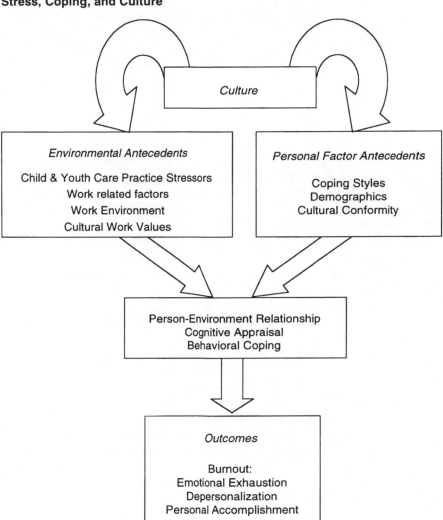

In the present research, all these methods are employed to delineate as clearly as possible the connections between burnout and environmental conditions, personal factors, and culture.

BURNOUT AND CULTURE

Finally, there is preliminary evidence that cultural factors are related differently to the separate burnout subscales (Savicki, 1999b, 1999c). Only a few studies have compared different cultures on the burnout scales. These studies fall into two categories: methodological and cross-cultural.

Methodological studies sought to confirm that the factors of burnout measured by the Maslach Burnout Inventory (Maslach, Jackson, & Leiter, 1996) were applicable in other cultures. Confirmation of the three-factor structure of the Maslach Burnout Inventory was found in countries such as Germany, Finland, Sweden, The Netherlands, Ireland, the United Kingdom, Estonia, and New Zealand (Büssing & Perrar, 1992; Green, Walkey, & Taylor, 1991; Schaufeli & Janczur, 1994; Schutte, Toppinen, Kalimo, & Schaufeli, 2000). Despite this confirmation, some caution was advised in interpreting Maslach Burnout Inventory score in differing cultures (Schaufeli & Van Dierendonck, 1995).

Cross-cultural comparisons of burnout have been conducted in these countries and others (Canada, Pakistan, Japan, and Jordan) on a variety of occupational groups such as forest industry employees (e.g., managers, clerks, foremen, and blue-collar workers), teachers, nurses, businessmen, social workers, and human service professionals (Armstrong-Stassen, Al-Ma'Aitah, Cameron, & Horsburgh, 1994; Etzion & Pines, 1986; Jamal, 1999; Shutte, Toppinen, Kalimo, & Schaufeli, 2000). No cross-cultural comparisons have been published using the child and youth care workers specifically. Thus, the current study fills a research gap concerning cross-cultural comparisons of burnout in the child and youth care field.

In addition to studying the effects of culture on burnout, another goal of this book is to test the generalizability of findings concerning the relationship of burnout to work environment and coping styles. Lee and Ashforth's (1996) meta-analysis of burnout research contained studies predominantly from North America. As the previous chapter illustrated, strong relationships of burnout to work environment did emerge. Other research has shown the relationship between burnout and coping (Leiter, 1991). For the current study, the question of generalizability and extension is, "Are the patterns found in North America of the relationship between burnout from work and coping replicated in other cultures?"

With the framework of culture in place, it is time to focus the lens of culture as a way to examine burnout. Does culture affect burnout? How do its effects operate? Are there patterns of burnout precursors across cultures? How do patterns of burnout differ across cultures? These and many other questions will be the focus of examination as we peer at burnout through the lens of culture.

PROCESS, PRACTICE, AND CULTURE COMPARISONS

Chapters in Part II set forth the structure of the research and some of the descriptive results with regard to cultural variability and characteristics of the research sample. Prior to testing the relationships of burnout and culture within the context of child and youth care work, some understanding of the range of cultural variability is useful; as is a sense of the similarities and differences in child and youth care practice in the research sample. Part II gives a bit of a macro view prior to focusing more tightly on burnout.

Chapter 4, "The Study: The People and the Process," is the methods section for the research study. The sample is defined, the procedures explained, and the measures described. In any research study, it is important for readers to understand the operational definitions that undergird the measurements made. All the key concepts—burnout, culture, coping, and work environment—are explained from this point of view. Later explanations and interpretations of the findings flow from a clear statement of these processes.

Chapter 5, "Thirteen Culture Comparisons," shows the variation of the thirteen cultures on the cultural work value dimensions. Significant differences between cultures abound. These differences are vital for the later explanation of how culture affects burnout. The goal is to give the reader a thumbnail sketch of the different cultures via their relative positions on the four cultural dimensions. The thirteen cultures separate themselves into various groupings depending on which of the cultural dimensions are considered. These similarities and differences provide context for later explanation of differences in burnout.

Chapter 6, "Thirteen Cultures of Child and Youth Care: Who They Are and What They Do," offers a description of the field of child and youth care work though cultural comparisons. Questions of who does what type of practice in what locations are answered. Although there seems to be quite a bit of communality in how child and youth care work practice is organized across the thirteen cultures, important differences also emerge. The sense of the range of people, places, and practices allows the reader to consider how these factors may relate to burnout. Later chapters incorporate demographic and work-related variables into their analyses. The broad brush descriptions offered by this chapter paints a larger context.

The overall goal of Part II is to set the stage for subsequent burnout analyses by defining methodology and describing the current research sample regarding both cultural variability and differences in the people and practices involved.

CHAPTER 4

The Study:
The People and the Process

Any research project must clarify its methods so that readers can understand the process behind the results. This chapter focuses on the people or, in methodological terms, the sample, as well as the procedures used to carry out the research. In addition, it will describe crucial information about the research questionnaire. For some readers, this kind of information excites high interest; for others, their eyes glaze over at the mention of research procedure. If you find yourself nodding off, feel free to skip over this chapter. If you find your heart rate accelerating, read on.

THE THIRTEEN CULTURES

The thirteen cultures included in this study are Australia (N = 37), Austria (N = 48), Canada-English (N = 48), Canada-French (N = 68), Denmark (N = 79), England (N = 89), Germany-East (N = 98), Germany-West (N = 47), Israel (N = 36), Poland (N = 42), Scotland (N = 56), the Slovak Republic (N = 80), and the United States (N = 97). Notice that in three cases, culture is defined in a manner so that one nation contains two different cultures: Canada contains French-speaking and English-speaking cultures; the United Kingdom contains English and Scottish cultures; and Germany contains the former East and former West sectors. German data were collected in 1996, six years after German reunification, so the data technically come from a single country, but from two regions with distinct recent histories. Such a definition of culture is quite consistent with issues concerning culture as discussed in Chapter 3. In Germany and the United Kingdom, the two cultures are separated geographically but share the same language. In Canada, the cultures share the same geography, but differ in preferred language. In all cases, history and customs differ significantly so that the presumption of different cultures was merited (Triandis, 1996).

With the exception of Israel and Australia, the cultures are drawn from North America and Northern Europe. The European sample has representatives from three of the five clusters of cultures in Europe: Anglo, Germanic, and Nordic. It is missing representatives from the Latin and Near East Europe clusters (Ronen & Shenkar, 1985). While this representation of cultures was more easily obtained, it is not representative of child and youth care globally. Thus, some care should be taken in extending the findings of this study to unrepresented European cultures as well as regions such as Asia, Africa, and Latin America. Future research should be extended to include this broader span of cultures. Such efforts made during the current study did not come to fruition.

The People: Description of the Sample

Across the thirteen cultures, an attempt was made to match samples to some degree. The 835 participants in this study were all treatment providers, educators, and managers who worked in day or residential treatment facilities dealing with children or youth who might be classified as emotionally disturbed or developmentally delayed. This meant that within such child and youth care service organizations, only custodians, cooks, and office personnel were excluded from the study. Such a restrictive sample controls for variation that might be introduced by studying participants from variety of industries or service sectors. However, this is not a precisely matched sample. Rather, it is a convenience sample; that is, it is the people who were willing to participate from the agencies or professional groups known to the primary research contact person in each culture.

In the typical procedure, the country contact person approached directors of child and youth care agencies to have all the treatment and management staff from the agencies respond to the research questionnaire. Both burnout and cross-cultural research have a long history of this type of sample (Maslach & Schaufeli, 1993; Van de Vijver & Leung, 1997). A major consideration for burnout research is that participants be currently functioning in a helping profession; that is, they are actually professionals doing real child and youth care practice under typical working conditions. Because of the nature of burnout development, it is not possible to conduct simulation studies of burnout. Such a restriction makes it difficult to find qualified participants. The current sample, while not randomly chosen or precisely matched, meets a standard frequently used in such studies.

Figure 4.1 shows the distribution by work primary role across the 13 cultures. For the most part the largest proportion of participants in any culture are child and youth care workers who deliver the major part of their care

Figure 4.1
Distribution of Primary Work Roles

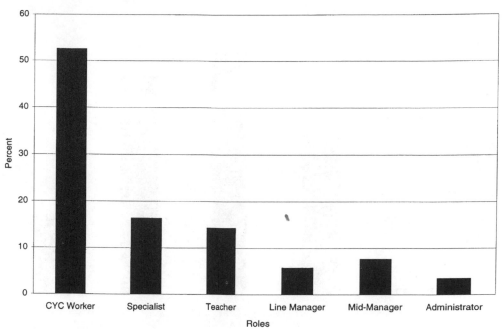

within the daily living milieu of needy children and youth. In several cultures (e.g., England and Israel), there was a larger proportion of teachers than in other cultures. To some degree, this result stems from the manner in which service is organized, with the classroom as a focal point of care; and to some degree it reflects a difference in the titles used to describe the primary care provider. In other cultures (e.g., Germany-West and Slovakia), the specialist role shows a higher proportion than in other cultures. Again, this may reflect a difference in how service is provided, with specialists more likely to meet one on one with clients rather than in groups. It also may reflect the role differentiation within cultures, with some cultures having a broader range of specialists (e.g., family therapists, drug and alcohol workers, community liaisons).

As far as basic demographics are concerned, the 835-person sample contained 63 percent women and 37 percent men. The average age in the total sample was approximately thirty-eight years. Figure 4.2 shows the distribution of age categories in the sample. The preponderance of workers were in the thirty- to fifty-year age range. As might be expected, a more detailed analysis showed that participants in the child and youth care worker role were significantly younger than persons in the other primary work roles; there was no difference in age between specialists, teachers, or any participants at the managerial level. Further description of the participants will appear in Chapter 6.

Figure 4.2
Distribution of Age

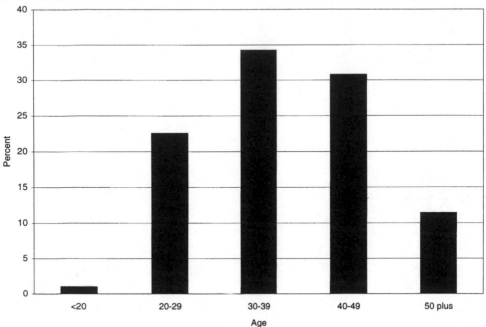

THE QUESTIONNAIRE

Each participant responded to a 166-item questionnaire. The length, though long, was a dramatically shortened version of the original questionnaire. Respondents took between thirty and forty-five minutes to answer the 166 items. Methodologically speaking, in burnout research, there is always a compromise between how much information a researcher wants to gather and the goodwill of respondents to complete the required questions. Respondents are real people doing real work; and so must take time away from their primary duties to respond to the questionnaire. The sample size would have been larger if the questionnaire had been shorter, but some research questions would have gone unanswered.

When a questionnaire needs to be translated into a different language, differences in meaning are likely to occur. But even using the same language (in this case, English), alterations in language to accommodate different meanings were required in certain cultures.

The questionnaire originated in U.S. English. The majority of the research scales were formulated in the United States. When translation was necessary, one of two standard methods were utilized. In the first, the back-translation method, the English questionnaire was first translated into the destination language. Then a different person translated it back into English to see if the retranslation matched the original. Adjustments were made to increase agreement if necessary. In the second method, a professional panel who knew the field and were bilingual worked to develop an accurate translation. Both of these methods are acceptable in cross-cultural research (Hofstede, 1980; Van de Vijver & Leung, 1997).

Several interesting linguistic and cultural translation issues arose. The idiomatic phrase, "I'm at the end of my rope," appears in the burnout inventory. Idioms always create a problem in translation since the literal meaning of the phrase is not a true reflection of the metaphoric meaning. With this item, either a culturally appropriate idiom was found in the destination language, or a phrase was substituted to indicate that personal resources were becoming exhausted. For example in German the comparable phrase was "Ich glaube daß ich nicht mehr weiter weiß," which in literal translation means "I think that I don't know how to go on any more," and in more idiomatic way communicates the meaning that the person is at their wit's end or is desperate. Thus it conveys a comparable meaning to being "at the end of my rope."

A major cultural difference in the meaning of the word "supervisor" arose. In the United States, a supervisor is someone who is in the next higher level of hierarchy in an organization and whose duty it is to consult with individual workers about how to do their jobs and to oversee compliance with the recommendations that the supervisor has made. In several cultures in Europe, the consulting and overseeing roles are separated, and two different individuals handle these duties. Thus a "supervisor" in Europe is someone who consults but has no authority to see that their recommendations are followed. The person with authority to oversee work performance is not the person whose responsibility it is to consult on cases. As you will see, the impact of the person one level up in the organizational hierarchy, or "line managers" as they were called in the United Kingdom, was an important component of this research, since it was part of the generalization aspect of the study. The problem of clarifying the appropriate cultural meaning of the term "supervisor" was one we spent a good deal of time sorting out.

Another interesting alteration to the original questionnaire was made in relation to the question concerning marital status. In the United States, categories such as "single, married, separated, and divorced" accounted for the range of marital status. However, in Europe, a larger proportion of individuals lived together while unmarried. In Denmark 25 percent of respondents fell into this category. Often these couples would set up households, have children, and make lifelong commitments to one another without officially getting married. A trend seemed to indicate that only when the children reached school age would the couple feel that marriage was necessary to ratify the family in the eyes of the law. Thus, another marital status category, "Unmarried and living together" was added. Across all cultures 12 percent of respondents selected this marital status category. It may also have allowed gay and lesbian couples to indicate a marital status more representative of their lifestyle. This is a substantial marital category.

A common measure of education level afforded some difficulty since educational systems across the cultures produced different educational degrees or certificates, demanding differing lengths of classroom or practical experience. For example, although the *diplom* from a traditional German university is the first level of university degree in that country, the *diplom* is equivalent to the master's degree, the second level university degree in the United States. Each demanded eighteen years of formal education. Therefore, rather than ask for degrees or certificates completed, the questionnaire asked for years of formal education. This shows some equivalency of education level, while at the same time avoiding the necessity to somehow standardize the results of widely differing educational systems.

Finally, the issue of salary caused some consternation. A simple conversion from U.S. dollars to the currency of the other culture was not a realistic method of determining salary. Very early in the research project, the Polish translator indicated that if such a simplistic currency conversion were to take place, then all of the Polish sample would appear in the lowest salary category. Not only did the currency vary, the economic levels of the various countries also varied widely. Therefore, each country was asked to determine a set of salary categories that spanned the range of salaries available to workers in the child and youth care field for their country. Two issues were considered in salary conversions. First, currency differences had to be accounted for. Second, the range of salaries in the country had to be considered. Thus, whatever salary data are presented represent the range of salaries within the specific country, and no attempt has been made to compare the absolute value of salaries across cultures.

In the end, the questionnaire versions were substantially equal in their meaning. There is always some slippage in such a project, but care was taken to account for both language and cultural variations.

RESEARCH SCALES

Four research scales were used in the questionnaire: burnout, cultural work values, work environment, and coping. These scales were selected first because of the desire to determine if results for burnout found in the United States were generalizable to other cultures. Second, the cultural work values scale was utilized to aid in interpreting any differences between cultures.

Maslach Burnout Inventory (MBI)

The factor-analyzed subscales for this measure include emotional exhaustion, depersonalization, and personal accomplishment (Maslach, Jackson, & Leiter, 1996).

Emotional exhaustion is the extent to which a worker feels worn out and drained by the job.

Depersonalization is the extent to which workers think about and treat children and youth and their families in an unfeeling and impersonal manner.

Personal accomplishment describes the extent to which workers feel successful in their work. This last scale becomes lower as workers become more burned out.

The MBI is a widely used instrument in human service professions. The scales have been established as reliable and valid in a number of studies (Maslach, Jackson, & Leiter, 1996). The internal consistency reliability for the scales reported in the current study are emotional exhaustion, 0.87; depersonalization, 0.69, and personal accomplishment, 0.74. In addition, the MBI has shown good reliability in cross-cultural settings. The theoretical relations and factor structure has shown consistency across cultures (Büssing & Perrar, 1992; Green, Walkey, & Taylor, 1991; Schaufeli & Janczur, 1994).

Hofstede's Cultural Work Value Scale (CWV)

Hofstede's (1980) landmark study of cultural work values resulted in four dimensions of cultural work values. These dimensions describe critical norms and understandings of cultures. The multiple-scale approach to measurement of culture allows a multivariate view into the character of a culture.

Individualism (IND) versus Collectivism (COL)

Individualistic cultures emphasize personal action and responsibility. Collectivist cultures emphasize interpersonal relatedness and group action.

Masculinity (Career Success [CS]) versus Femininity (Quality of Life [QL])

Masculine cultures emphasize autonomy, assertiveness, and the centrality of work. Feminine cultures emphasize social consciousness, nurturance, and the centrality of social connectedness. Although Hofstede (1998) defends his choice of the terms "masculinity versus femininity" as a description of culture, the current research will use Adler's (1997) terms "career success versus quality of life" for this scale because these terms capture important content of the scale, yet are less likely to be mistaken as indicators of gender.

Power Distance (PD)

Power distance between a boss and a subordinate in a hierarchy is the difference between the extent to which the boss can determine the behavior of the subordinate and the extent to which the subordinate can determine the behavior of the boss. In high power-distance cultures, bosses believe that they can dictate the behavior of the subordinate, and subordinates believe that they have little recourse but to follow, whether the behavior is agreeable or not. On the other hand, in low power-distance cultures, bosses understand that they must consult and collaborate with subordinates to direct their behavior, and subordinates understand that they can question and influence the boss's directives.

Uncertainty Avoidance (UA)

Uncertainty avoidance indicates the degree to which cultures establish rules, procedures, and rituals to buffer uncertainties of individual judgment and freedom. High uncertainty-avoidance cultures develop rules to cover a broad range of possibilities. Low uncertainty-avoidance cultures let individuals react more spontaneously and "go with the flow."

Because of the derivation of the CWV scales, internal consistency can only be calculated for individualism–collectivism and career success–quality of life scales. The reliability for these scales in this sample is 0.74 for each.

Work Environment Scale

Selected subscales from the Work Environment Scale (WES) (Moos, 1981) were used to measure seven different dimensions of an environmental characteristic called social climate. Subscales were included based on their relation to burnout as indicated in previous research. The 63, true–false items included seven 9-item scales:

Peer Cohesion (PC): the amount of friendliness and support that is perceived in co-workers.

Supervisor Support (SS): the support of management and the extent to which management encourages workers to be supportive of each other.

Autonomy (A): the degree to which workers are encouraged to be self-sufficient and to make their own decisions.

Task Orientation (TO): the extent to which the work environment emphasizes efficiency and good planning.

Work Pressure (WP): the extent to which the press of work dominates the job milieu.

Control (CTL): the extent to which management uses rules and pressures to keep workers under control.

Innovation (INN): the extent to which variety, change, and new approaches are emphasized in the work environment.

Internal consistency for the seven WES scales in the current sample is as follows: PC = 0.64, SS = 0.71, A = 0.57, TO = 0.65, WP = 0.70, CTL = 0.57, and INN = 0.76. Two items were dropped from the control scale to achieve the above level of reliability.

Coping Scale

This twenty-eight-item scale was developed to measure individual coping styles in the workplace (Latack, 1986). It is based on research that found more particular coping strategies could be categorized into these two major coping styles.

Control Coping (Control Cope)

Control coping consists of both actions and cognitive reappraisals that are proactive and take-charge in tone. They address the actual source of stress. This approach is sometimes called "problem-focused coping."

Escape Coping (Escape Cope)

Escape coping consists of both actions and cognitive reappraisals that suggest an escapist, avoidance mode. They are oriented to decrease the negative feelings of stress. This approach is sometimes called "emotion-focused coping."

Internal consistency for the coping scales for the current sample are 0.84 for control coping and 0.79 for escape coping.

SUMMARY

Service providers in child and youth care agencies from thirteen different cultures responded to a questionnaire measuring burnout, work environment, coping, and cultural work values. The majority worked in day or residential treatment settings with children or adolescents who were emotionally disturbed or developmentally delayed. Over 50 percent of respondents identified themselves as child and youth care workers providing care in the daily living milieu of their clients.

If you have not yet read the acknowledgments section of this book found in the Preface, please do so. This research could not have been completed without the enthusiasm, energy, and persistence of significant people within each of the cultures. Not only did they translate the questionnaire and arrange to collect the data, they also conferred with me to make sense of the results. Their perceptions and interpretations were my window into their culture. Someone from outside a culture can draw vastly erroneous conclusions without a participant from within that culture to give them perspective. My infinite thanks goes out to all of them.

CHAPTER 5

Thirteen Culture Comparisons

A logical first question when considering the impact of culture is, "Do the cultures to be compared differ in meaningful ways?" This chapter outlines important, measured differences between the thirteen cultures and begins to place the cultures in a culture-dimensional space in order to depict the differences and similarities more clearly. An understanding of cultural comparisons will form the background for later chapters that relate cultural dimensions to burnout. In addition, this chapter will provide some points of comparison with Hofstede's 1980 study of computer industry workers. Cultures are changing entities; therefore, it should not be expected that the descriptions of the cultures offered here will exactly match Hofstede's descriptions, nor descriptions of these cultures in the future (Fernandez, Stepina, & Nicholson, 1997). However, such descriptions give a point of reference to help explain later comparisons of cultures on burnout and associated environmental and personal variables.

A multiple analysis of variance showed that the thirteen cultures differed significantly when all four cultural work value dimensions were examined together ($F(12, 812) = 18.70$, $p < 0.0001$). That is, when power distance, uncertainty avoidance, individualism–collectivism, and career success–quality of life were considered at the same time, significant differences emerged across cultures overall. Table 5.1 shows the means and standard deviations for each culture on each dimension. The cultures are listed in ascending order for each dimension so the reader can see both the range of scores and how the cultures were ordered on each dimension. Scores are reported as standard scores (T-scores) with a mean of 50 and a standard deviation of 10 for easy comparison between cultural dimensions. A score of 50 represents the average score across

Table 5.1
Comparison of the Thirteen Cultures T-Score Means and Standard Deviations on Cultural Work Value Dimensions*

Power distance			Individualism-Collectivism[a]		
Culture	M	SD	Culture	M	SD
United States	46.135	8.104	Slovakia	46.362	12.688
Germany-West	46.361	10.233	Canada-French	46.927	9.652
Australia	47.091	10.591	England	47.240	10.160
Scotland	47.599	10.080	Germany-East	48.310	8.245
Germany-East	49.193	10.459	Australia	48.340	8.244
Canada-French	49.277	9.226	Poland	48.938	10.971
Denmark	49.458	10.547	Israel	50.704	11.233
Israel	51.094	8.833	Scotland	50.933	9.025
Canada-English	51.683	8.629	United States	52.641	5.197
England	52.476	9.475	Germany-West	52.729	9.244
Slovakia	52.886	9.825	Austria	53.031	9.753
Austria	53.776	9.285	Denmark	53.119	9.514
Poland	54.907	10.964	Canada-English	53.392	12.767

*Cultures appear in order from lowest to highest for each dimension.
[a]Low scores indicate collectivism, and high scores indicate individualism.

all cultures. Scores higher than 50 indicate a cultural work value score above the average of all cultures, while a score below 50 represents a lower-than-average score. Clearly, there are no right or wrong scores; they are merely descriptive of the cultures. Likewise, recall that each culture is represented by the child and youth care workers who chose to answer the research questionnaire. The child and youth care occupation as well as their voluntary participation should argue for caution in concluding that the results apply directly to the culture as a whole. Finally, results should be applied only to the cultures who participated and not extended beyond. With all these cautions stated, the comparisons made here are still interesting and potentially useful in describing child and youth care across cultures. The question, "Do the cultures to be compared differ in meaningful ways?" can be answered in the affirmative.

Uncertainty avoidance			Career success-Quality of life[b]		
Culture	*M*	*SD*	Culture	*M*	*SD*
Israel	42.354	10.736	Canada-French	45.587	9.174
Denmark	44.385	8.016	Slovakia	46.017	11.716
Australia	45.149	9.878	Germany-East	47.322	8.441
England	47.097	8.973	Canada-English	49.503	9.534
United States	48.006	9.892	Poland	49.854	7.501
Slovakia	48.168	8.866	Austria	50.292	12.769
Scotland	48.881	9.686	Scotland	50.529	9.564
Canada-English	50.632	9.589	Germany-West	51.330	11.019
Poland	52.520	9.966	United States	51.442	7.281
Germany-East	53.189	7.863	Denmark	51.796	9.094
Austria	54.082	8.953	Australia	52.865	9.356
Germany-West	55.458	8.583	Israel	53.007	10.559
Canada-French	59.673	7.387	England	53.468	10.649

[b]Low scores indicate quality of life, and high scores indicate career success.

SINGLE CULTURAL WORK VALUE DIFFERENCES FOR THE THIRTEEN CULTURES

First we will examine each cultural work value independently; then we will see how the scores relate to one another in an effort to compare cultures more fully. The clustering of cultures on each dimension is based on post hoc analyses following the determination of significant differences for each of the cultural work value dimensions. Please refer to Table 5.1 for a visual reminder of both the order and the intensity of each culture on each dimension.

Power Distance

For power distance, there was a significant difference across cultures ($F(12, 812) = 5.23$, $p < 0.001$). A group of cultures showed low power distance (the

United States, Germany-West, and Australia) and were significantly different than a group of cultures showing high power distance (Poland, Austria, Slovakia, England, and Canada-English). The middle group (Scotland, Germany-East, Canada-French, Denmark, and Israel) were mostly different from the extreme groups, but showed some overlap.

In general, the lower cluster of cultures were more likely to value equality and to minimize status differences, while the higher cluster was more likely to accent differences in hierarchy and to value larger differences between workers and bosses.

Please note with this and the following single-dimension comparisons that cultures do not clump themselves at the extremes of the dimensions, but rather array themselves broadly along them. Therefore, the characterization of the extremes of the dimensions is only meant to provide a general description of the cultural variation and not to imply that all cultures fit exactly within the verbal characterizations of the scale end points. Cultures in the midlevel clusters show more moderate responses. The descriptive language used may be more extreme than the actual characteristics of the cultures. Each culture is unique and these generalizations should be used as tentative descriptors.

Uncertainty Avoidance

For uncertainty avoidance, there was a significant difference across cultures ($F(12, 812) = 17.31$, $p < 0.001$). On this cultural work value, Canada-French was significantly higher than any other culture. Next highest was a group of cultures (Germany-West, Austria, Germany-East, and Poland) who were significantly different from a low cluster of cultures (Israel, Denmark, and Australia). The midlevel cluster of cultures (England, the United States, Slovakia, Scotland, and Canada-English) were mostly different than the other clusters but with some overlap.

In general, the lower cluster of cultures were more likely to value flexibility of action and spontaneity, while Canada-French and the higher cluster were more likely to value predictable methods of uncertainty reduction such as rules or rituals.

Individualism–Collectivism

For individualism–collectivism, there was a significant difference across cultures ($F(12, 812) = 5.00$, $p < 0.001$). On this cultural work value, an individualistic cluster of cultures (Canada-English, Denmark, Austria, Germany-West, and the United States) were significantly different from a more collectivist cluster (Slovakia, Canada-French, and England). The midrange cluster (Germany-East, Australia, Poland, Israel, and Scotland) were mostly different from the extreme cultures with some overlap.

In general, the lower collectivist cluster of cultures was more likely to value communal action and shared responsibility, while the higher individualist cluster was more likely to value individual freedom and accountability.

Career Success–Quality of Life

For career success–quality of life, there was a significant difference across cultures ($F(12, 812) = 4.90, p < 0.001$). On this cultural work value, a quality of life cluster of cultures (Canada-French and Slovakia) differed significantly from a career success set of cultures (England, Israel, Australia, Denmark, the United States, Germany-West, and Scotland). The middle cluster (Germany-East, Canada-English, Poland, and Austria) were mostly different from the extremes but with some overlap.

In general, the lower quality of life cluster of cultures was more likely to value a balanced life and socially conscious action, while the higher career success cluster was more likely to value career achievement and work-oriented self-identity.

Clearly, there are dramatic differences for the cultures on each of the cultural work value dimensions. Even a cursory glance at Table 5.1 shows that the rankings of the cultures can be quite different for each of the dimensions. While it may be possible to compare and contrast the thirteen cultures on each of the separate cultural dimensions, it is more useful to investigate how the dimensions operate in concert. Cultures, just like people, cannot be sliced apart. Researchers try to simplify the task of understanding culture through attempts at independent measurement of cultural factors; but, in truth, the factors operate all at once. Therefore, the following sections endeavor to illustrate the interactions between dimensions. First, a graph of all four cultural work value dimensions for all thirteen cultures at once will be presented. Second, a set of two-by-two comparisons is offered, just as Hofstede did in his original publication (1980). Then a statistically based analysis will be described which attempts to find the set of all four cultural dimensions that provided the most separation of the cultures in a multidimensional cultural space.

CULTURAL WORK VALUES GRAPH

Figure 5.1 is a graphic illustration of where the cultures stand on all four cultural work value dimensions. In this figure, the overall average for all cultures for each dimension has been set to zero. Therefore, bars extending to the right of the midline or zero point indicate above-average scores, whereas bars extending to the left indicate below-average scores. All dimensions are set to the same standard-score scale, called a z-score. Therefore, the reader can note visually not only whether a culture is higher or lower than the average on any one dimension, but also how the dimensions compare to one another in relative value.

At first glance, the graph may be difficult to understand. For example, there are cultures with extreme scores (e.g., Canada-French and Israel) and those with only modest variations from the average (e.g., Scotland). Most cultures have scores both above and below the average (e.g., the United States, England, Denmark) and one culture (Austria) has all scores above the mean.

Figure 5.1
Cultural Work Value Dimension Comparisons for Thirteen Cultures

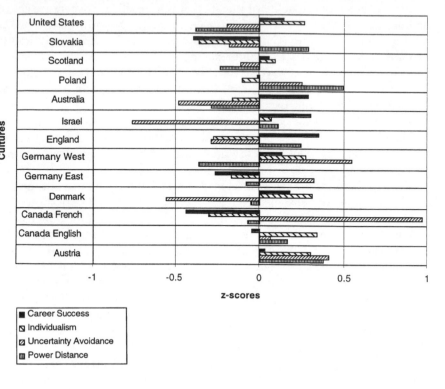

The key to interpretation of the graph is to note the relative configuration of cultural dimensions. For example, Poland was the highest of all cultures in power distance, about average in career success, moderately high in uncertainty avoidance, and moderately low in individualism (i.e., on the collectivist side). Taken together this configuration of cultural work-value scores describes a culture in which there was strong respect for hierarchy and status at work, a desire for structure in terms of rules to reduce work ambiguities, and a tendency to prefer group activity and shared responsibility. Such a description of each culture based on the configuration of the four cultural work values can be developed using the information from Figure 5.1 and Table 5.1.

TWO-BY-TWO CULTURAL DIMENSION COMPARISONS

To begin the process of examining how the dimensions may function together, it is instructive to note that the cultural work value dimensions were mostly independent from one another in the current sample. When comparing the average scores for all thirteen cultures, only uncertainty avoidance and career success–quality of life dimensions show a significant correlation ($r = -0.64$, $p < 0.05$). That is, there is a tendency for high uncertainty avoidance cultures to also score higher on quality of life, while low uncertainty avoidance cultures scored higher on career success. No other correlation approached significance. Therefore, with one exception, further interpretation of possible interactions between dimensions can be undertaken with the understanding that the cultural work value dimensions function independently from one another. Three illustrative comparisons follow. Again, clusters are based on post hoc analyses for both cultural work values.

Individualism–Collectivism and Power Distance

Figure 5.2 shows four clusters of cultures as they array themselves in the two-dimensional space of individualism–collectivism on the vertical axis and power distance on the horizontal axis. The thirteen cultures separate themselves neatly into four clusters, plus Denmark. In the individualistic–low power distance quadrant are the United States, Germany-West, and Scotland. These cultures value relative equality of status and the freedom of the individual. In

Figure 5.2
Thirteen-Culture Comparison on Power Distance and Individualism–Collectivism

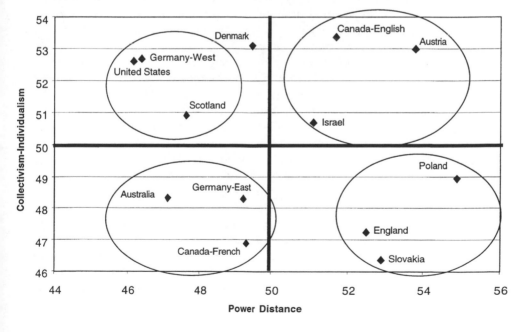

the opposite collectivist–high power distance quadrant are Poland, England, and Slovakia. These cultures value differences in hierarchical status and group action and shared responsibility. In the collectivist–low power distance quadrant are Australia, Germany-East, and Canada-French. These cultures value more collaborative–consultative leadership and collective action. Finally, in the individualistic–high power distance quadrant are Canada-English, Austria, and Israel. These cultures value high status differences and individual initiative and accountability.

Triandis (1995, 1996) describes a two-dimensional descriptive schema for cultures based on individualism–collectivism on one dimension and construal of self as same or different than others on the other. His resulting four-quadrant differentiation of cultures roughly corresponds to the four quadrants in Figure 5.2. The upper-left quadrant is equivalent to Triandis's horizontal–individualism category in which people see themselves as independent from although similar to others, valuing freedom and equality and deserving of fair rewards based on merit. The lower-right quadrant is equivalent to the vertical–collectivism category in which people see themselves interdependent yet differing in status, having both low freedom of action and low equality, and deserving of rewards based on communal sharing and the beneficence of authority figures. In the lower-left quadrant is the horizontal–collectivist category in which people view themselves as interdependent with others who are similar, as valuing high equality but not concerned with individual freedoms, and deserving of rewards relevant to the group and not oriented to individual performance. Finally, the upper-right quadrant is equivalent to the vertical–individualism category, in which people view themselves as independent from others who may differ in status, as valuing freedom but recognizing unequal status, and as deserving of rewards based on merit and the judgment of authority figures. The Triandis category descriptions may help to understand the cultures of the four different clusters found in the current study.

However, a caution regarding this correspondence between the Triandis categories and the current data should be noted. Hofstede also provided a two-dimensional comparison of individualism–collectivism with power distance. In his diagram (1980, p. 159), all the cultures common to his sample and the current sample appear in the low power distance–high individualism quadrant on his figure. The range of scores in his forty-culture study was wider; therefore, the variability on the cultural work value dimensions was much greater. Virtually all of the cultures in Hofstede's high power distance–collectivist quadrant were from Asia and South America. Clearly, the dimensions of power distance and individualism–collectivism gain broader scope when cultures from Asia and South America are considered.

Nevertheless, when restricting one's consideration of cultural differences to the cultures in the current sample, the differences described in Triandis's categories can be helpful in capturing important contrasts and comparisons.

Individualism–Collectivism and Career Success– Quality of Life

Figure 5.3 illustrates the relationship of the cultural work value dimensions of individualism–collectivism and career success–quality of life. Three clusters of cultures emerged from the simultaneous examination of these two dimensions. The largest cluster is in the career success–individualism quadrant. This cluster includes almost half of the cultures (Denmark, the United States, Germany-West, Austria, Scotland, Israel, and Canada-English). This cluster may be characterized by a strong value of work and work-related activities combined with the preference for individual effort and achievement. In the opposite quadrant is a set of overlapping clusters representing collectivism and quality of life. Cultures in this quadrant include Canada-French, Slovakia, Germany-East, and (somewhat related) Poland. This quadrant might be characterized as valuing balance in life of work, family, and other interests combined with a preference for communal action and shared accountability. Entirely by itself was the cluster of England and Australia in the career success– collectivism quadrant. This cluster might be characterized as being actively

Figure 5.3
Thirteen-Culture Comparison on Individualism–Collectivism and Career Success–Quality of Life

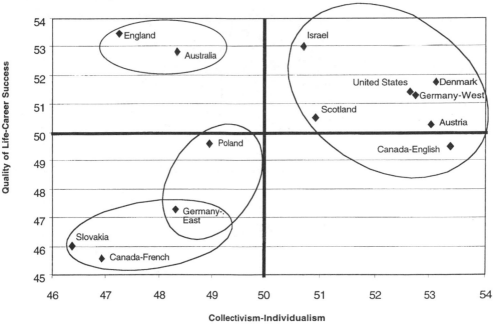

identified with work and career while preferring group-oriented approaches to work.

It is interesting to note that all former East Bloc cultures (Germany-East, Poland, and Slovakia) fall in a quadrant that bears some connection with the idealistic values of the former Communist regimes, that is, collective action and social consciousness (More discussion on this is provided in Chapter 12).

Hofstede (1997) is of the opinion that individualism increases as economic development increases. Similarly, Triandis (1995) believes that individualism increases with increased complexity in society and "looseness" in the norms and sanctions for social behavior and its violations. Certainly the individualistic–career success quadrant in Figure 5.3 is consistent with both of these conceptions. England and Australia provide an exception to the rule. However, with a wider range of cultures, even England and Australia would probably fall on the individualistic side of the comparison.

Power Distance and Uncertainty Avoidance

The final two-by-two comparison is between power distance and uncertainty avoidance. Figure 5.4 indicates that except for Canada-French, which stands alone, and the cluster of Denmark and Israel that spans the power

Figure 5.4
Thirteen-Culture Comparison on Uncertainty Avoidance and Power Distance

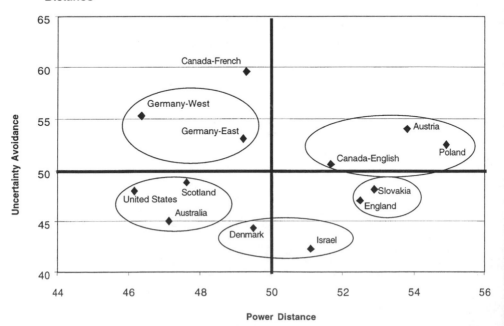

distance mean, the cultures again divide themselves into four clusters roughly representing the four quadrants of the diagram. In the upper right, Austria, Canada-English, and Poland comprise the high power distance–high uncertainty avoidance cluster. This combination might be characterized as both preferring status differences in the work hierarchy and wanting the structure of rules and rituals in order to contain work ambiguities. The low power distance–low uncertainty avoidance cluster of the United States, Scotland, and Australia is in the opposite quadrant. In these cultures equality of status is preferred, and work uncertainties are dealt with more on a case-by-case basis rather than referring to extensive rules and regulations. In the upper-left quadrant, in addition to Canada-French, which is most extreme on uncertainty avoidance, is the high uncertainty avoidance–low power distance cluster of Germany-West and Germany-East. These cultures may be characterized as wanting clear structures and rules to stave off workplace uncertainties while at the same time preferring more egalitarian status differentiations in the work hierarchy. In the lower-right quadrant is the high power distance–low uncertainty avoidance cluster of England and Slovakia. This cluster is likely to prefer clear status differences at work but to dislike extensive, fixed rules and regulations. Denmark and Israel, as a separate cluster, are more balanced in their view of work hierarchy, but clearly prefer to react more spontaneously to events rather than have too many preset procedures in place.

Hofstede (1980) also offered a power distance and uncertainty avoidance comparison (p. 214). Again, the span of cultures in the current study all fell in the lower half of the power distance dimension in Hofstede's sample. Further, cultures in the current study did not extend to the upper reaches of the uncertainty avoidance scale as documented in Hofstede's study. Also, cultures that extended beyond the levels of the current sample on both power distance and uncertainty avoidance were primarily from Asia and South America. Generalization of the current findings should be restricted to the cultures sampled.

MULTIPLE DISCRIMINANT ANALYSIS
OF CULTURAL WORK VALUE DIMENSIONS

Two-by-two comparisons certainly capture more of the complexity of the cultures than does consideration of only one dimension at a time. However, it would be even more enlightening if we could consider all four dimensions at the same time. A statistical method to accomplish this is called multiple discriminant analysis. It is a method that seeks a statistical way to find the greatest separation between cultures while considering all four cultural work value dimensions at once. The resulting discriminating factors usually combine the effects of the original measurement scales by adjusting for possible overlap of the scales. The following section describes such an approach to capture the descriptive power of all four cultural work values.

Figure 5.5 shows the two discriminant functions that were found to account for 83 percent of the variance between the thirteen cultures when all four dimensions were considered at the same time (χ^2 (33) = 144.61, $p <$ 0.0001). Each function combines components of the four cultural work values; therefore, the significant functions will be described by the major work values that contributed to its significance. Once again, clusters were defined by post hoc analysis.

Function 1, accounting for 60 percent of the variance, is related mostly to high uncertainty avoidance and quality of life. On the extreme high end of this function is Canada-French which is different from all other cultures on the two-function interpretation. At the low end (i.e., low uncertainty avoidance and career success) there is a cluster of Israel, Denmark, and Australia. This cluster is not only different from the other cultures on Function 1, but also the grouping represents a unique cluster when Function 1 and Function 2 are considered together.

Function 2, accounting for 23 percent of the variance, is related primarily to low power distance and individualism. On the high end is the single culture of Germany-West and the cluster of the United States and Scotland. At the

Figure 5.5
Two-Function Discriminant Analysis

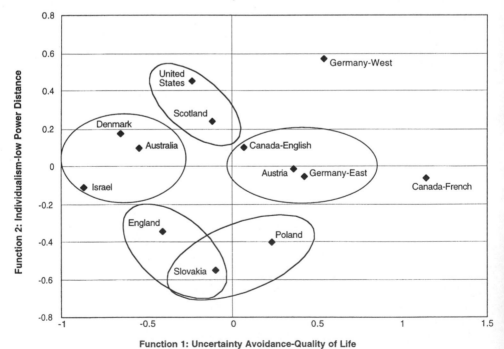

Function 1: Uncertainty Avoidance-Quality of Life

low end (i.e., high power distance and collectivism) is the set of overlapping clusters including Slovakia, England, and Poland.

Another cluster of Canada-English, Austria, and Germany-East occupies the center of the two-factor graph. These cultures show moderate scores on both of the discriminant functions.

Function 1 (Uncertainty Avoidance and Quality of Life) emerged as a result of the significant first-order correlation of these two cultural work value dimensions, as mentioned earlier. Since they were related in this sample, a single, statistically derived scale seemed to account for the majority of the variance in the previously separate scales. The uncertainty avoidance–quality of life function captures a real difference in cultural variation which reflects both a desire to reduce workplace uncertainties and to maintain a balance in the pressures from various aspects of life. In cultures with a higher emphasis on balance in life, it may be logical to presume that methods to reduce workplace ambiguities would be valued as a way to constrain the impact of work on other aspects of life. At the other end of the function, a value of work and career may be seen as focusing a worker's motivations such that rules and structures were not as valued in dealing with work ambiguities since they may detract from job flexibility.

After the variance from Function 1 was accounted for, the low power distance–individualism Function 2 emerged. In cultures with high regard for individual action and responsibility, consultative or collaborative leadership would seem to accent the role of the individual. Rather than waiting for someone in authority to tell them what to do, workers in individualistically oriented cultures would be more likely to use their own initiative. On the other end of the function (high power distance–collectivism), workers with a sense of shared responsibility and group orientation might find it congenial to defer to authority figures rather than taking individual initiative.

Figure 5.5 shows interesting differences and similarities between cultures. The Denmark, Israel, and Australia cluster has one culture from each of three different continents. England was in a different culture than any of the other English-speaking cultures. Of English-speaking cultures, only the United States and Scotland were in the same cluster. No two cultures from the same political nation-state were in the same cluster; that is, Germany-West and Germany-East were significantly different, as were Canada-English and Canada-French and Scotland and England. It seems clear that culture has its own logic and must be considered as unique when considering differences on other variables such as burnout.

CONCLUSIONS

The cultures in the current study differ in meaningful ways. When cultural dimensions are considered singly, in pairs, and with all four dimensions together, significant differences and similarities emerge among the thirteen cultures. The language of Hofstede's (1980) conceptualization of culture can be useful in describing these differences and similarities. In later chapters linkages will be made between cultural work value dimensions and the phenomenon of burnout.

Although the cultures showed substantial variation on the cultural work value dimensions, it is useful to remember that the range of cultures is somewhat restricted. Comparisons to Hofstede's original forty-culture study show that the dimensions can extend well beyond the variability of the current sample. However, if generalizations are confined to the cultures included in this study and comparable cultures, the findings here can extend our understanding of cultural differences and similarities.

CHAPTER 6

Thirteen Cultures of Child and Youth Care: Who They Are and What They Do

Now that we have examined how the thirteen cultures differ on the cultural work values dimensions, it is time to compare the cultures on other factors that may give some understanding of how the cultures conduct their daily business of child and youth care work. Because the sampling method was not random, the results for each culture may not be exactly representative. However, enough points of comparison exist to draw out themes and explore ideas that will help to understand child and youth care work from a more international framework.

To construct an international framework, cross-cultural comparisons will be made on several different categories of information. First, demographic information (e.g., age, gender, education level) will be compared to see if the people working in child and youth care are different across cultures. Second, work-related features of the individual will be explored (e.g., primary job role, hours worked per week). Third, characteristics of child and youth care organizations will be compared (e.g., size of agency, age of clients served). Finally, questions of where and how child and youth care service is provided will give a glimpse into the manner of service delivery (e.g., location, modality). It is hoped that differences and similarities in these variables will help to describe not only general themes of child and youth care work, but also unique cultural contributions. However, be aware that the sample in this study is restricted to mostly North America and Northern Europe. Generalizations about child and youth care drawn from this sample may not extend to cultures in Latin America, Asia, and Africa.

Most of the cross-cultural comparisons are displayed as graphs. Graphs have the advantage of being immediately and visually understandable without the intermediate step of comparing numbers such as those that may be presented in tables. Because the number of respondents is different for each country, the graphs will show percentages of respondents for each culture in the specific categories being discussed. When demographic and other variables in this chapter are correlated with cultural work value variables, the cultural work value scores reflect the means of the separate cultures.

DEMOGRAPHICS

Various demographic factors showed significant differences across the thirteen cultures. Some of these differences showed interesting relationships to cultural factors. When significant difference probabilities are reported, they are based on one-way analysis of variance and the Fisher's PLSD post hoc test.

Age

Figure 6.1 shows percentages of workers in various age categories by culture. A quick glance at the graph shows that there are substantial differences in age of workers by culture ($F(12, 812) = 8.42$, $p < 0.001$). On the young end, Israel, with an average of 29.1 years, was significantly younger than all other cultures ($p < 0.01$). On the old end, Canada-French and the United

Figure 6.1
Age by Culture

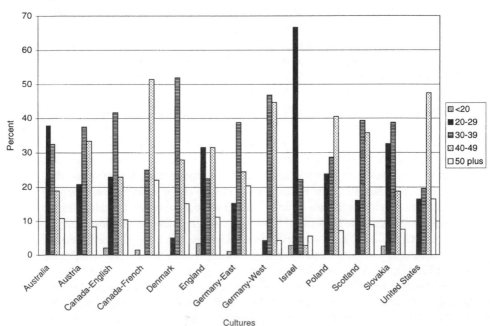

States were significantly older than the other cultures and had a combined average age of 42.3 years ($p < 0.05$). In the middle were two clusters. The mid-young cluster (Slovakia, Australia, England, and Canada-English) had a combined average age of 35.5 years. The mid-old cluster (Austria, Poland, Scotland, Germany-East, Germany-West, and Denmark) had a combined average age of 38.8. As we will see later, average age is related to the number of teachers and managers responding in each culture. The larger proportion of child and youth workers, the younger the average age. A role diversity index was calculated for each culture based on the proportion workers serving different roles. When role diversity and age were correlated, it was found that a culture that provides more different kinds of specialized service roles beyond the entry level position is more likely to have older workers ($r = 0.14$, $p < 0.001$), since entry level child and youth workers have room to move to more specialized jobs while, at the same time, remaining within the field.

Age of workers was significantly positively correlated to uncertainty avoidance ($r = 0.20$, $p < 0.001$) and inversely correlated to power distance ($r = -0.16$, $p < 0.001$). Thus more formal cultures with a higher degree of rules and regulations were more likely to have a larger proportion of older workers, and those cultures who valued status and hierarchy were more likely to have younger workers. Workers in high uncertainty avoidance cultures may have felt less free to shift jobs and careers thus stayed in the field longer. A cultural work value of collaboration and consultation also seemed to help workers stay longer in the field. Those cultures with less structure and more status differential were likely to have younger workers.

Gender

Figure 6.2 shows the proportion of men and women in each culture. Again, significant differences appear ($F(12, 808) = 2.78$, $p < 0.01$). Israel was the only culture with a larger proportion of men than women in child and youth work positions. Several cultures indicated an approximate balance between men and women, with women being slightly more prevalent (England, Canada-French, Scotland, Germany-West, and Germany-East). The largest group of cultures show substantially more women than men in child and youth care positions (the United States, Denmark, Slovakia, Australia, Canada-English, Poland, and Austria). By and large, child and youth care seems to be more of a female profession, similar to other professional fields such as teaching and social work. However, some cultures seem to have achieved a closer balance than others.

Marital Status

Marital status categories by culture showed significant differences ($\chi^2 (60) = 131.76$, $p < 0.001$). For most cultures, the largest proportion of child and

Figure 6.2
Gender by Culture

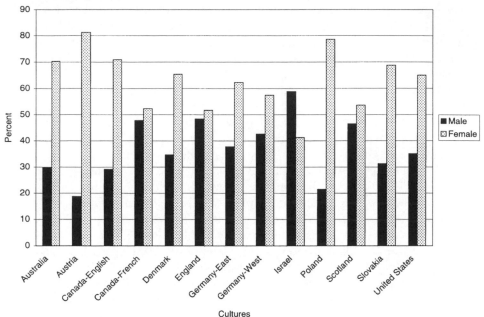

youth care providers are either married or single. For most cultures, married persons outnumber singles, with the exception of Australia and Israel. The divorced category was elevated in Australia, the United States, Slovakia, and Canada-French. The unmarried and living together category was elevated in Denmark, Australia, Canada-French, and Germany-West.

Of the cultural values, only power distance was related to marital status ($F(5,816) = 2.44$, $p < 0.05$). People in the divorced and the unmarried and living together categories came from lower power distance cultures. It is unclear how status and hierarchy preferences relate to marital status, but violations of the traditional married and single statuses might be more allowable in cultures that preferred collaboration rather than large status differences. Low power distance cultures also tend to be less paternalistic.

Number of Children

Across all cultures 48 percent of respondents indicate that they have no children, 25 percent indicate only one child, 26 percent indicate two to three children, and only 2 percent indicate four or more. In ten of the thirteen cultures, the largest proportion of respondents indicate that they have no children. The only exceptions are Denmark and Poland, who indicate the largest proportion of two- to three-children families. The number of children is consistent with the proportion of respondents indicating that they are young and single, with the exception of Denmark which has a larger proportion of unmarried and living together families. As might be expected, age and number of children is significantly correlated ($r = 0.15$, $p < 0.001$). Within certain parameters, it takes time to conceive more children. However, the trend for families in Northern Europe and North America to have small families is illustrated by the results.

There was a slight inverse correlation between number of children and the career success cultural value ($r = -0.08$, $p < 0.05$). Cultures with a stronger value of work and work-related identity tended to have fewer children. However, this was not a dramatic trend.

Level of Education

Figure 6.3 shows the years of formal education of respondents by culture. Because educational systems and requirements are different in the different cultures, large differences exist in years of formal education completed. At first glance, Slovakia has the highest proportion of highly educated workers and Israel the lowest. However, when looking at average education level across cultures, the largest contrast is between Israel (average 12.6 years) and the United States (average 17.1 years). In Israel, many child and youth workers move directly from high school into required military service and directly from that service into child and youth care jobs without an opportunity for advanced education. In the United States, a substantial proportion of workers hold master's degrees (eighteen to nineteen years of formal education), thus raising the average for that culture. In general, former East Bloc countries (Slovakia, Germany-East, and Poland) have higher average education levels than do former European West Bloc countries (Austria, Denmark, Scotland, England). There had been a trend for higher education requirements in the former East Bloc countries. In many countries, the average years of formal education are directly related to education requirements for being employed as a child and youth care worker. In Austria, for example, child and youth care workers cannot get a job in the field until they complete a standard set of courses leading to a specific degree or certification, thus the large spike in the thirteen- to fourteen-year category of years of education for Austria. Also, there was a slight positive correlation between age and education level, with older workers showing slightly higher levels of education than younger workers as might be expected. However, as we shall see, significant exceptions to the general age–education relationship exist.

In terms of cultural work values, a combination of lower power distance and higher quality of life values was related to higher years of formal education ($R^2 = 0.07$, $p < 0.001$). Canada-French and Germany-East epitomize this combination of cultural values; they ranked second and fourth in the years of

Figure 6.3
Years of Formal Education

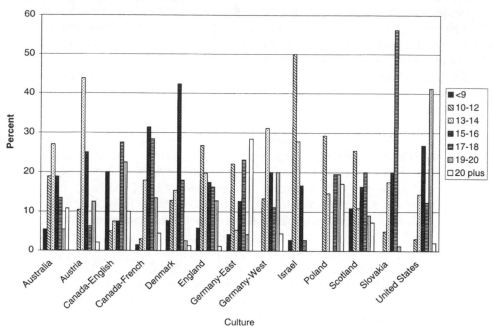

formal education, while England and Israel fall in the opposite quadrant of cultural values and rank twelfth and thirteenth in education. For low power distance cultures, education may be seen as a status equalizer. For high quality of life cultures, spending more time in education may be more likely to take precedence over work than in career success–oriented cultures.

WORK-RELATED FACTORS

Various work-related factors showed significant differences across the thirteen cultures. Some of these differences showed interesting relationships to cultural factors. Again, when significant difference probabilities are reported, these are based on one-way analysis of variance and the Fisher's PLSD post hoc test.

Length of Time in Current Position

The overall average of time child and youth care workers have spent in their current position was approximately 5.5 years. Figure 6.4 shows the tremendous variation around that average ($F(12,811) = 14.77, p < 0.0001$). Please note that the time categories in this figure are not equal, but rather show smaller units (months) at the low end and larger units (years) at the high end. Figure

Figure 6.4
Length of Time in Current Position

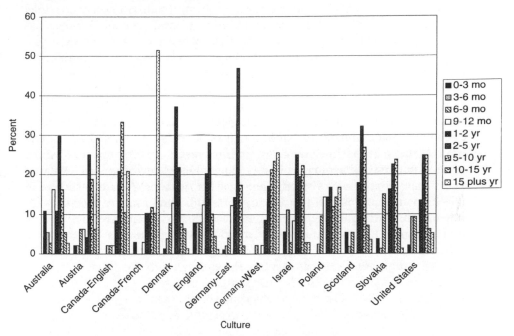

6.4 shows Canada-French having more than half of their workers in their current position for fifteen or more years. On the other extreme, Australia, England, and Slovakia show roughly one-third of their workers in their current position for one year or less. This range may be related to longevity in the child and youth care field, which is examined next, or to opportunities for advancement or changing responsibilities within a culture's child and youth care practice. On average, across cultures there seems to be a bulge of workers serving from two to five years. The five-year mark may be a significant point in career development where position shifts occur (Shirom & Mazeh, 1988). On the other hand, the five- to ten-year category and the fifteen or more year category were also large; overall, roughly 39 percent of workers have stayed in their positions five years or more. Thus it might be said that if workers stay in a position beyond the five-year mark, there is a good chance that they will continue in that position for a long time.

The strongest relationship between length of time in position and cultural work values was with uncertainty avoidance ($r = 0.36$, $p < 0.001$). Workers in high uncertainty avoidance cultures tend to stay longer in their job positions. The formality of the culture and the regulations guiding job changes may be more complex in those cultures. In addition, work changes may be seen as risky and are therefore discouraged.

Length of Time in the Field

Beyond time spent in any one position, it is interesting to observe how long workers remain in the child and youth work field in general. Turnover has been a problem that has plagued the field in the United States (Krueger, Laurerman, Beker, Savicki, Parry, & Powell, 1987). However, Figure 6.5 indicates substantial longevity within the field for certain cultures. Canada-French shows over 70 percent of workers have remained in the field for fifteen or more years. At the other end, Israel shows roughly 33 percent of workers with two or fewer years in the field. Length of time in the field can be influenced by a wide number of factors such as salary, status in the culture, and opportunities for advancement. Another interesting contributor may be the level of uncertainty avoidance in the culture. Uncertainty avoidance showed significant correlations with both length in the field ($r = 0.25$, $p < 0.001$) and length in current position ($r = 0.35$, $p < 0.001$). The formality and strict adherence to role requirements of higher uncertainty avoidance cultures may make it easier to stay and more difficult to switch positions or careers once they have been established. As with length of time in current position, discussed earlier, the five-year mark seems to be critical for longevity in the

Figure 6.5
Length of Time in the Field of Child and Youth Work

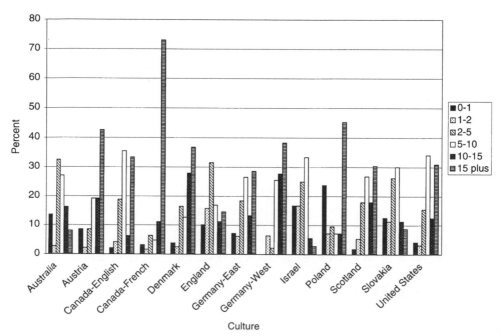

field. Roughly 67 percent of workers overall have stayed five or more years in the field.

The combination of high uncertainty avoidance and individualism was related to length of time in the field ($R^2 = 0.12$, $p < 0.001$). Representative cultures combining these cultural features were Germany-West and Austria which ranked second and third on length in the field, while in the opposite quadrant were Australia, England, and Slovakia, ranking tenth, eleventh, and twelfth, respectively. Within a culture that values structure and order in the workplace, workers were likely to remain longer in the field if their culture also valued individual expression and aspiration. It may be that career paths were more clearly defined and expectations for advancement more clearly stated in such cultures. Thus, the avenues to future jobs within the field were less ambiguous for those striving to express their individual achievement.

Primary Job Role

Figure 6.6 illustrates both similarities and contrasts in primary job role distribution across cultures. On average, over 50 percent of respondents were child and youth care workers engaged in daily contact with children and youth

Figure 6.6
Primary Job Role by Culture

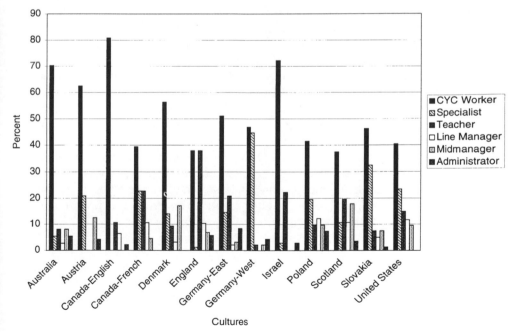

in their living units. Teachers (14%) and specialists (16%) made up the rest of the direct care staff. Specialists might hold a variety of positions such as family worker, drug and alcohol counselor, or community liaison. Line managers (direct supervisors) (6%), midmanagers (8%), and administrators (3%) made up the rest of the job role spectrum. Figure 6.6 shows interesting deviations from the overall averages. Australia, Austria, Canada-English, Denmark, and Israel all show larger percentages of child and youth care workers. Austria, Canada-French, Germany-West, Slovakia, and the United States show more than 20 percent of specialists. This percentage may represent a variety of positions available for job advancement and diversification. England shows the largest proportion of teachers, followed by Canada-French, Germany-East, and Israel. To some degree, the proportion of teachers may reflect the structure and funding of child and youth care practice in the cultures.

To probe the effects of role diversity a bit more carefully, a role diversity index was calculated by comparing the percentages of workers employed in roles of specialist, teacher, line manager, midmanager, and administrator to the percentage of child and youth care workers. That is, the index was the sum of the ratios of the percentage of child and youth care workers in the denominator and other job categories in the numerator. This single number captured the complexity of role structures in each culture. Scotland, England, Canada-French, and the United States showed the highest level of workers in diverse roles, while Canada-English, Israel, and Australia showed the lowest level of workers in diverse roles. Role diversity was modestly related to a number of demographic and work related variables. As mentioned earlier, cultures with higher role diversity had more older workers ($r = 0.16$, $p < 0.001$). Role diversity was also related to higher proportions of males versus females ($r = -0.12$, $p < 0.01$), and longer time in the child and youth work field ($r = 0.09$, $p < 0.05$), but not time in the current position. It was also related to higher salary ($r = 0.21$, $p < 0.001$) and less work done in the milieu ($r = -0.10$, $p < 0.05$). All these relationships support the hypothesis that workers who have an opportunity to move into different roles within the field of child and youth work were more likely to reap the benefits and thus remain longer in the field.

Role diversity was slightly related to higher uncertainty avoidance and higher collectivism. This relationship was somewhat complicated and was probably anchored by Canada-French on one end and Israel on the other. It was not clear how these cultural factors related to role diversity. Further investigation should be done following this work-related factor.

Number of Employees Supervised

There is a strong positive correlation between primary job role and number of employees supervised ($r = 0.56$, $p < 0.001$). It is logical that as workers move away from 100 percent direct care responsibilities, they would assume duties to consult with and oversee the work of others. Line managers, midmanagers, and administrators shoulder more responsibility to direct and evaluate the work of others. Even more interesting is the finding that 21 percent of workers who identify their primary job title as child and youth care worker also indicate that they supervise others. There is a moderate correlation of age to number of employees supervised ($r = 0.12$, $p < 0.001$), indicating that older, experienced workers may be called upon to supervise the work of others even though their primary duties focus on providing direct care for children and youth.

Hours per Week Worked

In most cultures, child and youth practitioners work between thirty and forty hours per week. Exceptions to this norm in Israel, Austria, and Slovakia where the larger proportion of workers spend forty to fifty hours at work. In Israel, the structure of the work setting contributes to longer working hours, since the child and youth workers reside in the same facilities in which they work. Under such circumstances it is difficult to draw a strict boundary between on-duty and off-duty hours. Therefore, it is quite usual for workers to be called upon even when they are not supposed to be working. In Austria, the situation is a bit different in that the law requires one worker be present for every four children. However, there are no funds to hire replacements for sick or vacationing workers; therefore, workers put in overtime to cover for absent colleagues, resulting in a longer-than-average workweek. In addition, a modest correlation exists between hours per week worked and the cultural work value of career success ($r = 0.13$, $p < 0.001$). This relationship suggests that cultures that emphasize job and career will create the circumstances for longer working hours and that workers will be more willing to fill those extra hours.

ORGANIZATIONAL FACTORS

Various work organizational factors showed significant differences across the thirteen cultures. Some of these differences showed interesting relationships to cultural factors. Again, when significant difference probabilities are reported, these are based on one-way analysis of variance and the Fisher's PLSD post hoc test.

Size of Agency

Figure 6.7 shows the range of agency sizes by culture. The average number of children or adolescents in treatment facilities varies quite widely. On the high side, Poland averages eighty-five clients per agency. On the low side, Denmark averages twenty-two clients per agency. The size of the primary

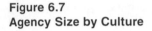

Figure 6.7
Agency Size by Culture

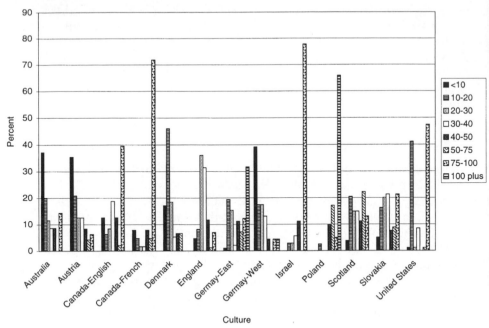

unit for children may vary even within larger overall agencies. In Israel and the United States, for example, larger overall units (e.g., children's villages) are subdivided into cottages with smaller numbers of children in each. In Poland and Canada-French, however, larger units are the norm with subdivisions less isolated from the larger mass of clients. In most cultures, the trend seems to be moving toward smaller units.

Gender of Clients

Except for rare exceptions, most child and youth care agencies across the thirteen cultures serve both boys and girls. Only in Scotland are their more male-only agencies, and only in Canada-English are there a substantial portion of agencies serving girls only. For the most part, mixed-gender treatment facilities are the norm, even if separate units within the agencies focus only on boys or girls.

Age of Clients

For the most part, across the thirteen cultures adolescents (ages 13–25) comprise a larger proportion of clients (64%) than do children (ages 3–12)

(36%). Notable exceptions are Austria, Israel, and the United States where the reverse is true. These exceptions stem from specific circumstances, such as the laws and regulations governing treatment of children in Israel and special funding opportunities in the United States.

PROVISION OF CHILD AND YOUTH CARE SERVICE

Both specific types of child and youth care work practice and their location of delivery showed significant differences across the thirteen cultures. Some of these differences showed interesting relationships to cultural factors.

Location of Service

Figure 6.8 shows the responses to a series of questions concerning where child and youth care providers delivered their care or service. Respondents were to take 100 percent of their work time and divide it across locations of milieu, individual meetings, school, home, and community in a pattern that reflected how much time they spent working in each location. The results show remarkable similarities across cultures. For the most part, the most common workplace was the child's daily living space in the agency (45%), fol-

Figure 6.8
Location of Service by Culture

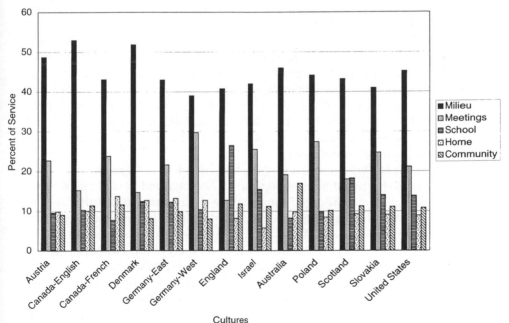

lowed by client meetings in the agency (21%), schools (13%), the community (11%), and client's homes (10%). Such a distribution reflects typical day and residential treatment service arrangements. Proportions of employees in different job roles also reflect the overall purpose of child and youth care agencies to care for children and youth away from their homes.

However, Figure 6.8 also shows interesting differences. These differences seem to reflect different program emphases that may exist in the different cultures. Caution must be taken to avoid overinterpreting these differences, since the organizations sampled for each culture may not necessarily have been representative of child and youth care practice in the culture as a whole.

For the milieu, Canada-English, Denmark, and Austria showed the highest percentage of work done in the child or adolescent's daily living environment within the agency or program. At the other end of the spectrum, Germany-West, England, and Slovakia show the lowest percentage of work done in the milieu. Because the percentages assigned to the various service locations are interrelated, as percentage of work done in one location goes up, percentage of work done in others go down. As we will see, Germany-West apportions more time to meetings, England to school, and Slovakia more evenly to both meetings and school. Such choices of where to provide service probably reflects specific treatment philosophies, personnel patterns, and funding requirements.

For individual, group, or family meetings within the agency, Germany-West and Poland rank highest, and Canada-English, Denmark, and England rank lowest. Clearly in Canada-English, Denmark, and Germany-West, there was a trade-off between milieu and meeting service delivery locations.

For the school location, England's percentage was significantly higher than all other cultures, although Scotland and Israel also showed high activity in this location. On the low percentage end were Canada-French and Australia. The major agencies participating in this research from England had a treatment program that emphasized academic activities by certified teachers. For the most part, these classrooms were within the agency grounds and treatment was integrated with academics in that location. Thus, England's high percentage of service in the school may reflect both a philosophy of care and a manner of service delivery which chose to identify with education rather than child care or mental health.

For visits to the homes of clients, Canada-French, Germany-East, and Germany-West ranked highest, and Israel, England, and Poland ranked lowest. Although some child and youth care workers reported that they met in clients' homes, the major job role associated with this location was specialists. Just as teachers were more likely to report working in schools, specialists were likely to report visiting clients' homes. Thus a variety of roles within an agency was likely to be associated with service spanning several locations.

Finally, for work in the community, Australia ranked significantly higher than all other cultures, with Germany-West, Denmark, Austria, and Germany-East ranking lowest. In most cases, midmanagers and administrators were most likely to be involved in community-based activities. However, some child and youth care workers also reported working in the community. This was especially true for Australia where organizational structures emphasizing collective, consultative leadership allowed more individuals to take on differing tasks. Therefore, a larger percentage of workers made community contacts despite not having a specific role assigned for that duty.

Clearly, child and youth care practice can occur at many locations. In general, the emphasis was on care in the child's living milieu within a day or residential agency. Beyond the milieu, agencies could emphasize one location over another (e.g., meetings for Germany-West, school for England, home for Canada-French, and community for Australia). In other cultures, for example Slovakia and Germany-East, a balanced approach to service beyond the milieu occurred. For most cultures, it is clear that child and youth care is no longer confined by the walls of the agency. However, much can yet be done to extend child and youth care to other venues.

Mode of Service

The modality of service results in Figure 6.9 follows a format similar to location of service. That is, respondents were to take 100 percent of their

Figure 6.9
Type of Service by Culture

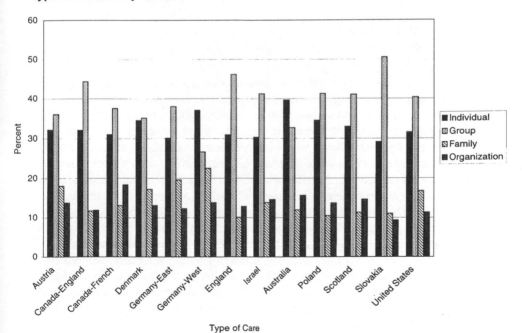

Type of Care

work time and divide it across modalities of client contact or treatment (one-to-one individual contact, group work, family work, or contact with organizations) in a pattern that reflected how much time they spent using each service mode. The results show remarkable similarities across cultures. Across all cultures, group contact was the most common modality (39%), followed by individual (33%), family (14%), and organization (13%). Clearly dealing with groups of children and youth in the milieu ranked highest. However, it is also clear that one-to-one contact was not the sole preserve of specialists. Child and youth care workers also used this modality substantially.

For the group modality, Slovakia and England ranked significantly higher than all other cultures in the percentage of time devoted to this mode. Germany-West, Australia, and Denmark ranked lowest. For Slovakia, group practice was based in the agency milieu, but for England a large proportion was based in the classroom. As with location of service, modalities of treatment vary in relation with one another. Germany-West, Australia, and Denmark emphasized other modalities and thus showed lower percentages of group work.

For the individual modality, Australia, Germany-West, Poland, and Denmark showed the largest proportion of this mode. Slovakia, Germany-East, and Israel showed the lowest. The emphasis on one-to-one contacts may reflect a philosophy of care, a response to funding requirements, or an evaluation of the needs of clients. In Germany-West staffing patterns indicate a high proportion of specialists who were more likely to use the individual contact modality. In Slovakia, a high proportion of specialists also existed, but their emphasis was on group work. In Australia, however, the proportion of specialists was low while individual contact was high. Child and youth care workers in Australia employed individual contact more than did child and youth care workers in other cultures since the treatment philosophy in some of their facilities deemphasized group work.

For the family work modality, Germany-West, Germany-East, and Austria showed the highest proportions of work done with families. England, Poland, Slovakia, and Scotland showed the lowest. Overall, there is a sharp dropoff of percentage of service delivered to families, from 39 percent for groups and 33 percent for individuals to 14 percent for families. To some degree this lower level of family work reflects the fact that most of the children and adolescents served were in care away from home. The main business of day and residential treatment is dealing with the people present: the children and youth. On the other hand, a reduction of service to families by almost two thirds from group work may reflect a treatment philosophy that views parents and families as both complicated to deal with and somehow adversarial.

For the organizational modality, Canada-French, Australia, and Scotland ranked highest in proportion of this modality. Slovakia, the United States, and Canada-England ranked lowest. Child and youth care service has broadened to many different sites. It is no longer restricted to the bricks and mortar of the child and youth care agency.

CONCLUSION

This brief snapshot of the people, places, and practices of child and youth care work shows that there were both remarkable similarities and remarkable differences between the thirteen cultures on who child and youth care workers were, how they organized their work, and how their agencies were structured. The primary objective of providing care for children and youth away from home was fulfilled, although variations in style and manner of fulfillment related to cultural work value dimensions.

CULTURE AND THE
DETERMINANTS OF BURNOUT

Part III is the heart of the research upon which this book is based. This part includes a pan-cultural analysis of aspects of burnout and also a configural analysis that attempts to consolidate findings about burnout. Both the pan-cultural and configural analyses will relate aspects of burnout to the work environment, working conditions, demographic characteristics, and personal styles of coping with stress.

Chapter 7, "The Impact of Environment, Coping, and Culture on Burnout," examines each scale of the Maslach Burnout Inventory with regard to its contributors. This is a pan-cultural analysis in which all cultures are considered together in attempt to find overarching themes. The categories of contributors to burnout considered include work environment, coping styles, cultural conformity, and general cultural work values. In addition, various demographic and work-related variables are considered. The idea is to find which package of precursors to burnout combine to relate to higher or lower levels of emotional exhaustion, depersonalization, and personal accomplishment. On the basis of the statistical analysis, themes are suggested that may relate to burnout regardless of the culture considered. These generalizations are further tested in Chapter 8.

Chapter 8, "Burnout Configurations," goes beyond the analysis of single burnout scales to propose a single measure of high and low burnout. The configuration of higher than average emotional exhaustion, higher-than-average depersonalization, and lower-than-average personal accomplishment form the high burnout configuration. The low burnout configuration consists of lower-than-average emotional exhaustion, lower-than-average depersonalization, and higher-than-average personal accomplishment. Although some fineness of analysis is lost through this configuration analysis, broader generalizations can be made about the extremes of burnout. Definitive patterns of contributors to burnout show a strong discrimination between the high and low configurations. These themes seem to echo and expand the patterns developed in Chapter 7.

The goal of these pan-cultural analyses is to find general themes concerning burnout and its precursors that span different cultures to form widely applicable themes.

Pan-Cultural Analysis of the Impact of Environment, Coping, and Culture on Burnout

This chapter will consider the generalizability of findings concerning the relationship of burnout to work environment and coping styles. Lee and Ashforth's (1996) meta-analysis of burnout research contained studies predominantly from the United States. In that statistical overview of burnout research, strong relationships did emerge (see Chapter 2 for a more extensive review). For the current study, two questions of generalizability and extension are relevant. First, are the patterns of relationship of burnout to work environment and coping found in the United States replicated across cultures? Second, do cultural dimensions contribute to those patterns? A pan-cultural analysis focused on the three burnout subscales will attempt to answer these questions.

In theory, culture provides another layer of environmental influence at a more general level. Work environment is clearly the proximal environmental condition for burnout, while cultural is more distal. For the purposes of analysis, the effects of culture as an environmental variable can be construed to impact all members of the culture relatively equally. In the current analysis, the influence of the cultural environment will be operationalized as the average score on cultural work values for each culture; that is, each member of a culture has an identical score. Even though cultural influence may be general, theorists have also suggested that individuals internalize cultural influence as a "structure of habits" (Triandis, 1995) and as mental programs or "software of the mind" (Hofstede, 1997). Thus, culture may be carried as a personal variable used in the cognitive appraisal and coping processes described by Lazarus (1999). For the purposes of analysis, the effects of culture as a personal mental program will be different for each individual depending on the level of conformity with or deviance from the overall cultural norm of his or her culture. In the current analysis, the influence of individual conformity to cultural norms will be operationalized as the deviation of the individual's response from the average of the culture to which the person belongs. Less deviation is indicative of higher cultural conformity.

No matter how its influence is conceptualized, if cultures differ in significant ways, one can conjecture that those differences may affect burnout. In this analysis the impact of culture will be represented both by the impact of general culture as an environmental variable and by the individual's subscription to cultural work as an internalized representation of the culture. Thus, the first research question is, "Does culture relate to burnout in child and youth care workers?" The second research question is, "How does culture impact the patterns of work environment and coping that are related to burnout?"

CROSS-CULTURAL DIFFERENCES IN BURNOUT

As in Chapter 5, the cultures represented in this study do indeed differ significantly on the four cultural work value dimensions. The logical next step in considering the impact of culture on burnout is to determine whether the thirteen cultures in this study differ on burnout as well. If they do not differ on burnout, then cultural work value differences are not relevant to this affective reaction to work. As Figure 7.1 illustrates, the overall levels of burnout for the thirteen cultures differed significantly ($F(36,2433) = 5.73$, $p < 0.001$). Levels of separate emotional exhaustion, depersonalization, and personal accomplishment subscales for each of the thirteen cultures can be seen as patterns indicating the overall intensity of burnout. Higher emotional exhaustion and depersonalization and lower personal accomplishment are indicative of greater overall burnout and vice versa. In this graph, by using z-scores, the pan-cultural mean was set to zero so that bars extending to the right of the midline indicate scores higher than the mean, and bars extending to the left of the midline indicate scores lower than the mean.

An analysis of burnout subscale scores by culture indicates substantial differences between them. Differences for each subscale reach the 0.001 level of statistical significance. At the extremes, for emotional exhaustion the United States was highest and Denmark lowest. For depersonalization Germany-West was highest, and Israel was lowest. For personal accomplishment the United States was highest, and Slovakia was lowest.

Figure 7.1 shows dramatic differences in the patterns of burnout subscales between cultures. For example, the United States, England, and Australia show all three subscales above the mean, while Slovakia and Germany-East show them all below the mean. Scotland, Israel, Denmark, Canada-English, and Canada-French show an overall configuration of subscale scores indicating lower burnout (i.e., low emotional exhaustion, low depersonalization, and

Figure 7.1
Emotional Exhaustion, Depersonalization, and Personal Accomplishment
Scores for Thirteen Cultures

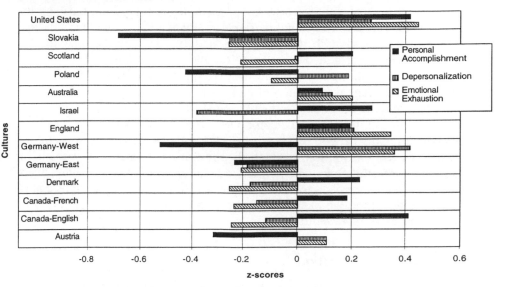

high personal accomplishment). In contrast, Germany-West and Austria show the reverse configuration indicating higher overall burnout. When considering this figure, it is important to recognize that there is no absolute level of subscale scores which indicates that the condition of burnout has been reached. Further, the figure displays an analysis in which the cultures are compared to each other. With more or fewer cultures or with a different set of cultures the comparison mean for each subscale would be different. Therefore, consider these results with some caution.

With the finding of significant differences across cultures in burnout, we can now address the question of the impact of the cultural variables.

PAN-CULTURAL ANALYSIS OF BURNOUT SUBSCALES

In the following sections each burnout subscale will be considered separately. As the manual for the Maslach Burnout Inventory suggests, each subscale has a unique contribution to make in understanding the general concept of burnout (Maslach, Jackson, & Leiter, 1996). Although some previous research has attempted to derive a single burnout score from the three subscales (Wright & Bonett, 1997), the current analysis follows the majority of burnout research and considers them separately (Lee & Ashforth, 1990).

In order to test for the contributions to burnout of work environment, coping styles, and culture, a specific statistical method called hierarchical multiple regression was used. In this method, variables of interest were added in clusters to test their contributions to explaining the burnout subscales, each cluster building on the explanatory power of the previous cluster. Specifically, work environment factors were added in the first step since the majority of previous research has found work environmental factors to have substantial explanatory strength (Maslach & Schaufeli, 1993). In the second step, coping styles were added in order to test the contribution of this personal variable in explaining the burnout subscales. In step three, individual conformity to the average work values of participant's culture was added. Finally in step four, culture as an environmental variable was added by using the averages for each culture as an indicator. Only after the explanatory power of the proximal factors of work environment and coping was assessed was culture tested for its contribution, through the addition of the personal variable of cultural conformity and the environmental variable of cultural norms. This is a conservative approach to testing the impact of culture, yet it seems called for since the other two factors have already been shown to have an impact in research based in the United States.

Emotional Exhaustion

Table 7.1 shows the hierarchical regression for emotional exhaustion with work environment, coping, and cultural work values. At step one, work environmental factors show a significant relationship with emotional exhaustion ($F(7,811) = 20.65$, $p < 0.001$). Higher work pressure combines with lower supervisor support and lower innovation to account for this significant relationship. Thus, spanning all thirteen cultures, considering work environment alone, a work situation with a high work load, an unsupportive immediate manager, and an atmosphere in which new ideas and practices are restricted sets the stage for feelings of emotional fatigue.

In step two, coping styles are added to the model in order to show which coping styles combined with environmental factors account for the variance in emotional exhaustion. Step two is also statistically significant ($F(9,809) = 24.58$, $p < 0.001$) with higher escape coping showing a significant contribution. That is, given the work environment conditions mentioned in the previous paragraph, workers showing increased attempts at reducing the unpleasant feelings associated with stress are more likely to experience emotional fatigue.

In step three, personal conformity to cultural work values is added to the work environment and coping variables to test whether or not deviation from cultural norms adds to the explanation of emotional exhaustion when the other variables are already accounted for. Again the result is statistically significant ($F(13,805) = 17.96$, $p < 0.001$). Individual deviation above the cultural work value of uncertainty avoidance contributed significantly to the model. Thus, given these work environment and coping results, individuals who in their culture showed a higher than average value for reducing workplace ambiguity and uncertainty by means of rules and rituals show higher emotional exhaustion.

Finally, in step four the environmental impact of cultural work values are added to the previous variables to test whether general cultural work value norms increases the explanation of emotional exhaustion when the other variables are already accounted for. Again the result is statistically significant ($F(17,801) = 15.73$, $p < 0.001$). When adding the influence of cultural work value norms to the model, cultures who show higher values for career success over quality of life had higher emotional exhaustion.

As indicated by the schematic representation below, when taken all together, emotional exhaustion (EE) was related to work environments with high pressure to work (WP), low support from bosses (SS), and low encouragement for changes and new ideas (INN); to dealing with stress by trying to reduce only its unpleasant side effects (escape coping); to an above-average work value of avoiding ambiguity and uncertainty (UA deviation); and to a general cultural norm that emphasizes work and career above other aspects of life (career success).

$$EE = \uparrow WP + \downarrow SS + \downarrow INN + \uparrow escape\ coping + \uparrow UA\ deviation + \uparrow career\ success$$

With regard to the question of generalizability of findings raised in the beginning of this chapter, it is clear that the patterns of work environment and coping do correspond with those specified in Lee and Ashforth's (1996) meta-analysis. Higher pressure to work shows the strongest relationship to emotional exhaustion in both studies. Lower supervisor support and lower innovation both load in the same direction. Also, results for escape coping are consistent with other research (Leiter, 1991; Riolli-Saltzman & Savicki, 2001a, 2001b); higher escape coping relates to emotional exhaustion. It seems that many findings regarding the relationship of work environment and coping can be generalized though the current pan-cultural analysis.

From a personal point of view, worker deviation from the uncertainty avoidance norms of their culture showed higher or lower emotional exhaustion depending on the direction of the deviation. The relationship of uncertainty avoidance and emotional exhaustion seems meaningful from two separate viewpoints. First, Hofstede (1980) indicates that in cultures high on uncertainty avoidance, individuals are likely to have a higher level of anxiety in general and higher job stress in particular (p. 132). Thus, individuals subscribing to high uncertainty avoidance may be more prone to stress, even though they attempt to reduce that stress through rules and other structural or procedural methods aimed at avoiding stress. The higher level of escape coping related to emotional exhaustion may be another demonstration of a higher base anxiety level. Second, Hofstede articulates the difference between good rules and bad rules as attempts to deal with ambiguity (p. 115). Although rules and standard operating procedures can relieve workers from anxiety-provoking decisions, they also can take on a life of their own and create additional anxiety when they restrict flexibility and inhibit innovative responses. Cherniss (1995) cites difficulties with bureaucratic restrictions as a major stressor for his sample. The perception of a lower level of innovation associated with emotional exhaustion may coincide with the restrictive effects of subscription to higher than normal uncertainty avoidance. Hofstede notes that fear of failure, lower risk taking, and intolerance for rule breaking are characteristics of high uncertainty avoidance cultures. These features seem consistent with the perception of lower support for innovation in the work environment.

Finally, culture as a more generalized environmental influence shows a strong relationship with emotional exhaustion through the work value of career success. All the variables mentioned may be intensified in an atmosphere in which work is a major source for self-identity and self-realization. Hofstede (1980) indicates that higher career success cultures emphasize greater work centrality, higher achievement motivation, and achievement defined in terms of recognition; additionally, they experience higher job stress (p. 200). In contrast, emphasis on quality of life relates to lower emotional exhaustion. Such a work value may dampen work-related stressors by construing work as less central to people's lives (p. 20). Workers may focus less on the products and outcomes of employment than on the processes and relationships both at work and elsewhere.

Depersonalization

Table 7.1 shows the hierarchical regression for depersonalization with work environment, coping, and cultural work values. At step one, work environmental factors show a significant relationship with depersonalization ($F(7,811)$ = 7.03 $p < 0.001$). Higher work pressure combines with lower supervisor support and lower task orientation to account for this significant relationship. Thus, spanning all thirteen cultures, considering work environment alone, a work situation with a high work load, an unsupportive immediate manager, and an atmosphere in which work is not efficiently organized sets the stage for feelings of emotional separation and distance from clients.

In step two, coping styles are added to the model in order to show which coping styles combined with environmental factors account for the variance in depersonalization. Step two is also statistically significant ($F(9,809) = 15.29$, $p < 0.001$) with higher escape coping showing a significant contribution. That is, given the work environment conditions mentioned in the previous paragraph, workers showing increased attempts at reducing the unpleasant feelings associated with stress are more likely to close off emotional contact.

In step three, personal conformity to cultural work values is added to work environment and coping variables to test whether deviation from cultural norms adds to the explanation of depersonalization when the other variables are

Table 7.1
Hierarchical Multiple Regression of Emotional Exhaustion, Depersonalization, and Personal Accomplishment with Work Environment, Coping, and Cultural Work Values

Variables	Emotional exhaustion	Depersonalization	Personal accomplishment
Step 1: Work environment	$R^2 = .151$	$R^2 = .057$	$R^2 = .065$
	$F(7,811) = 20.65{*}{*}{*}$	$F(7,811) = 7.03{*}{*}{*}$	$F(7,811) = 7.72{*}{*}{*}$
Peer cohesion	$\beta = -.036$	$\beta = -.033$	$\beta = .088{*}$
Supervisor support	$\beta = -.102{*}$	$\beta = -.104{*}$	$\beta = .001$
Autonomy	$\beta = .049$	$\beta = .054$	$\beta = .036$
Task orientation	$\beta = -.060$	$\beta = -.117{*}{*}$	$\beta = .051$
Work pressure	$\beta = .312{*}{*}{*}$	$\beta = .109{*}{*}$	$\beta = .023$
Control	$\beta = .029$	$\beta = .007$	$\beta = .071$
Innovation	$\beta = -.084{*}$	$\beta = -.520$	$\beta = .138{*}{*}$
Step 2: Coping style	$R^2 = .215$	$R^2 = .145$	$R^2 = .208$
	$F(9,809) = 24.58{*}{*}{*}$	$F(9,809) = 15.29{*}{*}{*}$	$F(9,809) = 23.67{*}{*}{*}$
Control coping	$\beta = -.019$	$\beta = -.057$	$\beta = .403{*}{*}{*}$
Escape coping	$\beta = .259{*}{*}{*}$	$\beta = .311{*}{*}{*}$	$\beta = .017$
Step 3: Cultural conformity	$R^2 = .225$	$R^2 = .156$	$R^2 = .215$
	$F(13,805) = 17.96{*}{*}{*}$	$F(13,805) = 11.24{*}{*}{*}$	$F(13,805) = 16.93{*}{*}{*}$
Power distance	$\beta = -.009$	$\beta = -.058$	$\beta = .007$
Uncertainty avoidance	$\beta = .099{*}{*}$	$\beta = .063{*}$	$\beta = -.011$
Individualism	$\beta = -.018$	$\beta = -.020$	$\beta = .081{*}{*}$
Career success	$\beta = .020$	$\beta = .049$	$\beta = -.009$
Step 4: Culture as environment	$R^2 = .250$	$R^2 = .173$	$R^2 = .226$
	$F(17,801) = 15.73{*}{*}{*}$	$F(17,801) = 9.85{*}{*}{*}$	$F(17,801) = 13.76{*}{*}{*}$
Power distance	$\beta = -.601$	$\beta = -.045$	$\beta = -.068{*}$
Uncertainty avoidance	$\beta = .052$	$\beta = .074$	$\beta = -.035$
Individualism	$\beta = -.039$	$\beta = .001$	$\beta = .061$
Career success	$\beta = .195{*}{*}{*}$	$\beta = .165{*}{*}{*}$	$\beta = -.005$

$*p < 0.05$; $**p < 0.01$; $***p < 0.001$

already accounted for. Again the result is statistically significant ($F(13,805)$ = 11.24, $p < 0.001$). The cultural work value of higher uncertainty avoidance again contributes significantly. Individual deviation above average for the culture on uncertainty avoidance contributed significantly to the model. Thus, given these work environment and coping results, individuals who in their culture showed a higher than normal value for reducing workplace ambiguity and uncertainty by means of rules and rituals showed higher depersonalization.

Finally, in step four the environmental impact of cultural work values are added to the previous variables to test whether general cultural work value norms adds to the explanation of depersonalization when the other variables are already accounted for. Again the result is statistically significant ($F(17,801)$ = 9.85, $p < 0.001$). When adding the influence of cultural work value norm to the model, cultures who show higher values for career success over quality of life had higher depersonalization.

As indicated by the following schematic representation, when taken all together, depersonalization (DP) was related to work environments with high pressure to work (WP), low support from managers (SS), and inefficient, disorganized work structure (TO); to dealing with stress by trying to reduce only its unpleasant side effects (escape coping); to higher-than-average sub-scription to the cultural value of avoiding or reducing work ambiguity through rules (UA deviation); and to a generalized cultural value of work and career above a more balanced approach to life (career success).

DP = ↑ WP + ↓ SS + ↓ TO + ↑ escape coping + ↑ UA deviation + ↑ career success

With regard to the question of generalizability of findings raised in the beginning of this chapter, it is clear that the patterns of work environment and coping do correspond with those specified in Lee and Ashforth's (1996) meta-analysis. Again, higher pressure to work shows a strong relationship to depersonalization in both studies. Lower supervisor support and lower task orientation both load in the same direction. Lower task orientation is represented by role ambiguity and role conflict in the Lee and Ashforth study. Also, results for escape coping are consistent with other research (Leiter, 1991; Riolli-Saltzman & Savicki, 2001b, 2001c); higher escape coping relates to depersonalization. For depersonalization also, culture appears to have a significant impact.

From a personal point of view, workers who valued higher than average uncertainty avoidance showed a greater tendency to withdraw emotionally than did those with lower than average uncertainty avoidance. This deviation from the norm probably works together with the work environmental condition of lower task orientation. That is, workers who work in somewhat chaotic or unpredictable settings and at the same time value structure to control their anxiety seem more prone to insulate themselves from the resulting conflict between environment and their value by building emotional barriers between themselves and their clients.

With regard to the question of the impact of culture as an environmental factor, the value of higher career success enhanced the explanation of depersonalization. The impact of an emphasis on one's career over a more balanced quality of life seems fairly straightforward. As Hofstede (1980) indicates high career success cultures emphasize the achievement ideal in which people "live to work" rather than "work to live" (p. 205) Without balance in one's life, a worker can narrow his or her focus of attention in a way that excludes personal contact with others, especially clients. Particularly under conditions of high workload and chaotic work organization, a worker focused primarily on career success may find it difficult to attain such success. Reducing emotional availability may be perceived as a way of streamlining work responses. Paradoxically, it may result in precisely the opposite outcome.

Personal Accomplishment

Table 7.1 shows the hierarchical regression for personal accomplishment (PA) with work environment, coping, and cultural work values. At step one, work environmental factors show a significant relationship with personal accomplishment ($F(7,811) = 7.72, p < 0.001$). Higher innovation and peer cohesion combine to account for this significant relationship. Thus, spanning all thirteen cultures, considering work environment alone, a work situation with support and encouragement for new ideas and practices and in which there is a supportive team or set of coworkers is related to feelings of goal attainment at work.

In step two, coping styles are added to the model in order to show which coping styles combined with environmental factors account for the variance in personal accomplishment. Step two is also statistically significant ($F(9,809) = 23.67, p < 0.001$) with higher control coping showing a significant contribution. That is, given the work environment conditions mentioned in the previous paragraph, workers showing increased attempts at directing efforts to reduce the source of stress itself showed a higher sense of achievement and goal attainment.

In step three, personal conformity to cultural work values is added to the previous variables to test whether deviation from cultural norms adds to the explanation of personal accomplishment when the other variables are already accounted for. Again the result is statistically significant ($F(13,805) = 16.93, p < 0.001$). The cultural work value of higher individualism (IND) contributes significantly to the model. Thus, given these environmental and coping results, individuals within a culture who more highly value the importance of self and individual action also show higher personal accomplishment.

Finally, in step four the environmental impact of cultural work values are added to the previous variables to test whether general cultural work value norms adds to the explanation of personal accomplishment when the other variables are already accounted for. Again the result is statistically significant ($F(17,801) = 13.76, p < 0.001$). When adding the influence of cultural work value norm to the model, cultures that show lower values for power distance had higher personal accomplishment.

As indicated by the schematic representation below, when taken all together, personal accomplishment (PA) was related to work environments with high cohesion and teamwork with one's coworkers (PC) and an atmosphere that encourages new ideas (INN); to dealing with stress by taking direct action to reduce the source of stress (control coping); to a higher-than-average work value of emphasizing individual, independent behavior over concerns for collective action (IND deviation); and to a general cultural value that favors equity and approachability between workers and managers (PD).

$$PA = \uparrow PC + \uparrow INN + \uparrow \text{control coping} + \uparrow IND \text{ deviation} + \downarrow \text{power distance}$$

Several areas of research indicate generalizability of findings. Social support from one's coworkers shows a relationship to personal accomplishment (Lee & Ashforth, 1996). Job design theory (Hackman & Oldham, 1980) suggests that innovation results from a well-organized work environment. Also, results for control coping are consistent with other research (Leiter, 1991; Riolli-Saltzman & Savicki, 2001b); higher control coping relates to personal accomplishment. For personal accomplishment, culture also appears to have a significant impact.

Deviation from the cultural work value of higher individualism enhanced the explanation of personal accomplishment beyond coping and factors in the immediate work environment. It is easy to see how innovation might be supported by an individualist orientation. Hofstede (1980) suggests that high individualism emphasizes "freedom and challenge" in one's work; likewise, "individual initiative is socially encouraged" (p. 166). In addition, taking independent action to diminish stressors as a method of coping might be supported by individualism. However, at first glance, it is difficult to understand how having good relations with one's coworkers relates to individualistic values. Given past research (Savicki, 1993) it might be speculated that most child and youth care workers function in teams. Therefore, teamwork and good coworker relationships impact not only one's sense of belonging, but also one's ability to perform well. Much of child and youth care practice occurs through interdependent actions with others. Therefore, good teamwork is likely to produce good results, while poor teamwork may create frustrations in actual job performance. Successes arising from team action are more likely to be perceived as expression of individual freedom within an individualistic culture, while even in more collectivist cultures, success can be connected with individual action in the sense of not burdening one's team. Thus, higher-than-average individualism may connect individual action and a sense of accomplishment through different meanings depending on the overall cultural norms (Triandis, Bontempo, Leung, & Hui, 1990).

With regard to more general cultural effects, lower power distance can be seen to enhance individual achievements that have been supported by innovation, control coping, and higher-than-average individualism. Cultures that view individuals as inherently equal regardless of placement in the organizational hierarchy allow individuals at any level more permission to act on their own without fear of running afoul of those with higher status. As Hofstede (1980) states, "People at various power levels feel less threatened and more prepared to trust people" (p. 94). Recognition for achievement is based on what one is able to accomplish rather than their status. Thus individual action is more likely to lead to perceptions of achievement and accomplishment. Cherniss (1995) recounts that individuals in his sample who recovered from burnout were able to do so in part because they engaged in some unique activity for which they could feel a sense of accomplishment.

CONCLUSION

In general, the research questions posed earlier in the paper can be answered in the affirmative. First, culture does seem to relate to burnout. Both general environmental measures and individual cultural conformity measures showed significant contributions to all of the burnout subscales. Second, patterns of work environment and coping related to burnout found in the United States did seem to generalize across the thirteen cultures.

Several important themes related to burnout in child and youth care workers emerged from the pan-cultural analysis of burnout across the thirteen cultures. Each theme will be discussed briefly.

Social Support

For all three aspects of burnout, some type of social support emerged as significant. Lack of supervisor support contributed to emotional exhaustion and depersonalization and the presence of peer cohesion contributed to personal accomplishment. Much of the research literature on stress and coping generally (Lazarus & Folkman, 1984; Thong & Yap, 2000) and on burnout specifically (Lee & Ashforth, 1996) have found social support to be an important buffer against psychological distress. These results seem to have broader meaning when considering the span of cultures found in the present study.

Work Structure

The structure of work played a significant role particularly for the negatively toned emotional reactions of burnout (emotional exhaustion and depersonalization). Feelings of being overloaded, or pressured by the amount of work contributed to both emotional exhaustion and depersonalization. For depersonalization the addition of disorganized or chaotic work structure exacerbated this reaction to work overload. Some of the strongest research findings related to these themes with work overload and aspects of role ambiguity and conflict showing high levels of significance in previous research (Lee & Ashforth, 1996).

Work Enhancement

An aspect of work enhancement, innovation, showed significant relationships to burnout, with emotional exhaustion being negatively related and personal accomplishment being positively related. Opportunities for workers to feel free to try out new ideas and to feel support for doing so both alleviated a sense of emotional fatigue and enhanced a feeling of accomplishment. Such findings are consistent with theories of job redesign (Hackman & Oldham, 1980) and work motivation (Steers & Porter, 1991).

Coping

Coping patterns which sought to relieve the emotional distress of stressful situations (escape coping) were related to both emotional exhaustion and depersonalization. A general style that seeks to reduce the unpleasant feelings associated with a stressful situation did not seem to have been effective in the long run. On the other hand, a problem-focused style of coping in which direct action was taken to alleviate the source of stress was related to a sense of achievement at work (personal accomplishment). In general, both coping styles can have positive benefits (Lazarus, 1999; Folkman and Moskowitz, 2000). That is, actions that bring brief respite from unpleasant feelings may set the stage for more problem-focused attempts. However, it seems that a consistent differential preference for escape over control coping is related to increased burnout, whereas consistent use of control over escape coping is related to lower burnout.

Culture

It is fascinating to note the contribution of culture above and beyond the strong, proximal contributions of work environment and coping. Culture enhances the prediction of burnout based on proximal factors alone. When examining cultural conformity, higher uncertainty avoidance added to predictions of both emotional exhaustion and depersonalization, while higher individualism contributed to the prediction of personal accomplishment. Cultural conformity reflects the tendency of the individual cultural member to emphasize or deemphasize a cultural norm. While it represents the person's position on that norm with regard to the culture, a question arises: "Why would a person deviate from the cultural norm?" With uncertainty avoidance, it may be possible that individuals with higher levels of anxiety may accentuate this norm because it promises to soothe that anxiety. With individualism it may be that the person is more egocentric (Triandis, 1995) and finds individual interpretations of behavior more appealing. In any event, deviations from the cultural norm did relate to aspects of burnout; individual variations in adherence to cultural norms cannot be ignored.

With culture as an indicator of a more general environmental influence, higher career success related to both emotional exhaustion and to depersonalization, while lower power distance related to personal accomplishment. These relationships emerged powerfully enough to explain variation after all of the other variables had been accounted for. Such a result clearly shows the impact of culture as an important factor in understanding burnout. Career success may make work so important to child and youth care workers that the difficulties they face on the job take on immense proportions. Without balance or other facets of life to counteract work-related stress, it may be that workers in high career success cultures feel trapped by their jobs without a venue for discharge of accumulated work stressors. Low power distance cultures offer an opportunity for workers to have more influence and control at work; thus they may feel a greater sense of accomplishment because they are more directly responsible for their actions, as opposed to being required to wait for direction by a boss or supervisor.

It is somehow reassuring that the patterns described in this chapter did emerge, given the span of cultures accounted for as well as the variety of specific work situations in which participants were involved. As yet to be tested, however, is the extent to which these findings generalize to cultures that may be found outside of Northern Europe and North America. The preponderance of cultures in this study come from those areas. Even though there are significant cultural differences in this sample, other cultures are not represented which may extend and alter these findings.

CHAPTER 8

Burnout Configurations

How can we develop an overall picture of burnout as it is experienced across cultures? Burnout has been most often defined as a syndrome in which a worker feels emotionally exhausted or fatigued, withdraws emotionally from their clients, and perceives a diminution of their achievements or accomplishments at work. The de facto standard of measurement for burnout is the Maslach Burnout Inventory (MBI), which contains three subscales purported to measure the three factors identified in this definition. Clearly, there is much information to be gained by looking at the three classic burnout subscales individually. Emotional exhaustion, depersonalization, and personal accomplishment each play an important role in understanding the quality of the burnout experience. In addition, the pan-cultural analysis of Chapter 7 indicates that there are different relationships between the three burnout subscales and work environment, coping, cultural conformity, and culture.

To the consternation of some researchers, there is no single score that inevitably indicates the overall burnout condition. Rather it is the configuration of burnout subscales that in theory characterizes someone suffering from burnout. The highest levels of burnout are experienced by someone with high emotional exhaustion, high depersonalization, and low personal accomplishment (Maslach, Jackson, & Leiter, 1996; Savicki & Cooley, 1983). Conversely, someone experiencing low burnout would show low emotional exhaustion, low depersonalization, and high personal accomplishment. Those individuals who show moderate scores or a mixture of high and low scores on the three subscales might be moderately burned out, or they may have one or two high subscale scores offset by other low subscale scores.

Previous research has sought to derive a single indicator of burnout and its intensity. Savicki and Cooley (1987) developed a simple arithmetic formula which added emotional exhaustion and depersonalization scores, and subtracted personal accomplishment scores. The resulting single number was supposed to represent an overall burnout score. Subsequently, those authors abandoned the formula because it obscured information about burnout that could only be garnered through examination of the separate burnout subscales. Likewise, the latest manual for the Maslach Burnout Inventory (Maslach, Jackson, & Leiter, 1996) suggests maintaining separate scoring for the subscales. Golembiewski and Munzenrider (1988) developed a phase model of burnout which was supposed to indicate an individual's movement from lower to higher burnout by virtue of the configuration of low and high scores on the three burnout subscales. Although there was some agreement on the end points of the phase progression, the middle points were less clear. Thus very high and very low burnout were easier to conceptualize than was moderate burnout.

Both Cherniss (1995) and Maslach and Leiter (1997) clearly distinguished between high and low burnout. High burnout results in physical and psychological difficulties at work and elsewhere, which lead to lower productivity and eventual harm to the individual and to the organization. In contrast, low burnout results in individuals thriving and growing in their work. The challenges of work stress invigorate and energize the worker to produce more and to become innovative. Again, the end points of high versus low burnout show dramatic differences, while it is more difficult to characterize the more confused midpoints of the continuum.

Summing the import of the previous studies, it seems that an analysis that captures the end points of the burnout continuum might be helpful. Such an analysis may be able to answer questions about which environmental and personal factors are associated with high and low burnout. However, rather than computing a single score, the subsequent analysis will rely on configurations of the three burnout subscales.

Configuration Procedure

In order to derive burnout configurations, several procedural steps were taken. First, a median score was computed for all participants in the total sample across all thirteen cultures. Thus the cut point for high versus low burnout on each subscale represented the entire sample, not each separate culture. The object was to be able to make not only individual but cultural comparisons. Second, the configuration of above-median scores for emotional exhaustion and depersonalization and a below-median score for personal accomplishment was labeled as high burnout. Conversely, configuration of below-median scores for emotional exhaustion and depersonalization and an above-median score for personal accomplishment was labeled as low burnout. All participants whose burnout scores did not meet the previous criteria were labeled as mixed burnout; they had some combination of above- and below-median scores. Cutting the sample at the median point for each subscale is a very rough criteria for high or low burnout, but it is at least partially indicative of the intensity of individual reaction. At the same time, having a three-scale configuration criterion is somewhat restrictive since only a relatively small proportion of participants would meet the high and low burnout configuration standard. In any event, this categorization allows probing differences in overall burnout in a way not possible when considering the three burnout subscales separately.

Proportions of High, Mixed, and Low Burnout Configuration Classification

Before looking at how the thirteen cultures faired in burnout configurations, let us examine the results of the categorization process itself. Of all participants, 21 percent were classified in the high burnout category. Only 17 percent fell into the low burnout category. The overwhelming majority (62%) were classified in the mixed burnout category. Thus we might expect that roughly one in five people working in the child and youth care field might be experiencing the deleterious effects of burnout. This is not a trivial proportion of workers. As we will see, we cannot expect that these high burnout workers are randomly distributed across all organizations. However, it is possible that in the moderately sized agency of fifteen treatment workers, teachers, and managers, three workers might be suffering from high burnout. From what we have already learned about the impact of high burnout, we know that there may be serious consequences for individual workers and for the organization if this potential incidence of burnout is left unattended.

On the other hand, almost one in five workers show low burnout. Thus, individuals who have mastered working conditions and demands may be available as models and advisers to those who may need help in preventing, staving off, or recovering from burnout. The following analysis will also shed some light on the process of protection, treatment, and restoration.

Finally, the 62 percent of participants in the mixed burnout category could be quite a varied group. There may be those whose scores on all three burnout subscales hover quite close to the median. There may be others who have extreme scores that offset each other. This is the critical problem with attempting to devise a single measure of burnout from the three burnout subscales. There may be unique configurations of burnout scores that are related to specific environmental conditions and personal factors. What we gain in ability to examine the extremes of burnout, we lose in understanding the mixed and middle range. The current methodology is only the most recent in the ongoing saga of searching for a unidimensional measure of burnout.

Burnout Configuration Results by Culture

Figure 8.1 shows the proportions of high, mixed, and low burnout configurations for each of the thirteen cultures. One first impression from the graph

Figure 8.1
Burnout Configurations for Thirteen Cultures

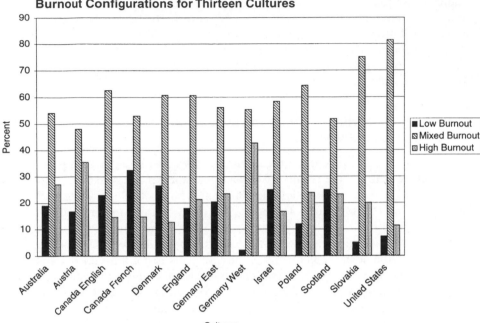

is that some cultures have a larger proportion of mixed burnout participants than do others. For example the United States, Slovakia, Poland, and Canada-English show more individuals with mixed burnout patterns than do Austria, Scotland, and Canada-French. For cultures with higher percentages of mixed burnout individuals, there were fewer extremes in terms of burnout configurations. On the other hand, some cultures had substantial differences between high and low burnout configurations:

More Low than High	Approximately Equal	More High than Low
Canada-French	Scotland	Germany-West
Denmark	Germany-East	Austria
Israel	England	Slovakia
Canada-English	United States	Poland
		Australia

For example Germany-West and Austria have larger proportions of high versus low burnout configuration workers. In contrast, Canada-French and Denmark have larger proportions of low versus high burnout configuration workers. In general, when mixed burnout is not considered, the cultures with proportionally lower burnout are Canada-French, Denmark, Israel, Canada-English, and Scotland. The cultures with proportionally higher burnout are Germany-West, Austria, Slovakia, Poland, Australia, the United States, England, and Germany-East.

Beyond the examination of proportions of high, mixed, and low burnout configurations, it is useful to consider what environmental and personal aspects may contribute to these patterns.

NONSIGNIFICANT CONTRIBUTORS TO HIGH AND LOW BURNOUT CONFIGURATIONS

Before discussing the environmental and personal factors that are strongly related to high and low burnout configurations, it may be enlightening to identify those factors that do not show significant relationships. That is, sometimes finding out that certain variables do not relate to levels of burnout gives us a more focused picture of the relative importance of specific types of differences that do seem to have an impact. The following results (significant and nonsignificant) are based on a multiple analysis of variance procedure in which the three groups were found to be significantly different from one another ($F = 3.65$, $p < 0.001$). Separate variables are reported based on their univariate significance levels. See Table 8.1 for the relevant statistical results.

Several demographic variables did not relate to high or low burnout configurations. These variables include salary, hours per week worked, education level, length of time in one's current position, and length of time in the child and youth care field generally. In addition, no cultural work value related to burnout configurations. Even though cultural work values related to separate burnout subscales, as discussed in Chapter 7, when the subscales were combined as a configuration, no single cultural work value emerged as significant. Some fineness of analysis was lost with regard to culture when the configurations were created.

With regard to salary, logically, the more a worker is paid, the more that worker might feel rewarded and find sources of satisfaction in work. Historically, however, burnout and job satisfaction do not relate to salary level (Daley, 1979). Lower paid workers may find fulfillment and satisfaction in their work in spite of pitiful pay; while higher paid workers may encounter working conditions that introduce unacceptable levels of stress. Salary and emotional reactions to work have been found to be unrelated as long as the salary meets a minimal level to support the needs of the worker.

With regard to hours per week worked, previous research indicates that increasing hours are related to higher burnout if the worker perceives those hours as representing increased workload or pressure to perform. Later, we will see that this relationship between perceived work pressure and burnout exists for child and youth care providers in the current study as well. However, two factors may explain the lack of relationship between hours per week

Table 8.1
Work Environment and Coping Means for High, Mixed, and Low Burnout Configurations

Variables	Low	Mixed	High	F
Peer cohesion	6.47	5.92	5.46	8.92***
Supervisor support	6.15	5.57	4.97	9.43***
Task orientation	6.58	5.91	5.54	9.75***
Work pressure	4.31	5.07	5.30	6.96***
Autonomy	6.23	5.93	5.44	4.77**
Innovation	5.89	4.99	4.52	11.86***
Control coping	52.13	48.20	45.76	9.28***
Escape coping	21.00	21.62	25.18	14.85***

$**p < 0.01$; $***p < 0.001$.

worked and burnout configurations. First, the key to the experience of work pressure is the perception that the work tasks may exceed the personal resources of the worker to accomplish them. Under these conditions, according to Lazarus (1999), the worker feels threatened, and all of the negative stress-related physiological reactions spring forth. However, if the worker believes that his or her personal resources may be able to cope with the pressures of work in a way that will allow him or her to accomplish meaningful goals, then the worker feels challenge which is invigorating. Such invigoration may actually reduce burnout (Riolli-Saltzman & Savicki, 2001c). Thus, as Lazarus repeatedly asserts, the key to understanding reactions to objective environmental stressors such as hours per week worked depends on the combination of the stressors themselves and the individual worker's perceptions of them, not on the objective stressors alone. A second reason for lack of relationship between hours per week worked and burnout is that there is very little variation in hours per week worked. With a few exceptions, most child and youth care providers work between thirty-one and forty hours per week. Thus variations in hours worked is generally not large enough to produce significant statistical relations to variations in burnout.

Education level does not relate to overall burnout because people with differing educational backgrounds are exposed to similar levels, if not similar types, of stress. Educational level is significantly related to the primary role performed in the child and youth care organization. Teachers, specialists, and managers have higher educational levels than do child and youth care workers, but each role has individuals with both high and low burnout configurations. Thus, with regard to burnout, all education level seems to do is put people in contact with slightly different job stressors. It does not buffer against burnout.

Finally, burnout configurations were not related to length of time in one's current position or to length of time worked in the child and youth care field generally. As we will see later, age is inversely related to burnout. One might expect then that the two length-of-time variables would also be related to burnout. However, a study by Shirom and Mazeh (1988) indicates that levels of burnout vary across one's career. These researchers found that job satisfaction cycled from high to low to high over approximately five-year periods. Thus, increasing lengths of time in one's current position or in the field generally are not related to burnout. Rather, one's place in the five-year cycle may be more relevant.

Finally, a few other demographic and work-related variables are not related to high or low burnout. These factors will be merely mentioned since there is no reason to suppose that they should relate. They are marital status, number of children in one's own family, primary job role, agency size, age of children served, and gender of children served.

SIGNIFICANT CONTRIBUTORS TO HIGH AND LOW BURNOUT CONFIGURATIONS

Now that we have ruled out several variables, we can focus more cleanly and intensely on those environmental and personal factors that do relate significantly to high and low burnout configurations. First, we will examine two demographic variables: age and gender. Second, we will describe significant work environment conditions. Finally, we will look at personal variables in the form of coping styles.

Demographic Variables

Both age and gender related to burnout configurations, but in substantially different ways. Figure 8.2 shows that men seemed to show greater intensity of burnout response, both high and low, than did women. A larger proportion

Figure 8.2
Burnout Configurations by Gender

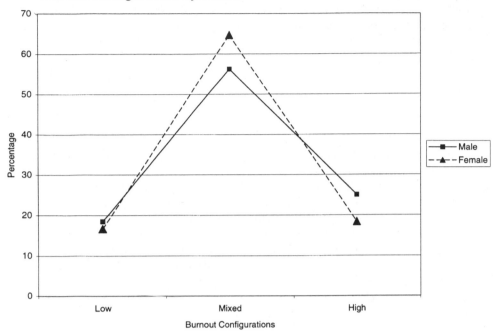

of women appeared in the mixed configuration. It is difficult to conceptualize this result. It could be that women are better able to control conditions related to one or more of the burnout subscales. Indeed, women did show significantly less depersonalization than did men. Women's ability to reduce this aspect of burnout may have prevented them from showing beyond-the-median scores for all three subscales, thus making it more likely that they would fall in the mixed configuration category. One hypothesis concerning women's lower depersonalization focuses on the general finding that women respond more effectively to the socioemotional aspects of interpersonal interaction. Thus they stay more empathic and emotionally connected to clients and co-workers than do men (Savicki, Kelley, & Oesterreich, 1998). More research needs to be done to understand this result.

Fortunately, the relationship between burnout and age is much clearer. People in the low burnout configuration group were significantly older than both the high and mixed burnout configuration groups. Clearly, age gives an advantage in dealing with burnout-related situations. This relation of older workers to lower burnout is a quite consistent research finding (Savicki & Cooley, 1987). Several possible explanations exist for this relationship. First, it might be that only people inherently prone to lower burnout remain in the field after a few years. Those prone to higher burnout leave to find more congenial jobs. There may be some truth to this idea. Cherniss (1995) found that some of his longitudinally studied research subjects had indeed left the field under the pressure of high stress in their early years in a helping profession career. Another idea is that older workers move to jobs with lower levels of stress. That is, early entry level jobs may be inherently more stressful because of the high percentage of client contact. However, any occupational role in the child and youth care field carries its own stressors (Savicki, 1993, 1999a). Thus, being promoted out of one position may only change the sources of stress, not eliminate them. Finally, a more probable explanation for the higher age–lower burnout finding is that workers learn how to reduce the effect of stressors and increase the energizing, growth-oriented aspects of work. Cherniss (1995) gives many examples of this process. Initial disillusionment and anxiety change to commitment and feelings of competence as workers learn from their mistakes. They focus not only on personal skills and qualities that help them reduce stress, but also take control of their work environment to construct a more engaging, supportive, and challenging job.

Environmental Variables

In previous research, work environment variables have shown the strongest relationships to burnout (Maslach & Schaufeli, 1993). In order to orchestrate the kind of metamorphosis mentioned in the previous paragraph, workers need to focus on the aspects of work that really make a difference. This section will examine environmental aspects of social support (peer cohesion and supervisor support), work structure (work pressure and task orientation), and job enhancement (autonomy and innovation).

Social Support

Two aspects of social relationships in the workplace show an association to burnout configurations: peer cohesion and supervisor support. In both cases each of the three burnout configuration groups is significantly different from all others. High burnout shows the least peer cohesion and supervisor support, and low burnout shows the most, with the mixed configuration in the middle. This finding is consistent with much of the research on burnout (Lee & Ashforth, 1996), which has found that support from others in the workplace buffers the effects of stress. Clearly one's coworkers and those who oversee one's work are very important interpersonal contacts for child and youth care service providers.

With peers, social support may take the form of a sympathetic shoulder to cry on and an understanding ear to talk to. In addition, roughly 70 percent of child and youth care providers indicated that they spent some part of their service delivery day in a milieu context. That is, they often did their work in an environment in which they functioned as a team member working together with others within the living environment of the children or youth they served. During this teaming process, group cohesion is very important because team members rely upon each other for successful job performance. Thus peer cohesion affects not only how one feels about the stressors at work, but also how successful one feels in job performance. Social support in this context is doubly important.

Work Structure

Work can be structured to increase or decrease the level of stress to which workers are exposed. Two important work structure features reviewed here are work pressure and task orientation. High work pressure or workload has been found to contribute to burnout in much of the previous burnout research (Lee & Ashforth, 1996). This study is no exception. Child and youth care providers in the high and mixed burnout configuration groups reported significantly more work pressure than did those in the low burnout configuration group. Work overload does present a significant threat to many workers. Too much work to do and not enough time or resources to do it successfully can overwhelm even the best intentioned and talented practitioners. Clearly, those workers who gained some control over their workload were able to modulate the effects of work so that they could fall within the low burnout configuration.

Task orientation reflects the degree to which work is organized efficiently. In other studies, variables such as role ambiguity, role clarity, and role conflict tap some of what is represented by task orientation; workers are just not sure what they should be doing. For this variable all burnout configuration groups were significantly different from each other. The high burnout configuration showed the lowest levels of task orientation, the low burnout group the highest, with the mixed configuration falling in-between. Knowing what to do, when to do it, and how to do it are important factors in performing efficiently at work. Efficient performance increases predictability and decreases anxiety and worry caused by ambiguity. Milieu environments are especially prone to some level of disorganization and chaos, since much of the care flows in and around daily events. Effective care presupposes that responding to critical incidents within the milieu takes precedence over a rigid schedule. However, too little structure can also be damaging. A balance must be struck. Lack of planning or deterioration into chaos sets the stage for burnout.

Job Enhancement

Beyond merely doing one's job, workers may find support or restrictions to making their jobs more fulfilling. Two aspects of job enhancement will be addressed: autonomy and innovation. Some theorists have speculated that autonomy is an indispensable condition for satisfaction in one's job (Hackman & Oldham, 1980). The ability to control important aspects of one's work assignment helps to increase involvement in the job. Some job aspects that may aid in a sense of autonomy include scheduling activities, assigning cases, arranging breaks and days off, choosing modes of care, requesting support, and consultation. In the current sample, the high burnout configuration group is significantly lower in autonomy than are the other two groups. In Hackman and Oldham's model of job redesign, it is impossible to have job satisfaction without autonomy. Cherniss (1995) emphasizes that low burnout workers acquire a sense of efficacy or mastery in their jobs. Autonomy seems to be a prerequisite for the development of the self-attribution of efficacy. Such a model may reflect an individualistic cultural bias. Even though the cultural groups in the current sample show a range of scores on the individualism–collectivism continuum, the sample is quite restricted on this dimension. Asian and Latin American cultures in general show dramatically higher collectivism (Triandis, 1995). It would be interesting to see if lack of autonomy was related to higher burnout in more classic collectivist cultures. Nevertheless, lower autonomy does relate to burnout in the current, predominately North American and Northern European sample.

The final significant work environment factor related to burnout configurations is innovation. On this scale all configuration groups are significantly different from all others, with the high burnout group scoring lowest in innovation; the low burnout group scoring highest; and the mixed group falling in-between. The innovation scale taps the work environment's receptiveness to and encouragement of new and different ways of operating. Low innovation environments would rely on fixed, standard operating procedures which could not easily be challenged or loosened. High innovation environments in contrast would allow experimentation and variation in approach to one's work. It seems clear that higher innovation would support job enrichment and a sense of efficacy. Classic theories of management tout job enrichment as imperative for high work motivation (Herzberg, 1966). In addition, rigid bureaucracies seem to stifle job creativity and satisfaction (Cherniss, 1995). Again, the individualism–collectivism dimension may alter the interpretation of these results for innovation.

Personal Variables

According to the cognitive-mediational theory of stress (Lazarus, 1999), reactions to stress, such as burnout, derive from the combination of objective environmental events (stressors) and personal variables within each individual such as coping styles. Both coping styles measured in this study, control coping and escape coping, showed significant differences between the burnout configuration groups. Coping styles may be related to burnout both through the success or failure of the individual worker to reduce stressful events or reactions and also through the process of appraisal. That is, individuals who have had past successful stress-reducing experiences may evaluate current and future environmental stressors as less demanding than those who have had unsuccessful experiences. This evaluation is part of the appraisal process that mediates between the actual stressor and the individual's reaction to it.

Control Coping

Control coping focuses the individual's attention at the source of stress. The worker using a control coping strategy is more likely to deal with stress actively and attempt to reduce the stressful situation itself, not just the reactions to it. On this scale each configuration group was significantly different from all others, with the high burnout group scoring lowest on control coping, the low burnout group scoring highest, and the mixed group falling in between. Previous studies have also shown this pattern (Leiter, 1991). Obviously a strategy of active stress reduction seems to pay off in lower burnout. As yet to be examined are the types of stressors toward which control coping is aimed. It may well be that some stressors are more amenable to direct action than others. Control coping may function better with day-to-day hassles (Kanner, Coyne, Schaefer, & Lazarus, 1981) than with larger, structural issues. Nevertheless, successful control coping reduces the overall level of stress. This strategy has much to recommend it.

Escape Coping

Escape coping focuses the individual's attention on the unpleasant effects of stress. That is, the worker using escape coping attempts to deal with their emotional reactions to the stressful situation rather than the situation itself. In the current sample, the high burnout configuration group is significantly higher on escape coping than are the other two groups. One would expect that individuals experiencing a high level of burnout would attempt to decrease the disagreeable feelings associated with it. Much of the literature focused on treatment of burnout suggests strategies such as meditation and exercise. These activities do not change the stressful situation, but rather relieve the build-up of noxious physiological and emotional reactions. However, following the notion that coping strategies may be active in the appraisal process, individuals who emphasize escape coping may overlook avenues to actually reduce or remove stressors. Thus, the escape coping strategy, injudiciously applied, may actually perpetuate the stress it is supposed to alleviate. Further research needs to be focused on this potential paradox.

A Multivariate View

Although we have examined work environment and coping variables separately for the sake of clarity, individual workers cannot be cavalierly sliced into logic-tight compartments. They react as organismic wholes. Following the "person–environment relationship" conceptualization (Lazarus, 1999), it is important to discover how environmental and personal variables function in concert. Figure 8.3 shows the results of a multivariate approach to discriminating which of the variables separate the high, mixed, and low burnout groups in a significant manner. As the result of a multivariate discriminant analysis, a single discriminant function separated the groups accounting for 86 percent of the variance (*Wilks lambda*$(16) = 0.877, p < 0.0001$). The major distinction was between the high and low burnout configuration groups. Table 8.2 shows that the environmental and personal variables have relatively even weight when considered together. Work pressure and autonomy related slightly less to the discriminant function, but this difference is probably not meaningful. In other words, all of the variables examined should be considered relatively equally when describing the differences between high and low burnout configuration groups.

Figure 8.3
Discriminant Analysis Centroid Scores Incorporating All Significant Work Environment and Coping Scales for High, Mixed, and Low Burnout Configuration Groups

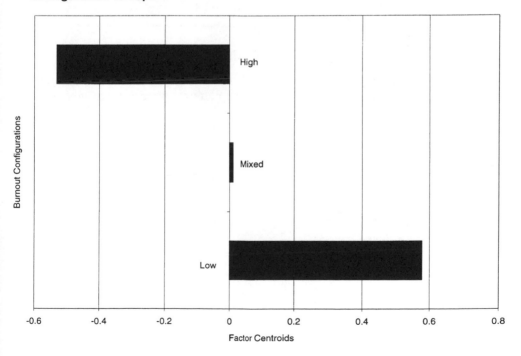

Table 8.2
**Correlations of Work Environment and Coping Scales to
Discriminant Function Separating High, Mixed, and Low
Burnout Configuration Groups**

Environmental and personal variables	Correlations to the discriminant function
Peer cohesion	.455
Supervisor support	.473
Task orientation	.454
Work pressure	-.375
Autonomy	.343
Innovation	.477
Control coping	.451
Escape coping	-.473

CONCLUSION

Strong patterns of contributors to burnout emerged from the configural analysis. The following summarizes these patterns of work environment and coping:

High Burnout
Lower
- Peer cohesion
- Supervisor support
- Task orientation
- Autonomy
- Innovation
- Control coping
Higher
- Work pressure
- Escape coping

Low Burnout
Higher
- Peer cohesion
- Supervisor support
- Task orientation
- Autonomy
- Innovation
- Control coping
Lower
- Work pressure
- Escape coping

For this analysis, high burnout was considered as a single score representing a configuration of high emotional exhaustion, high depersonalization, and low personal accomplishment. This high burnout configuration was related to lower social support, more intense and chaotic work structures, less opportunity to enhance one's work life, and styles of coping which emphasize reducing only the emotional distress of stressors rather than dealing directly with the source of stress. The reverse was true for the low burnout configuration. Thus, both organizational, environmental, and personal factors combined in this cross-cultural study in a way that affirmed many of the findings demonstrated in research from the United States. Just as burnout as a phenomenon seems to generalize to other cultures, so do some of the major contributors to burnout.

Surprisingly, culture as a variable did not add to the explanatory power of the configural analysis. Neither cultural work values generally nor individual conformity to cultural norms showed significant differences between the high and low burnout configurations. To some degree, this result may stem from the somewhat crude fashion in which the configurations were determined. Sensitivity may have been lost by combining the high and low groups on the single burnout subscales. The pan-cultural analysis of Chapter 7 retains that sensitivity.

Although, as we will see in the following chapters, contributors to burnout vary between cultures, the current configural analysis has the benefit of drawing conclusions about burnout as a single phenomenon across all cultures. Certainly there will be overgeneralizations. However, the broad trends that did emerge gain some validity from their consistency with previous research. The configural analysis combined with the pan-cultural analysis of the previous chapter form the basis for a description of emerging themes regarding burnout as elaborated in Chapter 14 and for a set of recommendations for burnout prevention, treatment, and recovery in Chapter 15.

PART IV

CROSS-CULTURAL COMPARISONS

A series of culture comparisons follows a more classic cross-cultural research format. Although Part III looked for general themes spanning cultures, Part IV examines the specific details of contrasts between cultures. In order to highlight the notion that culture has profound effects, comparisons are made that pit cultures that could be seen as similar against one another. The one-country, two-culture comparisons test the power of culture by showing the differences between two cultures within a single geopolitical unit.

In Chapter 9 England and Scotland, which belong to the United Kingdom, are compared. In Chapter 10 the former East and West Germany, which now exist within reunified Germany, are compared. These cultures also shared a common country prior to the lowering of the Iron Curtain. In Chapter 11 French- and English-speaking Canadians, who have shared the same country since the 1700s, are compared. Fortuitously, several Central European cultures, Poland, Slovakia, and the former East Germany, could be contrasted with Western countries such as Denmark, Austria, England, Scotland, and the former West Germany in Chapter 12 to test whether the ideology promoted by Communist regimes has continued to affect culture in the former East Bloc. Finally, in Chapter 13 all the English-speaking cultures are compared to determine if language and former and current relations with England create a similarity of culture in those cultures.

Within the context of possible similarities, these cross-cultural comparisons show that finer cultural distinctions can be drawn from this level of analysis. Not only are comparison made in terms of general cultural work values, but also the contributors to burnout are compared. The work environment, coping, demographic, and work-related variables show different relationships to burnout in the different cultures. Each culture is unique and must be considered when thinking about the precursors to burnout.

CHAPTER 9

===============

The United Kingdom—
Scotland and England:
One Country—Two Cultures

The Union Jack, the flag of the United Kingdom, is an apt representation of the relationship between England and Scotland. It was created in 1603 by King James VI of Scotland when he assumed the throne of England. The flag combines England's red cross of St. George with Scotland's white cross of St. Andrew. The design shows the amalgamation of the two kingdoms, yet the two separate kingdom flags are clearly visible. Both independence and cooperation are embodied in the design.

The defeat of Bonnie Prince Charlie at the bloody Battle of Culloden Moor in 1745 marked the end of Scotland's military efforts to pull away from England (Linklater, 1965). However, today Scotland is pulling away politically through their referendum supporting a separate parliament. The alliance has always been somewhat uneasy to some degree because of the cultural differences between the two peoples.

Although Scotland and England have a long history of both cooperation and difference, the emphasis in this chapter will be on differences between the cultures as expressed through child and youth care practice and burnout. To begin, Scotland and England will be compared on both culture and burnout measures. Given that differences do exist, the following two sections will address these differences from two points of view. First, individual demographic and work-related factors will be examined to discover distinctions between the two cultures that may be related to culture and burnout differences. Second, the relationship between burnout and work environment, coping, and culture will be examined for each culture separately.

CULTURE DIFFERENCES

Scotland and England differed on two of the four cultural work value dimensions: power distance and individualism (see Table 9.1). England showed higher power distance, which indicates that the English culture, on average, prefers hierarchical work relationships with distinct boundaries between managers and workers, whereas the Scottish culture on average prefers a more collaborative and consultative relationship between managers and workers.

Scotland scored higher on individualism, which indicates a cultural value of individual action and accountability, whereas England showed less individualism and more collectivism, which indicates a preference for group action and shared responsibility.

Taken together, the two significant cultural work value scales describe different beliefs concerning how individuals should act at work, and by implication, in life generally. According to these results, English culture favors looking for leadership from those with higher status and higher assigned roles within the work hierarchy. Within a specific level of hierarchy, English culture encourages collective approaches with communal accountability. Higher collectivism in the English sample may be related to the geographic area in which the data were collected. The mining region from which most participants came may have placed higher value on small work groups, based on experience in the coal mines, than do English participants in other regions. Scotland, on the other hand, favors individual behavior and accountability independent of the level of hierarchy. As one Scottish colleague explained, historically Scots thrived in a harsh physical environment, and they elected their kings. In contrast, English political history emphasized distinctions of status, aristocracy, and inheritance of royal titles. In England it was important to "know one's station." Distinctions between history and territory may help explain the cultural differences found in the current study.

BURNOUT DIFFERENCES

England and Scotland differed on only one of the three burnout subscales: emotional exhaustion. As Table 9.1 indicates, England was significantly higher on this subscale, which many consider to be the subscale most representative of the burnout phenomenon. In general, child and youth care workers in England were more likely than their Scottish counterparts to indicate that they were feeling emotionally worn down, fatigued, and depleted of personal resources in the face of daily work stressors.

DEMOGRAPHIC AND WORK VARIABLES

Demographic and work variables seem to add to the understanding of burnout differences between Scotland and England. First, Table 9.2 indicates that

Table 9.1
Comparison of Means for Cultural Work Values and Burnout between England and Scotland

Variable	England	Scotland	F	p
Cultural work values				
Power distance	52.476	47.599	8.667	.004
Uncertainty avoidance	47.097	48.881	1.277	ns
Individualism-Collectivism	47.240	50.933	4.943	.028
Career success-Quality of life	53.468	50.529	2.827	ns
Burnout				
Emotional exhaustion	53.430	47.881	9.035	.003
Depersonalization	52.078	49.890	1.274	ns
Personal accomplishment	51.916	52.001	0.003	ns

ns = no significant difference.

workers in the two cultures did not differ in terms of age, gender composition, education level, or age of clients served. However, several work-related variables did differ between the cultures. These differences may be related to the difference in burnout. As Table 9.2 indicates, child and youth care workers in Scotland have worked longer in the field, have held their current positions longer, work in larger agencies, work fewer hours per week, and get paid more than do their counterparts in England. Figures 9.1 and 9.2 show the distribution of longevity of English and Scottish workers in their current work positions and in their length of time in the child and youth care field. The majority of workers in the English sample had worked five years or less, while the majority of workers in the Scottish sample had worked five years or more. Although there were no differences in age between the cultures, Scottish workers seemed to stay longer in their jobs. Longevity in the position and the field is likely related to higher pay. In addition, Figure 9.3 indicates that England showed a much higher proportion of teachers and Scotland a higher proportion of specialists and midmanagers. This difference in job role may also influence hours per week worked, pay, and job longevity. Specialists often work only part time and are paid more. Usually, older workers show less burnout than do younger ones. However, a colleague in England indicated that some child and youth care workers had shifted from other, previ-

Table 9.2
Comparison of Demographic Factors for England and Scotland

Variable	England	Scotland	F	p
Age	36.34	38.48	1.437	ns
Gender			0.155	ns
Male	48%	46%		
Female	52%	54%		
Education level in years	14.4	14.5	0.001	ns
Length in current position in years	3.01	4.89	10.494	.002
Length in child care field in years	6.14	9.51	11.534	.001
Agency size	33.62	42.30	4.225	.042
Age of clients			0.349	ns
Children	13%	15%		
Adolescents	87%	85%		
Hours per week worked	40.69	38.24	4.250	.041
Salary per month in British pounds	306.07	345.85	8.636	.004

ns = no significant difference.

ous jobs, so that as child and youth care workers, they were older even though working in what is usually thought of as an entry level position. Thus, in this case, not age but longevity in the position and in the field might be related to lower burnout. In addition, working longer hours for less pay might set the stage for feelings of work overload, as is discussed in the next section.

CONTRIBUTORS TO BURNOUT IN EACH CULTURE

In this section, Scottish and English cultures will be considered separately. The focus will be on patterns of work environment, coping, and cultural conformity that were related to the three aspects of burnout within each culture.

Figure 9.1
Comparison of Length of Time in Current Position in England and Scotland

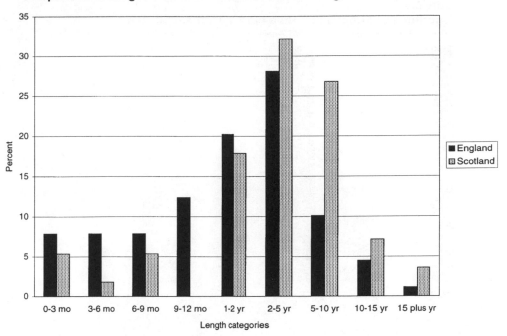

Figure 9.2
Comparison of Length of Time in the Child and Youth Care Field

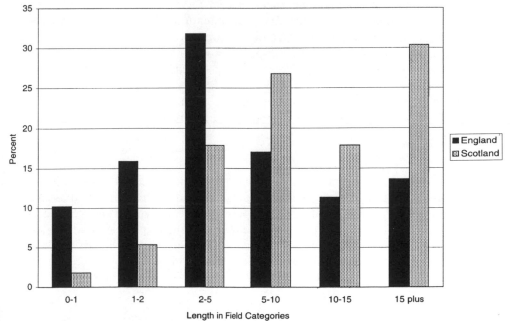

Figure 9.3
Proportions of Primary Job Roles in England and Scotland

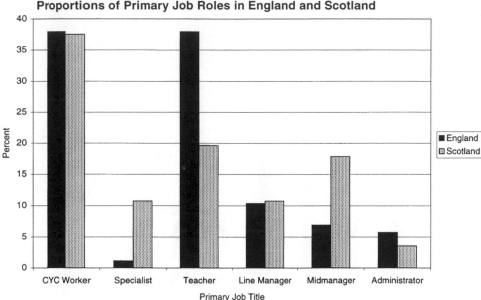

England

For England, significant relationships between work environment and coping occurred with both emotional exhaustion and depersonalization but not with personal accomplishment (see Table 9.3).

For emotional exhaustion (EE), a combination of higher work pressure (WP), higher escape coping, and lower control coping related to higher levels of this burnout subscale. Under conditions of work overload, those workers who acted to reduce the negative emotions associated with the stress and who reduced their attempts to deal directly with the source of stress were more likely to become emotionally fatigued and worn out. Variations of cultural conformity did not contribute to understanding emotional exhaustion.

$$EE = \uparrow WP + \uparrow \text{ escape coping} + \downarrow \text{ control coping}$$

For depersonalization (DP), a combination of lower control (CTL), lower control coping, and higher escape coping related to this burnout subscale. When workers perceived that management was not providing enough leadership and guidance, workers who acted to reduce the negative emotions associated with the stress and who reduced their attempts to deal directly with the source of stress were more likely to become emotionally distant and cut off from their clients. Variations of cultural conformity did not contribute to understanding depersonalization.

Table 9.3
Hierarchical Multiple Regression of Emotional Exhaustion, Depersonalization, and Personal Accomplishment with Work Environment, Coping, and Cultural Conformity in England

Variables	Emotional exhaustion	Depersonalization	Personal accomplishment
Step 1: Work environment	R^2= .341	R^2= .213	R^2= .082
	$F(7,81)$= 5.976***	$F(7,81)$= 3.141**	$F(7,81)$= 1.027
Peer cohesion	β = -.197	β = -.173	β = .163
Supervisor support	β = -.333	β = -.222	β = .150
Autonomy	β = .001	β = .060	β = -.159
Task orientation	β = -.005	β = -.031	β = .110
Work pressure	β = .330**	β = .123	β = .081
Control	β = -.012	β = -.244*	β = -.057
Innovation	β = .119	β = -.069	β = .119
Step 2: Coping style	R^2= .407	R^2= .333	R^2= .151
	$F(9,79)$= 6.02***	$F(9,79)$= 4.390***	$F(9,79)$= 1.563
Control coping	β = -.267*	β = -.308**	β = .309
Escape coping	β = .219*	β = .343***	β = -.135
Step 3: Cultural conformity	R^2= .414	R^2= .358	R^2= .205
	$F(13,75)$= 4.07***	$F(13,75)$= 3.216***	$F(13,75)$= 1.488
Power distance	β = .019	β = -.090	β = .186
Uncertainty avoidance	β = .049	β = .133	β = .058
Individualism	β = -.032	β = .051	β = .124
Career success	β = -.067	β = -.009	β = .114

$*p < 0.05$; $**p < 0.01$; $***p < 0.001$.

$$DP = \downarrow CTL + \uparrow \text{escape coping} + \downarrow \text{control coping}$$

Taken together these findings for England are consistent with general cultural values of expecting management to exert leadership and take care of employees, especially in the face of difficult work situations. Colleagues in England recounted that a major shift in work efforts had recently taken place. A majority of agencies sampled in England had changed their clientele from delinquent to severely emotionally disturbed children and youth as a result of funding shifts and other outside pressures. Given the higher power distance and lower individualism shown in English culture, workers probably expected more guidance from management on how to deal with this change. Likewise, they probably did not feel free to address sources of stress on their own. Awareness of cultural work values could have probably helped to frame the change effort in a manner which would have avoided increases in burnout.

Scotland

For Scotland, significant relationships between work environment, coping, and cultural conformity occurred with both emotional exhaustion and personal accomplishment but not with depersonalization (see Table 9.4).

For emotional exhaustion (EE), a combination of higher work pressure (WP) and higher deviation from the uncertainty avoidance cultural norm (UA deviation) was related to this burnout subscale. Under conditions of work overload, in comparison with their coworkers, those workers who believed that ambiguities at work should be reduced through rules or other standard procedures were more likely to become emotionally fatigued and worn out. Coping styles did not contribute to understanding emotional exhaustion.

$$EE = \uparrow WP + \uparrow UA \text{ deviation}$$

For personal accomplishment (PA), a combination of higher control coping and higher deviation from the career success cultural norm (CS deviation) was related to this burnout subscale. Workers who believed more strongly than their coworkers in the centrality of work as a way of defining themselves and who at the same time strove actively to reduce sources of stress were more likely to perceive themselves as achieving increased accomplishments at work. Work environment did not contribute to understanding personal accomplishment.

$$PA = \uparrow \text{control coping} + \uparrow CS \text{ deviation}$$

Taken together, the findings for Scotland are consistent with the more general cultural values that support individual action that is not overly restricted by hierarchical differences. Scottish workers who showed higher emotional exhaustion were more likely to deviate from the general cultural norm regarding dealing with work ambiguities. With higher workload, they seemed to believe that more structure regarding work was desirable. Such structure, while not necessarily provided by management, does place restrictions on individual action. Thus, those who deviated from the general cultural norm of individualism were more likely to experience burnout. The relations of coping and cultural conformity to personal accomplishment seem most informa-

Table 9.4
Hierarchical Multiple Regression of Emotional Exhaustion, Depersonalization, and Personal Accomplishment with Work Environment, Coping, and Cultural Work Values in Scotland

Variables	Emotional exhaustion	Depersonalization	Personal accomplishment
Step 1: Work environment	$R^2 = .235+$	$R^2 = .187$	$R^2 = .186$
	$F(7,48) = 2.101$	$F(7,48) = 1.580$	$F(7,48) = 1.568$
Peer cohesion	$\beta = -.269$	$\beta = -.084$	$\beta = -.020$
Supervisor support	$\beta = .052$	$\beta = -.333$	$\beta = -.036$
Autonomy	$\beta = .065$	$\beta = .135$	$\beta = .194$
Task orientation	$\beta = .012$	$\beta = .187$	$\beta = .132$
Work pressure	$\beta = .383*$	$\beta = .176$	$\beta = .304$
Control	$\beta = -.205$	$\beta = -.103$	$\beta = -.014$
Innovation	$\beta = .101$	$\beta = -.012$	$\beta = .317$
Step 2: Coping style	$R^2 = .272$	$R^2 = .213$	$R^2 = .376$
	$F(9,46) = 1.913$	$F(9,46) = 1.381$	$F(9,46) = 3.084**$
Control coping	$\beta = -.013$	$\beta = .044$	$\beta = .451***$
Escape coping	$\beta = .210$	$\beta = .167$	$\beta = -.128$
Step 3: Cultural conformity	$R^2 = .372$	$R^2 = .225$	$R^2 = .496$
	$F(13,42) = 1.911*$	$F(13,42) = .938$	$F(13,42) = 3.179**$
Power distance	$\beta = .043$	$\beta = .010$	$\beta = -.158$
Uncertainty avoidance	$\beta = .270*$	$\beta = .063$	$\beta = -.018$
Individualism	$\beta = -.176$	$\beta = -.039$	$\beta = .131$
Career success	$\beta = -.006$	$\beta = -.079$	$\beta = .264*$

$+p < 0.06$; $*p < 0.05$; $**p < 0.01$; $***p < 0.001$.

tive with regard to Scottish individualism. Within a culture that emphasized individual action, those workers who directly attacked stressors and perceived work as central to their sense of self seemed to gain a higher sense of self-realization from their work. The general cultural norm of individualism can be seen as supporting such direct, personal action.

CONCLUSION

In summary, cultural differences do seem to be reflected in child and youth care practice between England and Scotland. Significant differences in individualism and power distance seem to impact both the practice of child and youth care and in the manner in which workers in the two cultures experience burnout. Various demographic and workplace variables seemed to help explain the differentials in emotional exhaustion. Each culture had different patterns of burnout in relation to work environment, coping styles, and cultural conformity.

Several generalizations can be drawn. First, effective coping can be helpful. In both Scotland and England, control coping played a large role in burnout. Actively attempting to reduce the source of stress had beneficial outcomes, while decreasing such attempts was problematic. Second, work overload played a part in burnout in both Scotland and England. Work overload is the classic contributor to burnout (Lee & Ashforth, 1996). Clearly work needs to get done. However, the arrangement of work may have a large impact on how taxing it seems to individual workers. If work tasks can be paced to challenge and not overwhelm workers, they may experience more engagement with their work and find work invigorating in spite its difficulty or fast pace (Riolli-Saltzman & Savicki, 2001c).

CHAPTER 10

Germany—Former East and Former West: One Country—Two Cultures

Prior to 1872, Germany had been a collection of territories, duchies, and city-states only loosely affiliated in the sense of sharing a similar history stemming from Celtic and Teutonic origins and a somewhat similar language based on Indo-European roots. In 1872, Otto von Bismark unified this aggregate of entities into the political and geographic unit of Germany. For approximately seventy years it evolved as a nation-state that held sway in middle Europe. Through two world wars, it held together under a variety of challenges. Then, following World War II, it was split. This division lasted for approximately forty years.

In more recent history the former East (German Democratic Republic) and the former West (Federal Republic of Germany) were reunified in 1990. For the seventy years prior to 1949, Germany had shared a common language, a vivid history, and a common political system. With the advent of the German Democratic Republic and the imposition of the Iron Curtain, a new political system and ideology was introduced in the East, and a Western style economic system was accented in the West. Anecdotal reports indicated that although Germany had once again became a single country in 1990, some of the values and attitudes inculcated under the Communist regime persisted in the East and that values associated with capitalism grew stronger in the West. This research's treatment of Germany-East and Germany-West as separate cultures was based on the reports of differing worldviews between the two sections of the now single country. The obvious, initial question is, "Are the cultures different?" and if so, "In what way?"

As a fortuitous control over spurious regional differences in the German sample that may have entered into the comparison of the former East and West sectors, the German states from which most of the data were collected were Hessen in the West and Thüringen in the East. These two middle German states share a common border along which the Iron Curtain was located prior to reunification.

CULTURE DIFFERENCES

Germany-West and Germany-East differed significantly on two of the four cultural work value dimensions: individualism—collectivism and career success—quality of life (see Table 10.1). Germany-West showed higher individualism, which indicates that the Germany-West culture valued individual action and accountability, whereas Germany-East showed less individualism and more collectivism, which indicates a preference for group action and shared responsibility. Germany-East showed a higher score for quality of life, whereas Germany-West showed a higher preference for the value of career success. Thus in Germany-East, workers were more likely to show a moderation and balance in the value of work and career. In the Germany-West culture, the emphasis was more strongly on work and career as a compelling source of personal growth and identity.

Table 10.1
Comparison of Means for Cultural Work Values and Burnout between Germany-East and Germany-West

Variable	Germany-East	Germany-West	F	p
Cultural work values				
Power distance	49.193	46.362	2.360	ns
Uncertainty avoidance	53.189	55.458	2.491	ns
Individualism-Collectivism	48.310	52.729	8.428	.004
Career success-Quality of life	47.323	51.330	5.837	.017
Burnout				
Emotional exhaustion	47.912	53.575	14.111	.0001
Depersonalization	48.129	54.120	16.747	.0001
Personal accomplishment	47.654	44.747	3.773	.054

ns = no significant difference.

Taken together, the two significant cultural work value differences seem to reflect differing ideologies regarding a person's role at work and elsewhere. Ideologically, capitalism and communism (in its more theoretical form) make contrasting statements that seem to reveal themselves in the cultural differences between Germany-West and Germany-East. Collectivist action and social consciousness were key features of the communist ideology. In collectivist cultures there is more "we" consciousness, more emotional dependence on organizations and institutions, and a belief in group decisions (Hofstede, 1980, p. 171). The quality of life work value is demonstrated in ideals of service to others, interdependence, and orientation to people over things (p. 205). These characteristics were found in the Germany-East culture. In contrast, individual action and the centrality of work characterize the free-market, capitalistic ideology. The Germany-West culture showed a higher regard for individual initiative and autonomy; it also rated achievement, independence, and trying to be the best as important (p. 205). Thus, the Germany-West culture contains strong themes of capitalistic ideology. The forty years of separation under two different political and ideological systems seem to reveal itself in the cultural contrasts between Germany-West and Germany-East.

BURNOUT DIFFERENCES

Germany-East and Germany-West differed significantly on all three burnout scales (see Table 10.1). Germany-West was higher on emotional exhaustion and depersonalization; Germany-East was higher on personal accomplishment. Child and youth care workers in Germany-West were more likely to show the high burnout configuration of higher emotional exhaustion, higher depersonalization, and lower personal accomplishment.

Demographic and Work Variables

Demographic and work variables may shed some light on the differences in burnout between Germany-East and Germany-West (see Table 10.2). Although worker's average age did not differ between the two cultures, child and youth care workers in Germany-East had completed more years of formal education but fewer years in either their current job positions or in the field of child and youth care generally than did their Germany-West counterparts. Figures 10.1, 10.2, and 10.3 illustrate an interesting pattern regarding age, length of time in one's current position, and length of time in the field of child and youth work. The distribution of workers across age brackets in Germany-East was more even than it was in Germany-West. In Germany-West 91 percent of workers fell in the thirty to fifty age brackets, while in Germany-East there were substantially more younger (20–29) and older (50+) workers than in Germany-West. The averages do not reflect this difference in age distributions. Figure 10.2 illustrates a bimodal distribution of longevity in the child

Table 10.2
Comparison of Demographic Factors for Germany-East and Germany-West

Variable	Germany-East	Germany-West	F	p
Age	39.21	39.77	0.0001	ns
Gender			0.126	ns
Male	38%	43%		
Female	62%	57%		
Education level in years	16.03	15.5	11.249	.001
Length in current position in years	3.58	9.11	40.452	.0001
Length in child care field in years	8.7	11.3	7.945	.006
Agency size	60	26	39.833	.0001
Age of clients			1.090	ns
Children	33%	22%		
Adolescents	57%	78%		
Hours per week worked	37.7	34.8	4.718	.032
Salary per month in Deutsch marks	2428.06	3003.72	6.505	.012

ns = no significant difference.

and youth care field for Germany-East in contrast to a steady progression of longevity for Germany-West. Although Germany-East has 29 percent of its workers with fifteen or more years in the field, it also has 32 percent with five years or less. It seems that Germany-East may be in a period of change in the field of child and youth care. Figure 10.3 adds further support for the notion of changes afoot. Fully 81 percent of workers in Germany-East have occupied their current job positions for five years or less. In Germany-West, by contrast, 49 percent have occupied their current positions for ten years or more. The data in Germany were collected six years after reunification. This event seemed to have a stronger impact on child and youth care workers in the Germany-East than in Germany-West.

Germany-West showed higher salaries and shorter work hours. Germany-East workers indicated that they worked in significantly larger agencies. His-

Figure 10.1
Age Distribution Comparison for Germany-East and Germany-West

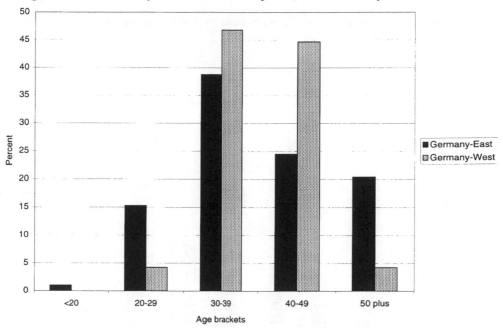

Figure 10.2
Length in the Field of Child and Youth Care Comparisons for Germany-East and Germany-West

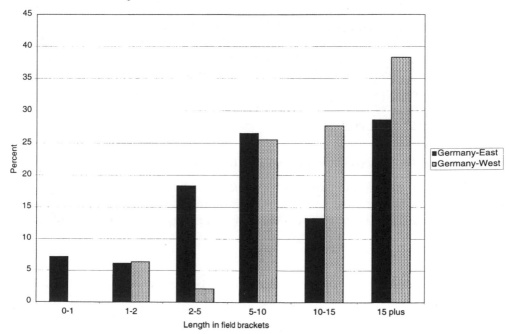

Figure 10.3
Length in Current Position Comparisons for Germany-East and Germany-West

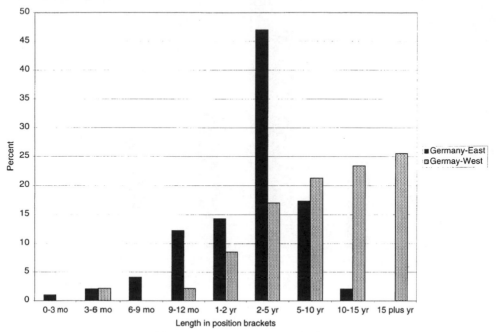

torically, salary and hours worked have not correlated highly with job satisfaction and burnout (Jayaratne & Chess, 1984); the current results affirm this trend. It may well be that higher education levels in Germany-East translated into a qualitatively different kind of work attitude or skill set than did the years of experience in Germany-West. Even though Germany-East indicated a larger number of children and youth per agency than did Germany-West, this difference appears unrelated to the differences in burnout.

Contributors to Burnout in Each Culture

Now let us consider Germany-East and Germany-West as separate cultures. The focus will be on patterns of work environment, coping, and cultural conformity that were related to the three aspects of burnout within each culture.

Germany-East

For Germany-East significant relationships between work environment, and coping occurred with all three burnout scales (see Table 10.3).

Table 10.3
Hierarchical Multiple Regression of Emotional Exhaustion,
Depersonalization, and Personal Accomplishment with Work Environment,
Coping, and Cultural Conformity in Germany-East

Variables	Emotional exhaustion	Depersonalization	Personal accomplishment
Step 1: Work environment	R^2= .136	R^2= .141	R^2= .311
	$F(7,90)=2.021+$	$F(7,90)= 2.119*$	$F(7,90)= 5.813***$
Peer cohesion	β = -.205	β = -.057	β = .377**
Supervisor support	β = .251	β = -.237*	β = -.141
Autonomy	β = -.086	β = .199	β = -.219*
Task orientation	β = -.189	β = -.193	β = .422***
Work pressure	β = .259*	β = .167	β = -.021
Control	β = -.123	β = .085	β = -.021
Innovation	β = .034	β = .141	β = .009
Step 2: Coping style	R^2= .155	R^2= .236	R^2= .347
	$F(9,88)= 1.787$	$F(9,88)= 2.964**$	$F(9,88)= 5.203***$
Control coping	β = -.119	β = -.190	β = .208*
Escape coping	β = .112	β = .298	β = .007
Step 3: Cultural conformity	R^2= .234	R^2= .324	R^2= .335
	$F(13,84)= 1.97*$	$F(13,84)= 3.097***$	$F(13,84)= 4.758***$
Power distance	β = -.091	β = -.169	β = .248*
Uncertainty avoidance	β = .110	β = .169	β = .171
Individualism	β = -.217*	β = -.172	β = -.048
Career success	β = .195+	β = .209*	β = .025

$+p < 0.06$; $*p < 0.05$; $**p < 0.01$; $***p < 0.001$.

Emotional exhaustion (EE) was related to higher work pressure (WP) and lower than the cultural average individualism (IND deviation) and higher than the cultural average for career success (CS deviation). Thus, those workers who deviated from the Germany-East cultural norm by expecting more collective action and by focusing more than average on work-related aspects of life suffered more emotional fatigue at work under conditions of work overload.

$$EE = \uparrow WP + \downarrow IND \text{ deviation} + \uparrow CS \text{ deviation}$$

Depersonalization (DP) was related to lower supervisor support (SS) and higher than the cultural average for career success (CS deviation). Workers who valued work and career more than their colleagues were more likely to emotionally distance themselves from their clients when their supervisors did not provide the assistance they wanted.

$$DP = \downarrow SS + \uparrow CS \text{ deviation}$$

Personal accomplishment (PA) was related to higher peer cohesion (PC), and task orientation (TO) and lower autonomy (A); to control coping; and to higher than average power distance (PD deviation). Thus, workers whose work lives featured a congenial work team, well-organized work, and a limited requirement to make independent decisions were able to feel more successful at work when they used direct action to deal with stress and valued clear distinctions between levels of hierarchy.

$$PA = \uparrow PC + \uparrow TO + \downarrow A + \uparrow \text{control coping} + \uparrow PD \text{ deviation}$$

To summarize, social support and cultural deviation showed strong effects for both emotional exhaustion and depersonalization. If Germany-East child and youth care workers deviated from their cultural norms under conditions of lack of coworker or supervisor respect, they were more likely to experience the unpleasant emotional aspects of burnout. Deviations are less well tolerated in collectivistically oriented countries (Triandis, 1995). Deviations toward higher than average emphasis on work caused special problems, perhaps because coworkers or supervisors were less inclined to respond to that emphasis.

The more complicated response from Germany-East child and youth care workers comes in relation to personal accomplishment. One the one hand, workers valued leaders who would tell them what to do and task structures that were well organized so that they did not have to make too many independent decisions; on the other hand, they valued their coworkers and were able to take direct action to relieve stress. Thus feelings of achievement at work were more likely to take place in the framework of a collectivist approach which also stressed following rules and structures rather than exerting individual initiative. Workers felt more successful while operating within an organized, collectivist framework. In this case personal accomplishment may be better described as person-within-a-social system accomplishment, since the individual would be less likely to feel a sense of achievement by virtue of independent action alone.

Germany-West

For Germany-West a significant relationship between work environment, coping, and cultural conformity occurred with depersonalization, and a marginally significant relationship existed with emotional exhaustion (see Table 10.4).

Table 10.4
Hierarchical Multiple Regression of Emotional Exhaustion, Depersonalization, and Personal Accomplishment with Work Environment, Coping, and Cultural Conformity in Germany-West

Variables	Emotional exhaustion	Depersonalization	Personal accomplishment
Step 1: Work environment	R^2= .251	R^2= .271	R^2= .165
Peer cohesion	$F(7,39)$= 1.87	$F(7,39)$= 2.067	$F(7,39)$= 1.101
Supervisor support	β = -.069	β = .087	β = .013
Autonomy	β = -.128	β = .288	β = -.017
Task orientation	β = .160	β = .309	β = .549
Work pressure	β = -.431*	β = -.394*	β = -.195
Control	β = .432*	β = -.046	β = .124
Innovation	β = .261	β = -.018	β = .318
	β = -.039	β = -.459	β = -.077
Step 2: Coping style	R^2= .329	R^2= .349	R^2= .208
	$F(9,37)$= 2.019+	$F(9,37)$= 2.199*	$F(9,37)$= 1.079
Control coping	β = -.303+	β = -.143	β = .239
Escape coping	β = .015	β = .344*	β = -.139
Step 3: Cultural	R^2= .419	R^2= .455	R^2= .276
conformity	$F(13,33)$= 1.833	$F(13,33)$= 2.121*	$F(13,33)-$ .969
Power distance	β = .194	β = .132	β = .056
Uncertainty avoidance	β = .269	β = .194	β = -.070
Individualism	β = -.055	β = -.291+	β = -.193
Career success	β = -.077	β = .056	β = -.164

*$p < 0.05$; **$p < 0.01$; ***$p < 0.001$.

Depersonalization (DP) was related to lower task orientation (TO), higher escape coping and marginally lower-than-average individualism (IND deviation). Germany-West child and youth care workers were more likely to emotionally distance their clients when they relied on a coping style that focused on reducing the unpleasant feelings in a somewhat disorganized work situation and when they valued collective action more than did their colleagues.

DP = ↓ TO + ↑ escape coping + ↓ IND deviation

For emotional exhaustion (EE), marginal significance was achieved with the combination of lower control coping, lower task orientation (TO), and higher work pressure (WP). That is, workers were more likely to experience fatigue and emotional depletion when they perceived that they had too much to do, that the work was not efficiently organized, and when they reduced their attempts to deal directly with the sources of stress. Marginal significance means that this result should be considered less strong and interpreted with caution, although it is consistent with previous research (Lee & Ashforth, 1996).

$$EE = \downarrow TO + \uparrow WP + \downarrow control\ coping$$

Taken together, styles of coping and the structure of work seemed to have a large effect on the unpleasant emotional aspects of burnout in Germany-West. In a culture that values predictability and tries to constrain uncertainty, a well-structured and efficient workplace could be seen as a central requirement for job satisfaction. The relationship of lower task orientation for both emotional exhaustion and depersonalization confirms this expectation. Given that events at work are sometimes unpredictable or confusing, the manner with which the Germany-West workers coped with this uncertainty also seemed to impact burnout. Particularly in the face of higher workload, increasing attempts to relieve the unpleasant feelings associated with the situation while decreasing attempts to change the sources of stress provided a combination that made it more likely that the stress would continue unabated, thus possibly perpetuating burnout.

CONCLUSION

Although the former East and former West Germany share much in terms of cultural values, the emphasis on individualism and work achievement in the former West and collectivism and social consciousness in the former East may have set the stage for remarkably different patterns of burnout and remarkably different factors contributing to burnout. In the former West, the configuration of much higher levels of emotional exhaustion and depersonalization and lower levels of personal accomplishment make it the culture with the most severe overall burnout. It seems as though workers who valued personal responsibility, career, and a more structured workplace, when put into a high-pressure, disorganized workplace, experienced not only greater distress, but also a diminished sense of achievement. In the former East, although there was no sense of heightened personal accomplishment, neither were the unpleasant effects of burnout very severe. In the context of a more collectivist orientation, workers felt more successful in situations with effective organization of work and with someone else to share responsibilities with (i.e., co-workers or managers). Likewise, both a coping strategy aimed at decreasing unpleasant feelings and work structures that decrease responsibility for workplace decisions seem to aid in lowering distress and increasing a sense of achievement.

In other burnout studies (Savicki, Cooley, & Gjesvold, in press) and in other cultures (e.g., Slovakia) the configuration of demographic variables seen in the Germany-West was consistent with workers who had reached the end of their ability to advance in an organization. With lower levels of education, such workers may feel trapped because they cannot improve their jobs, but they cannot afford to seek different jobs since they have good salaries that have risen as they have stayed longer in the field. In addition, they may feel that they have foreclosed their occupational choices by needing to support a family or by fear of embarking on a new career path. Especially in a high uncertainty avoidance culture, it may seem that work stressors are more potent to those workers who have followed the rules, but not developed a satisfying or personally rewarding career. One theory of the development of burnout (Golembiewski & Munzenrider, 1988) contends that a lowered sense of accomplishment at work leads to distress and intensifies burnout.

By contrast, the former East portrays child and youth care in transition away from large institutions in which there was little opportunity to exert individual influence, in which workers relied on bosses to structure work, and in which responsibility was spread among several team members. Although a personal sense of achievement was difficult to attain under those conditions, the distress felt was also lower. Better educated workers earlier in their careers may be better able to sustain themselves at work knowing that they can rely on the more collectivist orientation to buffer stressors.

CHAPTER **11**

Canada—French and English Speakers: One Country—Two Cultures

In 1759 British General Wolfe defeated French General Montcalm on the Plains of Abraham in the Battle of Quebec, and the Eastern Seaboard of North America came under British rule. Up until that time, both France and England had vied for control of that part of the New World. Adventurers, trappers, and colonists from each European country attempted to lay claim to a wild and rich territory. One might expect that with the imposition of a single political system, the losers of the war would flee or at least be absorbed by the dominant culture. However, in Canada, French speakers continued to survive and even thrive within the predominately English-speaking country that became Canada. Through the almost 250 years that followed, something about the francophone culture allowed it to sustain itself. That culture now shares the similar geography as its anglophone countrymen. In the current Canadian sample, francophone participants came entirely from Quebec; anglophone participants came from Quebec and Nova Scotia. The two cultures exist side by side in a sometimes uneasy coexistence. Through periods of repression, threats of succession, and shared prosperity, French- and English-speaking Canadians have dwelled on a common turf.

There is some debate about how the Canada-French culture could survive relatively intact while surrounded by the more prevalent Canada-English culture. Some authors (Garigue, 1973; Langelier, 1983) suggest that a clannishness and isolation spawned by the Catholic Church as well as a desire for a preservation of the unique culture made French-Canadians suspicious of outsiders and dedicated to perpetuating their lifestyle and values. The survival of the culture is sustained, these authors say, through use of the French language and a parallel system of cultural institutions such as schools, churches, and businesses. Baer and Curtis (1984), on the other hand, point to a change in the values underlying the Canada-French culture, as the economy has demanded more interaction outside of traditional French-Canadian in groups and as the younger generation has gained advanced education alongside their anglophone neighbors.

From the point of view of this book, the Canada-French and Canada-English differentiation provides an opportunity for cross-cultural contrast not available in any other comparison. The fact that French and English speakers have occupied the same geography while maintaining their separate languages and their separate cultures contrasts the impact of differences in history and language but not territory or politics. How are the cultures different? Are there parallel child and youth care service systems? What impact do such closely existing cultural contrasts have on burnout? These and many other questions will be tested in this one country–two culture comparison.

To begin, Canada-English and Canada-French cultures will be compared on both culture and burnout measures. Given that differences do exist, the following two sections will address these differences from two points of view. First, individual demographic and work-related factors will be examined to discover distinctions between the two cultures that may be related to culture and burnout differences. Second, the relationship of burnout to work environment, coping, and culture will be examined for each culture separately.

CULTURE DIFFERENCES

The Canada-French and Canada-English cultures showed significant differences on three of the four cultural work value scales (see Table 11.1). Canada-French was higher on uncertainty avoidance. Canada-English was higher on the individualism and career success dimensions. The Canada-English culture might be described as one in which individual action aimed at work-related issues is highly valued. A preference for preestablished rules and standard procedures fell within the average range for the thirteen cultures considered in the larger cross-cultural study. The Canada-French culture, however, had the highest value of all the thirteen cultures for reducing or avoiding ambiguity and uncertainty at work. Combined with a preference for group activity, shared responsibility, and a tendency toward social consciousness, a preferred mode of uncertainty reduction might take the form of verbal discussion and analysis with the goal of understanding and feeling comfortable with decisions. Such a mode of uncertainty avoidance matches anecdotal reports both for French-speaking Canadians and for Latin cultures generally (i.e., European French, Italian, Spanish). A point sometimes lost on more individualistically oriented cultures is that the goal in such discussions is not necessarily to come to a "logical" conclusion, but rather to reach a satisfactory comfort level so that action can be taken within the given circumstances. This distinction, to some degree, falls under the contrast between universal versus particularistic cultures. Universalistic cultures try to establish a rule or procedure that applies to all situations, whereas particularistic

Table 11.1
Comparison of Means for Cultural Work Values and Burnout between
Canada-English and Canada-French

Variable	Canada-French	Canada-English	F	p
Cultural work values				
Power distance	49.28	51.68	2.016	ns
Uncertainty avoidance	59.67	50.63	32.861	.0001
Individualism-Collectivism	46.93	53.39	9.642	.002
Career success-Quality of life	45.59	49.50	4.963	.028
Burnout				
Emotional exhaustion	47.64	47.51	.006	ns
Depersonalization	48.50	48.82	.034	ns
Personal accomplishment	51.83	54.07	1.722	ns

ns = no significant difference.

cultures feel compelled to consider the unique aspects of the current situation and especially the interpersonal relationships involved (Trompenaars & Hampden-Turner, 1998).

BURNOUT DIFFERENCES

Canada-English and Canada-French did not differ significantly on any of the three burnout subscales (see Table 11.1). Both cultures showed average burnout configurations consistent with lower burnout, that is, lower emotional exhaustion, lower depersonalization, and higher personal accomplishment. This lack of difference between cultures on burnout is a quite surprising result, given the dramatic differences in culture described above. Apparently, each culture has developed satisfactory methods of preventing, treating, and recovering from burnout.

DEMOGRAPHIC AND WORK VARIABLES

Prior to a separate consideration of how each Canadian culture deals with burnout, a few demographic and work variables will be considered to develop an understanding of how child and youth care looks in the two cultures. Table 11.2 lists some of the points of comparison. Despite the lack of differences in burnout, the practice of child and youth care was organized quite differently in the Canada-English and Canada-French cultures. The Canada-French child and youth care practitioners were substantially older, a higher proportion were male, and they had served longer in their current positions and longer in the child and youth care field generally. The Canada-English sample worked in smaller-sized agencies, had fewer years of formal education, worked longer hours, and got paid less. The Canada-French child care practice seems to retain its workers longer (see Figure 11.1), with over 70 percent working for fifteen or more years in the field; this is the longest of all

Table 11.2
Comparison of Demographic Factors for Canada-English and Canada-French

Variable	Canada-French	Canada-English	F	p
Age	43.7	36.4	35.212	.001
Gender			3.457	.06
Male	48%	29%		
Female	52%	71%		
Education level in years	16.2	15.7	.018	ns
Length in current position in years	10.44	7.83	5.142	.026
Length in child care field in years	12.96	9.17	24.659	.001
Agency size	73.5	53.4	7.946	.01
Age of clients			.830	ns
Children	9%	20%		
Adolescents	91%	80%		
Hours per week worked	33.9	37.6	6.819	.01
Salary per month in Canadian dollars	2963	2375	11.371	.001

ns = no significant difference.

Figure 11.1
Comparison of Length of Time in the Field of Child and Youth Care for Canada-English and Canada-French

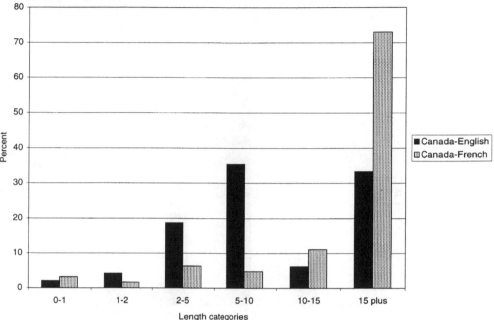

thirteen cultures in the larger study. On the other hand, the Canada-English culture, even though slightly above the average for the other thirteen cultures in the larger study, was still significantly lower in length of time in the field. In collectivist cultures workers show a stronger loyalty to and dependence on the organizations they work for than to workers in individualistic cultures. The differences in longevity in the Canada-French versus Canada-English cultures was consistent with their contrast on this cultural value dimension. Consistent with greater longevity were significantly older workers in the Canada-French culture whose average salary was higher than that of younger workers in the Canada-English culture. Contributing to these results is an unusually long history of professionalization of child and youth care in the French sector in Quebec that has resulted in more status for the field and better working conditions. Also, a French language university program that trains child and youth care workers in the educateur model has been in place for many years.

Although Canada-French workers were employed by larger-sized agencies, their hours per week worked were less, consistent with a stronger value of balance between work and other aspects of life. In contrast, Canada-English, with a higher career success orientation, showed a higher proportion of practitioners working more than forty hours per week (see Figure 11.2).

Figure 11.2
Comparison of Hours per Week Worked for Canada-English and Canada-French

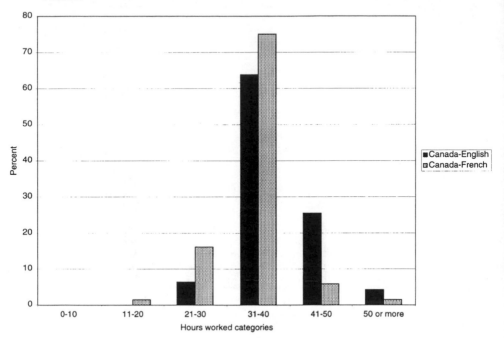

One other interesting finding was that the Canada-English culture had a much higher proportion of workers operating in the milieu of the child and far lower percentage working in individual meetings than did Canada-French. This is consistent with the distribution of primary job roles for the two cultures (see Figure 11.3). The Canada-English sample was overwhelmingly first-line child and youth workers, while the Canada-French sample showed more specialists, teachers, and managers.

In summary, the individualism–collectivism and career success–quality of life cultural differences may have had some impact on who worked as child and youth care workers and how their careers were structured. Longevity in one's career was probably affected not only by culture, but also by the opportunity for performing other roles while staying in the child and youth care field. In Canada generally, child and youth care services are regulated, job titles are protected, unions are strong, and working conditions overall are quite favorable.

CONTRIBUTORS TO BURNOUT IN EACH CULTURE

In this section, the Canada-French and Canada-English cultures will be considered separately. The focus will be on patterns of work environment,

Figure 11.3
Comparison of Primary Job Roles for Canada-English and Canada-French

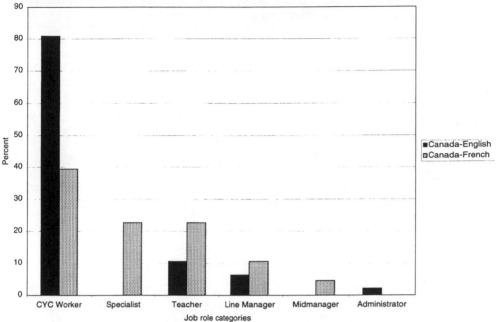

coping, and cultural conformity that were related to the three aspects of burn-out within each culture.

Canada-English

For the Canada-English culture, significant relationships between coping styles occurred with both emotional exhaustion and personal accomplishment, but not with depersonalization (see Table 11.3).

For emotional exhaustion (EE), only reduced control coping showed a significant relationship. No work environment or cultural conformity differences emerged as significant. Thus, workers in the Canada-English culture who felt emotionally drained from work were less likely to employ a coping style that aimed at directly changing the sources of stress.

$$EE = \downarrow \text{control coping}$$

For personal accomplishment (PA), a combination of higher control coping and lower escape coping related to higher levels of this burnout subscale. Workers who felt that they achieved more at work were more likely to rely on a coping style that emphasized direct action to reduce the sources of stress

Table 11.3
Hierarchical Multiple Regression of Emotional Exhaustion, Depersonalization, and Personal Accomplishment with Work Environment, Coping, and Cultural Conformity in Canada-English

Variables	Emotional exhaustion	Depersonalization	Personal accomplishment
Step 1: Work environment	R^2= .244	R^2= .171	R^2= .196
	$F(7,39)$= 1.801	$F(7,39)$= 1.151	$F(7,39)$= 1.354
Peer cohesion	β = .342	β = .598	β = -.082
Supervisor support	β = -.280	β = -.398	β = -.062
Autonomy	β = .195	β = .108	β = .301
Task orientation	β = -.193	β = -.057	β = .028
Work pressure	β = .158	β = -.183	β = .056
Control	β = .107	β = -.050	β = .295
Innovation	β = -.502	β = -.475	β = .223
Step 2: Coping style	R^2= .401	R^2= .304	R^2= .456
	$F(9,37)$= 2.757*	$F(9,37)$= 1.794	$F(9,37)$= 3.451**
Control coping	β = -.384*	β = -.341	β = .491**
Escape coping	β = .366*	β = .348	β = -.475**
Step 3: Cultural conformity	R^2= .479	R^2= .311	R^2= .503
	$F(13,33)$= 2.342*	$F(13,33)$= 1.145	$F(13,33)$= 2.568*
Power distance	β = .224	β = .065	β = .156
Uncertainty avoidance	β = .191	β = -.054	β = .089
Individualism	β = -.011	β = -.009	β = .169
Career success	β = -.006	β = -.058	β = .078

$*p < 0.05; **p < 0.01; ***p < 0.001.$

and avoid a coping style that only focused on reducing or avoiding the unpleasant personal feelings associated with stress.

$$PA = \downarrow escape\ coping + \uparrow control\ coping$$

Taken together, it seems that Canadian-English child and youth care workers employed differing coping styles with differing results in relation to burnout. With a direct approach to reducing sources of stress, there was an inverse relationship to differing aspects of burnout. Clearly, a positive outcome of a sense of achievement and accomplishment at work was related to increased utilization of the direct approach, while a negative outcome of feeling emotionally drained was related to a decreased utilization. At the same time, avoiding reliance on coping whose purpose was ameliorating the unpleasant emotions surrounding the stressful situation had the positive outcome of a greater sense of personal achievement at work. Neither aspects of the work environment nor individual differences in relation to cultural conformity were strong enough to add to the coping style results. It may well be that the individualistic cultural value of self-reliance in the Canada-English culture helped to accentuate the personal variable of coping styles above all other variables.

Canada-French

For the Canada-French culture, significant relationships between work environment, coping, and cultural conformity occurred with emotional exhaustion and personal accomplishment, but not with depersonalization (see Table 11.4).

Emotional exhaustion (EE) showed a relationship with higher work pressure (WP), escape coping, and uncertainty avoidance that was above average for the Canada-French culture (UA deviation). That is, under conditions of work overload, workers who suffered from higher emotional fatigue were more likely to value approaches that reduced ambiguity at work and more likely employ a coping style that focused on reduction of the anxiety and distress accompanying the stressful situation.

$$EE = \uparrow WP + \uparrow \text{escape coping} + \uparrow \text{UA deviation}$$

Personal accomplishment (PA) for Canada-French child and youth care workers was associated with higher levels of supervisor support (SS) and higher levels of control coping. Thus, workers felt a stronger sense of accomplishment at work when their immediate supervisors were encouraging of them and when the workers acted explicitly to reduce stress at its source.

$$PA = \uparrow SS + \uparrow \text{control coping}$$

In the Canada-French culture, work environment factors added to the understanding of two aspects of burnout. The impact of pressure to work is consistent with other findings regarding burnout (Lee & Ashforth, 1996; Savicki & Cooley, 1987). It may well be that the social support variable of support from one's supervisor was related to the differentiated job roles found in the Canada-French culture (Savicki, 1993, 1999a), or to more collectivist values that emphasize social over individual responsibility. The pattern of relationship between coping styles and burnout also resembled results from

Table 11.4
Hierarchical Multiple Regression of Emotional Exhaustion, Depersonalization, and Personal Accomplishment with Work Environment, Coping, and Cultural Conformity in Canada-French

Variables	Emotional exhaustion	Depersonalization	Personal accomplishment
Step 1: Work environment	R^2 = .294	R^2 = .091	R^2 = .207
	$F(7,60)$ = 3.575**	$F(7,60)$ = .873	$F(7,60)$ = 2.231*
Peer cohesion	β = .038	β = -.057	β = .019
Supervisor support	β = -.193	β = -.112	β = .493*
Autonomy	β = -.142	β = .111	β = -.107
Task orientation	β = -.009	β = -.109	β = .127
Work pressure	β = .288*	β = .233	β = .118
Control	β = -.089	β = -.076	β = .069
Innovation	β = -.214	β = -.174	β = .038
Step 2: Coping style	R^2 = .326	R^2 = .004	R^2 = .254
	$F(9,58)$ = 3.116**	$F(9,58)$ = 1.031	$F(9,58)$ = 3.534**
Control coping	β = -.045	β = .037	β = .369**
Escape coping	β = .241*	β = .203	β = .097
Step 3: Cultural conformity	R^2 = .423	R^2 = .208	R^2 = .424
	$F(13,54)$ = 3.045**	$F(13,54)$ = 1.09	$F(13,54)$ = 3.052**
Power distance	β = .201	β = -.087	β = -.203
Uncertainty avoidance	β = .252*	β = .212	β = .021
Individualism	β = .149	β = -.031	β = -.079
Career success	β = .050	β = .192	β = -.208

+$p < 0.06$; *$p < 0.05$; **$p < 0.01$; ***$p < 0.001$.

other studies (Riolli-Saltzman & Savicki, 2001c). Of special interest was the cultural conformity variable of uncertainty avoidance. The Canada-French culture as a whole has the highest uncertainty avoidance average of all thirteen cultures in the larger study. Individuals whose personal assent to this value was even higher than the cultural norm were more likely to feel drained from work activities, and those whose assent fell lower than the cultural average were less likely to experience this feeling.

In summary, although there were no differences in burnout between the Canada-French and Canada-English cultures, large differences appeared in cultural dimensions in the manner of child and youth care practice, and in the contributors to burnout in each culture. With three of the four cultural dimensions significantly different, dramatic differences in culture exist side by side in Canada, especially in Quebec Province. With regard to burnout, these differences seem to guide child and youth care practitioners in the two cultures to find ways to perform their duties without extensive burnout. When burnout does occur, each culture has a slightly different pattern of contributors.

It seems likely that the Canada-French and Canada-English child and youth care work institutions have been able to erect culturally sensitive organizations that meet the needs of their employees. Given the different cultural values, the formal and informal structures and processes in the child and youth care organizations are likely to look quite different. The more formal, relationship-focused, and collective Canada-French organizations with more specialization and greater worker longevity seem to meet the needs of the Canada-French workers. The more individual, informal, and career-focused Canada-English organizations respond better to the Canada-English workers. Each culture has found a solution for lower burnout in its child and youth care workers.

CHAPTER 12

East and West:
Burnout and the Fall of
the Iron Curtain

The political and ideological divisions that were imposed on and solidified in Europe after World War II set the stage for a stark delineation between cultures on either side of the Iron Curtain. Regardless of similarities or differences of the cultures prior to 1945, the Cold War struggle between communist and capitalist systems highlighted several of the features that Triandis (1995, 1996) suggests form the basis for cultural differences. Clearly the territory of the East Bloc and West Bloc countries was separated, and contact across that border was severely restricted. Ideological differences were highlighted in many aspects of the cultures; for example in schools, the arts, the press. Finally, the political and economic systems imposed radically different demands on the population; including, of course, child and youth care workers.

For these reasons, the partition into East and West separated by the Iron Curtain should have spawned cultural differences. Even after the fall of communism, the beginnings of free-market economies, and the restoration of freedom of movement and exchange between the formerly separated cultures, it is not logical to presume that forty years of history could be immediately erased, nor should cultures inevitably become more homogeneous. The research question to be examined in this chapter is, "Did 40 years of separation between former East Bloc and West Bloc countries make a difference in culture, burnout, and child and youth care service in those cultures?"

For the purposes of answering this question, only European cultures from the larger sample were included in this analysis. Former East Bloc countries included Germany-East, Slovakia, and Poland (total $N = 220$). Former West Bloc countries included Austria, Denmark, England, Germany-West, and Scotland (total $N = 319$). In previous chapters, we have seen that there was a good deal of variation across these European cultures; therefore, consistent differences that may emerge between the former East and former West Bloc cultures will have to be strong enough to overcome the variations within those groupings.

The following shows a contrast between capitalist and communist ideologies on several important factors (Sargent, 1996; Shay, 2000):

Ideological Factors	Capitalism	Communism
Role of the individual	Rational determination of self-interest and action (individualism)	Belief and action based on Party discipline (collectivism)
Definition of liberty	Freedom of choice, freedom from government interference (individualism, low uncertainty avoidance)	Freedom to act upon approved ideology and values (collectivism, high uncertainty avoidance)
Attitudes toward private property	Goods are a reward for successful, self-interested behavior (individualism, career success)	Private ownership abolished (collectivism, quality of life)
Definition of self-realization	Achievement and success in a competitive occupation (individualism, low power distance)	Attained through dedication to the Party (collectivism, low power distance, high uncertainty avoidance)
Definition of progress	Economic growth based on action of self-interested individuals (individualism, career success)	Movement toward a classless society (collectivism, low power distance)
Role of government	Protect individual and property rights (individualism, career success)	To advance the ideology until it is accepted, and then to disappear (collectivism, low power distance)
Acceptable procedures	Contracts, efficiency, pragmatism, compromise (individualism, low power distance)	Centralized planning and control, Party discipline (collectivism, high uncertainty avoidance)

The explanations are quite brief; however, included is a prediction concerning which cultural work values might be invoked in support of the ideology specified. Of the seven ideological factors contrasted, capitalism illustrates individualism in each of the seven, career success in three of the seven, low power distance in two, and low uncertainty avoidance in one. For communism, collectivism is illustrated in seven of seven, high uncertainty avoidance in three, low power distance in three, and quality of life in one. The assignment of cultural work value dimensions was based on the perceived match between the ideology and the cultural value. There may be debate about various of the conclusions embodied here; however, this forms a set of hypotheses that can be tested concerning the contrasts that may be found in the subsequent East–West comparison.

CULTURE DIFFERENCES

Table 12.1 shows that the former East and West Bloc cultures differ significantly on cultural work values ($F(9,498) = 10.091, p < 0.0001$). Former East Bloc cultures were significantly higher on uncertainty avoidance ($F(1,537) = 7.277, p < 0.001$). The former West Bloc cultures were higher on individualism ($F(1,537) = 13.749, p < 0.001$) and career success ($F(1,537) = 24.488, p < 0.001$). There was no difference on power distance. The combination of high individualism and a focus on career success seems to capture key features of the capitalist economic system which favors entrepreneurship, monetary achievement, and individual rewards. In contrast, the combination of collectivism and a focus on quality of life seems to reflect key features of the communist ideology which favors communal action, social consciousness, and rewards based on group membership rather than individual merit. A review of Figure 5.3 in Chapter 5 shows the two-by-two comparison of cultures on individualism–collectivism and career success–quality of life. Except for England, the East and West Bloc cultures organize themselves in opposing quadrants on this two-by-two comparison. Poland, Germany-East, and Slovakia were all in the collectivist–quality of life quadrant, and Denmark, Austria, Germany-West, and Scotland were in the individualist–career success quadrant. Thus, the overall distinctions between former East and West seem to capture meaningful cultural differences.

The higher score on uncertainty avoidance for the former East Bloc cultures seems to fit nicely with the contrasting ideologies, as does the absence of difference on power distance. There is considerable overlap between former East and West Bloc cultures on uncertainty avoidance with Germany-West and Austria being higher than any East culture and Denmark and England being lower (see the two-by-two comparison in Figure 5.4 of Chapter 5). However, on average, East Bloc cultures showed higher uncertainty avoidance. The ideology of communism supports removal of status differences, while in reality the tenets of centralized economy and centralized decision making common to the communist political system might suggest that power distance would be higher in the former East Bloc cultures. Indeed, Poland and Slovakia show quite high scores on this dimension; however, Germany-East is in the lower half of this scale. It may be that on average the formality of the process of making decisions in a centralized economy substituted for

Table 12.1

Comparison of Means for Cultural Work Values and Burnout between Former East Bloc and Former West Bloc European Cultures

Variable	East	West	F	p
Cultural work values				
Power distance	51.627	50.167	2.589	ns
Uncertainty avoidance	51.236	49.002	7.277	.007
Individualism-Collectivism	47.722	51.025	13.749	.0001
Career success-Quality of life	47.331	51.746	24.488	.0001
Burnout				
Emotional exhaustion	47.953	50.639	9.474	.002
Depersonalization	48.607	50.894	6.785	.009
Personal accomplishment	45.652	50.194	28.177	.0001

ns = no significant difference.

the value of acquiescence to central leadership. On a day-to-day basis, the rules, regulations, and bureaucracy imposed by central planning might have had more direct impact on the former East Bloc cultures than did the influence of individual leaders. Such a result is consistent with the "leadership substitutes" approach found in organizational psychology (Podsakoff, MacKensie, & Bommer, 1996), in which clear and consistent rules and procedures can render direction from leaders unnecessary.

Thus, cultural differences between former East and West Bloc cultures support the hypothesis that values from ideology and political and economic systems may have become embedded in the contrasting cultural groupings.

BURNOUT DIFFERENCES

East and West Bloc cultures were significantly different on all the burnout scales ($F(3,535) = 13.847$, $p < 0.001$). The former West Bloc cultures were higher on all the scales (see Table 12.1). The largest difference was in personal accomplishment ($F(1,537) = 28.177$, $p < 0.001$), followed by emotional exhaustion ($F(1,537) = 9.474$, $p < 0.01$), and depersonalization ($F(1,537) = 6.785$, $p < 0.01$). The pattern of higher negative aspects of burnout (emotional exhaustion and depersonalization) combined with higher positive reaction to work (personal accomplishment) fits nicely with the high individualism and career success values of the former West Bloc cultures. In this case, workers who emphasize the importance of work must shoulder the blame for whatever goes wrong at work; at the same time, they can also assume the credit for aspects that go well. In contrast, in former East Bloc cultures a value of communal action and shared responsibility combined with a lesser emphasis on work so that, although a sense of achievement at work was lower, so were the negative affective reactions. Although Hofstede (1980) found a linkage between high uncertainty avoidance and job stress, the reverse seems to be true in the current East–West comparison since the higher uncertainty avoidant East shows less emotional exhaustion and depersonalization than does the lower uncertainty avoidant West. In this comparison, it may be that the rules and standard procedures imposed to control work uncertainties both removed incentives for individual achievement, but also reduced personal responsibility for problems or failures. In addition, there were few consequences for poor performance, since workers were guaranteed employment regardless of their output.

DEMOGRAPHIC AND WORK VARIABLES

Several demographic and work-related variables show significant differences between the former East and West Bloc cultures ($F(9,498) = 21.704$, $p < 0.001$). Table 12.2 shows that the former East Bloc cultures were significantly higher in years of formal education ($F(1,532) = 43.239$, $p < 0.0001$), and average size of child and youth care agencies ($F(1,532) = 129.780$, $p < 0.0001$). The former West Bloc cultures were higher in years in the child and youth care field ($F(1,532) = 11.640$, $p < 0.001$), hours per week worked ($F(1,532) = 4.729$, $p < 0.05$), and salary distribution ($F(1,532) = 6.308$, $p < 0.05$).

Figure 12.1 shows that the modal education level for West Bloc cultures is thirteen to fourteen years. This corresponds with the vocationally oriented certification programs available in most West Bloc cultures. In contrast, the modal education level for former East Bloc cultures is fifteen to sixteen years, with a large percentage at the twenty or more years bracket as well. East Bloc cultures have historically required higher education levels. University diplomas seem more commonly required in the former East. Significantly higher proportions of graduate degrees also appeared. Often age or gender related to years of formal education, but in the two groups of cultures these correlations were near zero. The higher levels of formal education in the former East may reflect higher formality and constraints as indicated by higher uncertainty avoidance. Hofstede (1980) cites both "greater dependence of citizens on authorities" and "stronger accent on expertise" as characteristic of high uncertainty avoidance cultures (pp. 142–143). One way of demonstrating expertise and attaining status in the former East was through advanced education. In addition,

Table 12.2
Comparison of Demographic Factors for Former East Bloc and Former West Bloc European Cultures

Variable	East	West	F	p
Age	37.2	38.3	.467	ns
Gender			3.486	ns
Male	32%	39%		
Female	68%	61%		
Education level in years	15.5	13.8	43.238	.0001
Length in current position in years	4.24	4.96	1.058	ns
Length in child care field in years	7.78	9.28	11.640	.001
Agency size	58.5	30.1	129.78	.0001
Age of clients			2.887	ns
Children	38%	31%		
Adolescents	62%	69%		
Hours per week worked	37	38	4.201	.041
Salary distribution by salary bracket	3.7 Mid-low	4.2 Middle	6.308	.012

ns = no significant difference.

the formal requirements for degrees and certifications for comparable positions were higher. Such concerns would support higher levels of education.

Figure 12.2 shows East–West comparisons on years spent in the field of child and youth care. Former West Bloc cultures showed a consistent rise in percentage of workers in longer years-in-the-field brackets. Even though there was no significant difference between East and West on primary job role distribution, workers in the former West Bloc showed greater longevity. By contrast, the former East Bloc cultures showed a dramatic drop in the ten to fifteen years-in-the-field bracket. In the former East Bloc, it seems that workers may opt out of child and youth care some time after they reach the critical five-year mark. It would be interesting to discover if that dip in longevity was

Figure 12.1
Comparison of Education Levels of Former East Bloc and Former West Bloc European Cultures

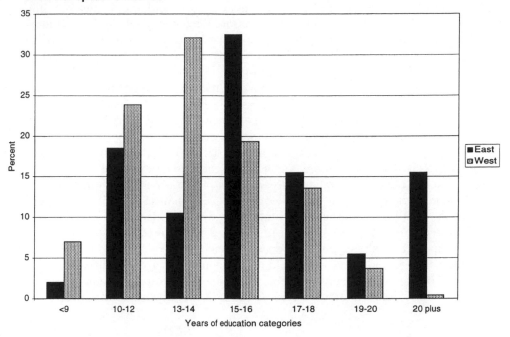

Figure 12.2
Comparison of Length of Time in the Field of Child and Youth Work in Former East Bloc and Former West Bloc European Cultures

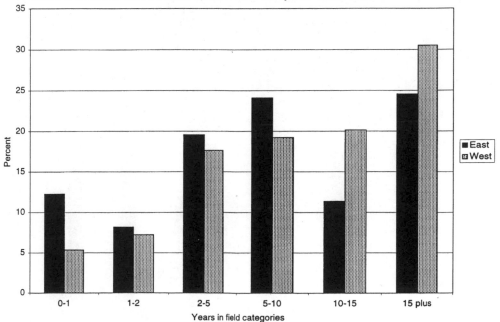

related to the fall of communism. Workers under the previous political system may have wanted to change careers but felt locked into the field of child and youth care. The opening up of options fomented by changes in political and economic systems may have spurred more defections from child and youth care than in previous times. The five-year mark is critical for this decision (see Chapter 6 for further explanation).

Figure 12.3 reveals the most dramatic difference between former East and West Bloc cultures with the comparison of agency size. In the West, the modal number of child and youth care workers were employed in organizations with ten to thirty clients; 45 percent of workers were employed by agencies in that size range. In contrast, the modal agency size in the East was in the seventy-five to one-hundred or more range; 40 percent of workers served in these large agencies. Larger, centralized organizations are consistent with the communist political system. At the time of data collection in 1996–1997, colleagues in the East indicated that deinstitutionalization was planned or under way in those cultures. In the West, that process had been already well established.

Figure 12.4 shows the differences in hours per week worked between the former East and West Bloc cultures. Although the average difference was only one hour per week (see Table 12.2), the distributions were interestingly different. The East showed a wider range of hours worked. More part-time

Figure 12.3
Comparison of Agency Size in Former East Bloc and Former West Bloc European Cultures

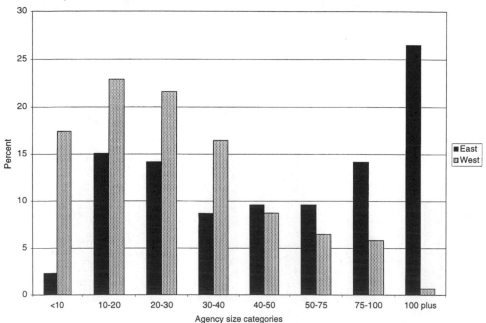

Figure 12.4
**Comparison of Hours per Week Worked in Former East Bloc and Former
West Bloc European Cultures**

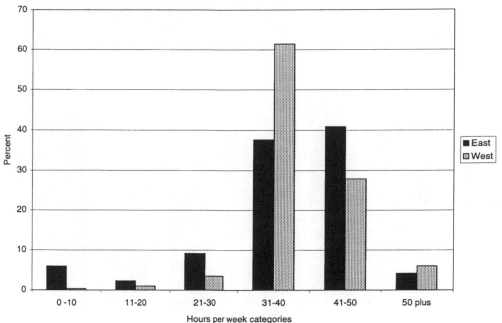

opportunities seemed to exist in the East. In the West roughly 90 percent of child and youth care workers labored between thirty and fifty hours per week. In several Western cultures this workweek was regulated by the state or through union-negotiated contracts. This larger proportion may reflect the stronger career success value shown in former West Bloc cultures.

Finally, Figure 12.5 shows the differences in the salary ranges between the former East and West Bloc cultures. Although the ranges are not comparable through conversion to a single currency, the salary brackets span the range of salaries available in the field of child and youth care within each culture. Thus, comparisons can be made in the distribution of salary if not in absolute amount. From other sources we can determine that the former East Bloc economies were not as strong as the former West, so that child and youth care workers were generally better paid in the West than in the East, if absolute monetary value is considered. Beyond absolute value, the ranges look remarkably different. Although each distribution is bimodal, the peaks appear in different salary brackets and show different intensities. In the former East Bloc cultures, slightly more than 40 percent or workers were in the mid-low bracket and 28 percent were in the highest bracket. Thus, 69 percent of all child and youth care workers in the East fell into these two salary brackets. There was a substantial gap between the two peaks. In the West, however, the

Figure 12.5
Comparison of Salary Distribution in Former East Bloc and Former West Bloc European Cultures

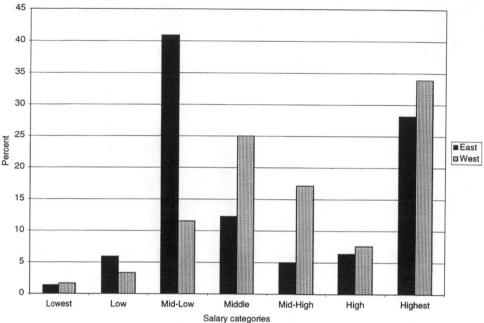

salaries were more evenly distributed. The first peak was in the middle salary bracket, and the second peak was in the highest bracket. In contrast to the East, however, the West showed 12 to 17 percent in the brackets surrounding the middle bracket. The larger salary differentiation in the former East Bloc could be related to the higher uncertainty avoidance value, since differentiations in the value of expertise and authority could be reflected in salary. In contrast, the more even distribution in the former West Bloc might relate to higher individualism with salary being more related to personal achievement and merit.

CONTRIBUTORS TO BURNOUT IN EACH CULTURE

In this section, former East and West Bloc cultures will be considered separately. The focus will be on patterns of work environment, coping, and cultural conformity that were related to the three aspects of burnout within each culture.

Former East Bloc

For former East Bloc cultures, significant relationships between coping and cultural conformity occurred with both emotional exhaustion and depersonalization. For personal accomplishment, both work environment and coping showed significant relationships (see Table 12.3).

For emotional exhaustion (EE), a combination of higher escape coping and deviations from cultural conformity that showed higher-than-average uncertainty avoidance (UA deviation) and collectivism (COL deviation) related to higher levels of this burnout scale. Workers who acted to reduce the negative emotions associated with work stress and whose values of formality and procedural rules combined with their view that work should occur in a communal fashion with shared responsibility, showed more emotional fatigue at work. Variations of work environment did not contribute to understanding emotional exhaustion.

Table 12.3
Hierarchical Multiple Regression of Emotional Exhaustion, Depersonalization, and Personal Accomplishment with Work Environment, Coping, and Cultural Conformity in the Former East Bloc European Cultures

Variables	Emotional exhaustion	Depersonalization	Personal accomplishment
Step 1: Work environment	R^2= .038	R^2= .020	R^2= .122
	$F(7,211)$= 1.174	$F(7,211)$= .630	$F(7,211)$= 4.196**
Peer cohesion	β = -.098	β = -.071	β = .157
Supervisor support	β = -.016	β = -.074	β = .009
Autonomy	β = .000	β = -.002	β = -.241**
Task orientation	β = .148	β = -.020	β = .169*
Work pressure	β - .059	β = .000	β = -.056
Control	β = -.048	β = .074	β = -.015
Innovation	β = -.140	β = .056	β = .139
Step 2: Coping style	R^2= .248	R^2= .236	R^2= .324
	$F(9,209)$= 7.670***	$F(9,208)$= 7.155***	$F(9,209)$= 11 125***
Control coping	β = .122	β = .015	β = .441***
Escape coping	β = .413***	β = .464***	β = .131*
Step 3: Cultural conformity	R^2= .414	R^2= .293	R^2= .329
	$F(13,205)$= 6.463***	$F(13,205)$= 6.531***	$F(13,205)$= 7.728***
Power distance	β = -.079	β = -.132+	β = .038
Uncertainty avoidance	β = .144*	β = .157*	β = -.043
Individualism	β = -.128+	β = -.146*	β = .044
Career success	β = .099	β = .101	β = -.036

+p < 0.06; *p < 0.05; **p < 0.01; ***p < 0.001.

$$EE = \uparrow \text{ escape coping} + \uparrow \text{ UA deviation} + \uparrow \text{ COL deviation}$$

For depersonalization (DP), a combination of higher escape coping and deviations from cultural conformity that showed higher-than-average uncertainty avoidance (UA deviation) and collectivism (COL deviation) and lower-than-average power distance (PD deviation) related to higher levels of this burnout scale. Workers who acted to reduce the negative emotions associated with work stress, and whose values of formality and procedural rules combined with their view that work should occur in a communal fashion with shared responsibility and that leadership should be consultative showed greater emotional insulation and loss of empathy at work. Variations of work environment did not contribute to understanding depersonalization.

$$DP = \uparrow \text{ escape coping} + \uparrow \text{ UA deviation} + \uparrow \text{ COL deviation} + \downarrow \text{ PD deviation}$$

For personal accomplishment (PA), lower autonomy (A) and higher task orientation (TO) combined with higher control coping to predict higher levels of this burnout scale. Under conditions of efficient task structure and low requirements to make decisions on their own, workers who dealt directly with sources of the stress were more likely to show a higher sense of achievement and accomplishment at work. Variations of cultural conformity did not contribute to understanding personal accomplishment.

$$PA = \downarrow A + \uparrow TO + \uparrow \text{ control coping}$$

Taken together, these findings for the former East Bloc cultures show an affirmation of the desire to have the work environment efficiently structured and nondemanding of individual initiative as might be expected given the overall cultural values of uncertainty avoidance and collectivism. As with the larger thirteen-culture sample, emotion-focused coping most strongly related to the negatively toned aspects of burnout, while problem-focused coping related to the positively toned aspect. Those workers who showed even higher collectivist and uncertainty avoidant values than their already high cultures reported more emotional exhaustion and depersonalization. Personal accomplishment in the former East Bloc cultures seems to be related less to individual accomplishment than to completing one's prescribed duties. Within collectivist and uncertainty avoidant cultures, not standing out and fulfilling one's prescribed roles may form the foundation for sense of accomplishment.

Former West Bloc

For former West Bloc cultures, significant relationships between work environment and coping occurred with all three burnout scales. Cultural conformity emerged as significant only for personal accomplishment (see Table 12.4).

Table 12.4
Hierarchical Multiple Regression of Emotional Exhaustion,
Depersonalization, and Personal Accomplishment with Work Environment,
Coping, and Cultural Work Values in Former West Bloc European Cultures

Variables	Emotional exhaustion	Depersonalization	Personal accomplishment
Step 1: Work environment	R^2= .246	R^2= .127	R^2= .073
	$F(7,307)= 14.339$***	$F(7,307)= 6.406$***	$F(7,307)= 3.459$**
Peer cohesion	$\beta = -.120$*	$\beta = -.156$*	$\beta = .032$
Supervisor support	$\beta = -.156$*	$\beta = -.130$	$\beta = -.049$
Autonomy	$\beta = -.006$	$\beta = .051$	$\beta = .111$
Task orientation	$\beta = -.148$**	$\beta = -.157$*	$\beta = .023$
Work pressure	$\beta = .333$***	$\beta = .118$*	$\beta = .041$
Control	$\beta = .078$	$\beta = -.033$	$\beta = .102$
Innovation	$\beta = .045$	$\beta = -.031$	$\beta = .192$**
Step 2: Coping style	R^2= .274	R^2= .185	R^2= .152
	$F(9,305)= 12.79$***	$F(9,305)= 7.701$***	$F(9,305)= 6.077$***
Control coping	$\beta = -.136$*	$\beta = -.028$	$\beta = .309$***
Escape coping	$\beta = .143$**	$\beta = .249$***	$\beta = -.052$
Step 3: Cultural	R^2= .280	R^2= .193	R^2= .167
conformity	$F(13,301)= 9.007$***	$F(13,301)= 5.538$***	$F(13,301)= 4.639$***
Power distance	$\beta = -.012$	$\beta = -.036$	$\beta = .059$
Uncertainty avoidance	$\beta = .078$	$\beta = .030$	$\beta = -.005$
Individualism	$\beta = -.000$	$\beta = .016$	$\beta = .107$*
Career success	$\beta = .048$	$\beta = .076$	$\beta = .032$

$+p < 0.06$; *$p < 0.05$; **$p < 0.01$; ***$p < 0.001$.

For emotional exhaustion (EE), a combination of higher work pressure (WP), lower task orientation (TO), lower supervisor support (SS), and lower peer cohesion (PC) combined with higher escape coping and lower control coping to relate to higher levels of this burnout scale. Under conditions of work overload with inefficiently organized work and poor relationships with one's supervisor and coworkers, those child and youth care workers who reduced their attempts to deal directly with stressors and increased their focus on diminishing the negative aspects of stress reported higher emotional fatigue. Variations of cultural conformity did not contribute to understanding emotional exhaustion.

$$EE = \uparrow WP + \downarrow TO + \downarrow SS + \downarrow PC + \uparrow \text{escape coping} + \downarrow \text{control coping}$$

For depersonalization (DP), the combination of higher work pressure (WP), lower task orientation (TO), and lower peer cohesion (PC) combined with higher escape coping to relate to higher levels of this burnout scale. In a situation in which workload was intense but poorly organized and in which coworker relationships were poor, child and youth care workers who only focused on reducing the emotional distress of the situation reported higher emotional alienation from clients.

$$DP = \uparrow WP + \downarrow TO + \downarrow PC + \uparrow \text{escape coping}$$

For personal accomplishment (PA) a combination of higher innovation (INN), higher control coping, and a higher-than-average value of individualism (IND deviation) related to this burnout scale. Thus, in an environment in which new ideas were valued, those workers who dealt directly with stressful situations and valued individual responsibility reported a higher sense of achievement and fulfillment at work.

$$PA = \uparrow INN + \uparrow \text{control coping} + \uparrow IND \text{ deviation}$$

Both work structure and social support in the work environment emerged as significant for the former West Bloc cultures. Moderate, well-organized work that was conducted with encouragement from supervisors and especially coworkers seemed to decrease reported burnout. Problem and emotion-focused coping contributed to burnout in predictable ways. Personal accomplishment showed a pattern most consistent with overall cultural values. Those workers with even higher individualist values within individualistic cultures reported a higher sense of fulfillment at work when they employed problem-focused coping in an environment which supported change and new ideas. The source of this accomplishment seems clearly strongly based in personal action and responsibility.

CONCLUSION

Cultural values seemed to have set the stage for differing levels of burnout, differing examples of demographic and work-related factors, and differing patterns of environmental, coping, and cultural conformity contributors to burnout. The cultural differences discovered were consistent with differences in the ideological, economic, and political values between the two sets of cultures solidified during the years following World War II.

Of interest is the strong contribution of work environment variables to explanations of burnout for former West Bloc cultures, but their virtual absence for former East Bloc cultures. Career-minded individualists may be more likely to seek explanations for their problems in the environment than from within themselves (Matsumoto, 1996). In contrast, collectivists with a high need for structure may presume that distress is more related to individual deviation from cultural norms. Opportunities to prevent or remediate burnout would need to take different forms for these two cultural clusters. An environmental change may be valued as directly on target in the West, but irrelevant in the East.

It would be instructive to return to these contrasting cultures in the near future to see whether political and economic changes instituted since the fall of communism are reflected in overall cultural values.

CHAPTER 13

Separated by a Common Language: Australia, Canada, England, Scotland, and the United States

At one time, it was true that the sun never set on the British Empire. Therefore, the English language was spread across many continents through Britain's formidable military and commercial might. Along with the British went their language, their culture, their values, and their laws. Over the centuries, the sun has set on the British Empire, but its influence was felt much longer through the British Commonwealth and continued trading ties with former colonies. This chapter attempts to document the degree to which a common English language and persistent commercial and cultural influence may still have an impact today.

Over and above the commonalties that language might imply, the various English-speaking cultures included in this study have distinct histories and varied relationships with England and the English culture from which the language has sprung. Scotland had a long and often bloody resistance to English influence, which ended with its incorporation into the United Kingdom. After centuries of affiliation with England, Scotland is today expanding its independence within the United Kingdom. In 1776, the United States separated from Britain through armed rebellion. Early conflicts have been followed by a closer relationship at the beginning of the twenty-first century. Australia began its English-language history as a penal colony. Individuals, usually of lower social status, who ran afoul of English laws were expelled from British soil to shift for themselves in a far-off land. Later, however, Australia became a part of the British Commonwealth and continues to this day to recognize the British monarch as its nominal head of state. Many citizens of English-speaking Canada had fled the rebellion in what is now the United States because they preferred a monarchy and maintained a strong allegiance to Britain. Canada continues to have strong ties to Britain, as they did from the beginning, and only established their own independent constitution in 1982. The British monarch still has the ceremonial duty of approving the governor general who presides over the National Parliament. Apart from the common language, the differences in histories and political systems of these cultures would seem to nurture dramatic differences from England and from each other.

The influences toward similarity and toward difference coexist. This chapter attempts to evaluate the degree to which both trends may influence burnout and the practice of child and youth care. As with previous cross-cultural comparisons, various statistical results will elaborate comparisons of culture, burnout, demographic and work variables, and contributors to burnout. The major burnout comparisons are based on the hierarchical regression procedure.

CULTURE DIFFERENCES

Substantial differences between English-speaking cultures exist on the cultural work value dimensions of power distance and individualism–collectivism, but not on uncertainty avoidance or career success–quality of life (see Table 13.1). For power distance, the five English-speaking cultures divided themselves into two separate clusters, with England and Canada-English in the high power distance cluster and Scotland, Australia, and the United States in the low power distance cluster. For individualism–collectivism, Canada-English and the United States form an individualist cluster, while England and Australia form a collectivist cluster. Scotland falls between the two clusters with some overlap with each.

Figure 13.1 shows the distribution of the five English-speaking cultures on the two cultural dimensions on which there were significant differences. England and Canada-English cultures differ from all other cultures in this two-dimensional display. Scotland, more moderate in individualism, overlaps with both the United States on the individualist end and Australia on the collectivist end. The cultures sort themselves roughly into the four groupings described by Triandis (1995) as explained in Chapter 5. England falls in the vertical collectivism quadrant. Canada-English falls in the vertical individualism quadrant. Australia falls in the horizontal collectivism quadrant. The United States and Scotland fall together in the horizontal individualism quadrant. Even remembering the cautions concerning the restricted range of cultures included in the study, the spread illustrated by Figure 13.1 documents the impressions of members of one culture who travel to the others that similarities based on shared language are overshadowed by differences embedded in the cultures though disparate paths through history. The phrase "separated by a common language" gives voice to this seeming paradox.

BURNOUT DIFFERENCES

Given these cultural differences, it seems logical to expect differences in burnout. However, the cultures differ only on emotional exhaustion but not on depersonalization or personal accomplishment (see Table 13.1). For emo-

Figure 13.1
English-Speaking Cultures Comparison on Power Distance and Individualism–Collectivism

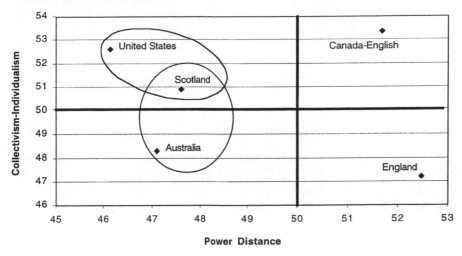

Table 13.1
Comparison of Means for Cultural Work Values and Burnout between English-Speaking Cultures

Variables	England	Scotland	United States	Canada-English	Australia	F	p
Cultural work values							
$F(16,1270) = 4.289$, $p < .0001$							
Power distance	52.476	47.599	46.136	51.683	47.091	7.248	.0001
Uncertainty avoidance	47.097	48.881	48.006	50.623	45.149	2.045	ns
Individualism-Collectivism	47.240	50.933	52.642	53.393	48.340	6.055	.0001
Career success-Quality of life	53.468	50.529	51.442	49.504	52.866	1.881	ns
Burnout							
$F(12, 953) = 2.649$, $p < .01$							
Emotional exhaustion	53.430	47.881	54.454	47.515	52.011	5.855	.0001
Depersonalization	52.078	49.890	52.699	48.821	51.266	1.258	ns
Personal accomplishment	51.916	52.001	54.125	54.071	50.919	1.968	ns

ns = no significant difference.

tional exhaustion, a high cluster of the United States and England contrasts with a low cluster of Canada-English and Scotland. Australia, falling in the middle, overlaps with both the high and low clusters. A reexamination of cultural differences in Figure 13.1 reveals that the clustered cultures on emotional exhaustion seem to come from entirely opposite quadrants on the two-dimensional comparison. There is no clear relationship between burnout and culture for the five English-speaking cultures based on individualism–collectivism and power distance. To some degree this lack of relationship is logical since, as was discussed in Chapter 7, the cultural dimension most strongly related to burnout in the overall thirteen culture sample was career success–quality of life (see Table 7.1). The five English-speaking cultures did not differ significantly on this cultural work value.

DEMOGRAPHIC AND WORK VARIABLES

Possibly differences in demographics and work-related variables may help to explain burnout results. The five English-speaking cultures differed significantly on the demographic variables of age and education level (see Table 13.2). For age, U.S. child and youth care workers were significantly older than all

Table 13.2
Comparison of Demographic, Work, and Organizational Factors between English-Speaking Cultures

Variables	England	Scotland	United States	Canada-English	Australia	F
Age	36.3	38.5	40.9	36.4	37.7	5.188***
Gender						ns
Male	48%	46%	35%	29%	30%	
Female	52%	54%	65%	71%	70%	
Education level in years	14.4	14.5	17.1	15.7	14.7	5.661***
Length in current position in years	3.01	4.89	4.64	7.83	3.74	7.781***
Length in child care field in years	6.14	9.51	9.35	9.17	6.51	6.347***
Agency size	33.62	42.30	52.32	51.94	28.11	6.756***
Age of clients						44.593***
Children	13%	15%	78%	20%	23%	
Adolescents	87%	85%	22%	80%	77%	
Hours per week	40.69	38.24	38.25	37.64	33.49	6.756***

ns = no signficant difference; *$p < 0.05$; **$p < 0.01$; ***$p < 0.001$.

other English-speaking cultures except Scotland. For education level, U.S. workers had more years of formal education than all other cultures except Canada-English. A correspondence between age and education level existed in the United States. In order for new U.S. child and youth care workers to enter the field, they had to meet a minimal educational requirement of four years of university study. In order for them to stay in the field and earn higher salaries, they had to obtain advanced degrees. Unfortunately, neither the undergraduate nor graduate degrees specifically focused on child and youth care practice. Rather, degrees in related disciplines of psychology, social work, or education were most commonly pursued. Child and youth care workers had to adopt a different profession in order to obtain graduate level education.

The five English-speaking cultures differed significantly from each other on the work-related variables of length of time in current position, length of time in the field of child and youth care work, and hours per week worked (see Table 13.2). Figure 13.2 shows the comparisons of the five English-speaking cultures on average length of time in a worker's current position and average length of time in the field of child and youth care work generally. On both measures England and Australia cluster together with less time in either variable than shown by the other cultures. Canada-English has the closest correspondence between the two measures, which may indicate both a low level of turnover and a low level of opportunities for job role changes within the field.

Figure 13.2
Average Length in Current Position and Length in Field of Child and Youth Care Work for English-Speaking Cultures

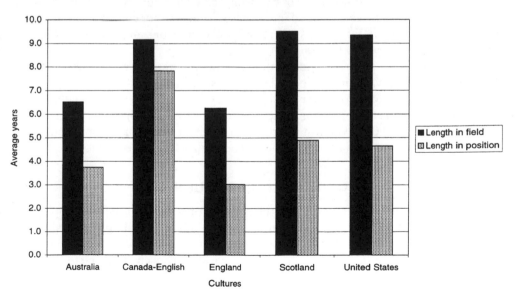

Scotland and the United States have the largest differences between the two variables which may indicate more opportunities for diverse job opportunities in the field, since they also have the greatest longevity in the field. For hours per week worked, England was significantly higher and Australia was significantly lower than all the other English-speaking cultures. The cluster of the United States, Scotland, and Canada-English fell in the midrange. Interesting correlations emerged between emotional exhaustion and education level ($r = 0.213$, $p < 0.001$) and hours per week worked ($r = 0.193$, $p < 0.001$). Emotional exhaustion seemed to increase with both hours per week worked and higher education levels. It may be that additional responsibilities derived from higher levels of expertise or conferred by educational status may be associated with longer work hours and thus linked to burnout. Neither age nor length in position nor length in the field was related to emotional exhaustion.

The five English-speaking cultures also differed significantly on two organizational characteristics: number of children or youth served by the worker's agency and age of clients served. The United States reported a significantly larger proportion of children (ages 3–12) than adolescents (ages 13–25) as compared to all other cultures. The other English-speaking cultures were not different from one another. This emphasis on younger children can be related to both the sample in the United States and to a recent funding emphasis on early identification and treatment of children and their families. For agency size, Australia showed a significantly lower number of children or youth in each agency. This stems from the small, community-based facilities sampled in Australia, which emphasized maintaining clients in their communities in noninstitutional settings. On the other end of the size spectrum were Canada-English, the United States, and Scotland. Facilities in these cultures were separate, more traditional day or residential care facilities. Typically, the large number of clients were divided into smaller living units or cottages, but shared common support facilities such as school, recreation, and dining. Agency size was unrelated to burnout.

For the most part, the wide variations in demographic, work-related, and organizational variables in the five English-speaking cultures do not relate to burnout. The exceptions, as explained earlier, were education level and hours per week worked. There is a modest correlation between these two variables ($r = 0.15$, $p < 0.05$), which supports the notion that additional responsibilities may be both the reward and the punishment for advanced education.

CONTRIBUTORS TO BURNOUT

Rather than documenting the relationship of work environment, coping, and cultural conformity to the burnout scales for all five English-speaking cultures, only the United States and Australia will be described here, since England, Scotland, and Canada-English have already been discussed in Chapters 9 and 11. In order to compare directly the differences in contributors to burnout for the five cultures, be sure to examine Tables 13.3, 13.4, and 13.5 for side-by-side comparisons of the hierarchical regressions. The remaining discussion will focus on the explanatory power of the various independent variables and how, through the interaction of cultural dimensions, one set of cultural work values may serve as a catalyst to potentiate the impact of another.

Table 13.3
Hierarchical Multiple Regression of Emotional Exhaustion with Work Environment, Coping, and Cultural Conformity in English-Speaking Cultures

Variables	England	Scotland	United States	Canada- English	Australia
Step 1: Work environment	$R^2 = .341$***	$R^2 = .235$+	$R^2 = .274$***	$R^2 = .244$	$R^2 = .346$
	$F(7,81) =$	$F(7,48) =$	$F(7,89) =$	$F(7,39) =$	$F(7,29) =$
	5.976	2.101	4.809	1.801	2.189
Peer cohesion	$\beta = -.197$	$\beta = -.269$	$\beta = -.031$	$\beta = .342$	$\beta = .164$
Supervisor support	$\beta = -.333$	$\beta = .052$	$\beta = -.009$	$\beta = -.280$	$\beta = -.102$
Autonomy	$\beta = .001$	$\beta = .065$	$\beta = .209$	$\beta = .195$	$\beta = -.286$
Task orientation	$\beta = -.005$	$\beta = .012$	$\beta = -.317$**	$\beta = -.193$	$\beta = .006$
Work pressure	$\beta = .330$**	$\beta = .383$*	$\beta = .545$***	$\beta = .158$	$\beta = .323$
Control	$\beta = -.012$	$\beta = -.205$	$\beta = .060$	$\beta = .107$	$\beta = -.094$
Innovation	$\beta = .119$	$\beta = .101$	$\beta = -.155$	$\beta = -.502$	$\beta = -.157$
Step 2: Coping style	$R^2 = .407$***	$R^2 = .272$	$R^2 = .290$***	$R^2 = .401$*	$R^2 = .590$**
	$F(9,79) =$	$F(9,46) =$	$F(9,87) =$	$F(9,37) =$	$F(9,27) =$
	6.02	1.913	3.96	2.757	4.322
Control coping	$\beta = -.267$*	$\beta = -.013$	$\beta = .061$	$\beta = -.384$*	$\beta = -.594$***
Escape coping	$\beta = .219$*	$\beta = .210$	$\beta = .100$	$\beta = .366$*	$\beta = .092$
Step 3: Cultural conformity	$R^2 = .414$***	$R^2 = .372$*	$R^2 = .298$**	$R^2 = .225$*	$R^2 = .607$*
	$F(13,75) =$	$F(13,42) =$	$F(13,83) =$	$F(13,33) =$	$F(13,23) =$
	4.07	1.911	2.712	.479	2.732
Power distance	$\beta = .019$	$\beta = .043$	$\beta = -.015$	$\beta = .224$	$\beta = -.069$
Uncertainty avoidance	$\beta = .049$	$\beta = .270$*	$\beta = -.013$	$\beta = .191$	$\beta = .154$
Individualism	$\beta = -.032$	$\beta = -.176$	$\beta = .091$	$\beta = -.011$	$\beta = -.080$
Career success	$\beta = -.067$	$\beta = -.006$	$\beta = .013$	$\beta = -.006$	$\beta = -.005$

+$p < 0.06$; *$p < 0.05$; **$p < 0.01$; ***$p < 0.001$.

Table 13.4
Hierarchical Multiple Regression of Depersonalization with Work Environment, Coping, and Cultural Conformity in English-Speaking Cultures

Variables	England	Scotland	United States	Canada-English	Australia
Step 1: Work Environment	R^2= .213**	R^2= .187	R^2= .124	R^2= .171	R^2= .266
	$F(7,81)$=	$F(7,48)$=	$F(7,89)$=	$F(7,39)$=	$F(7,29)$=
	3.141	1.58	1.794	1.151	1.497
Peer Cohesion	β = -.173	β = -.084	β = -.069	β = .598	β = -.139
Supervisor Support	β = -.222	β = -.333	β = -.041	β = -.398	β = -.1485
Autonomy	β = .060	β = .135	β = .110	β = .108	β = -.216
Task Orientation	β = -.031	β = .187	β = -.269	β = -.057	β = .112
Work Pressure	β = .123	β = .176	β = .098	β = -.183	β = .361
Control	β = -.244*	β = -.103	β = .056	β = -.050	β = .137
Innovation	β = -.069	β = -.012	β = -.161	β = -.475	β = .167
Step 2: Coping style	R^2= .333***	R^2= .213	R^2= .146	R^2= .304	R^2= .525**
	$F(9,79)$=	$F(9,46)$=	$F(9,87)$=	$F(9,37)$=	$F(9,27)$=
	4.390	1.381	1.649	1.794	3.312
Control coping	β = -.308**	β = .044	β = -.010	β = -.341	β = -.562***
Escape coping	β = .343***	β = .167	β = .165	β = .348	β = .336*
Step 3: Cultural conformity	R^2= .358***	R^2= .225	R^2= .242*	R^2= .311	R^2= .633**
	$F(13,75)$=	$F(13,42)$=	$F(13,83)$=	$F(13,33)$=	$F(13,23)$=
	3.216	.938	2.042	1.145	3.047
Power distance	β = -.090	β = .010	β = -.007	β = .065	β = -.238
Uncertainty avoidance	β = .133	β = .063	β = -.128	β = -.054	β = .162
Individualism	β = .051	β = -.039	β = .262*	β = -.009	β = -.203
Career success	β = -.009	β = -.079	β = -.192+	β = -.058	β = .373*

$+p < 0.06$; $*p < 0.05$; $**p < 0.01$; $***p < 0.001$.

Separate Culture Analyses

Australia

For all three burnout subscales, the most powerful contributor to burnout for Australian child and youth care workers was coping. For emotional exhaustion (EE), lower control coping alone was related to higher levels of emotional fatigue (see Table 13.3).

Table 13.5
Hierarchical Multiple Regression of Personal Accomplishment with Work Environment, Coping, and Cultural Conformity in English-Speaking Cultures

Variables	England	Scotland	United States	Canada- English	Australia
Step 1: Work environment	R^2= .082	R^2= .186	R^2= .054	R^2= .196	R^2= .229
	$F(7,81)$=	$F(7,48)$=	$F(7,89)$=	$F(7,39)$=	$F(7,29)$=
	1.027	1.568	.733	1.354	1.229
Peer cohesion	β = .163	β = -.021	β = -.006	β = -.082	β = .276
Supervisor support	β = .150	β = -.036	β = .043	β = -.062	β = -.312
Autonomy	β = -.159	β = .194	β = -.129	β = .301	β = .085
Task orientation	β = .110	β = .132	β = .106	β = .028	β = -.329
Work pressure	β = .081	β = .304	β = -.102	β = .056	β = -.092
Control	β = -.057	β = -.014	β = -.006	β = .295	β = -.081
Innovation	β = .119	β = .317	β = .213	β = .223	β = .211
Step 2: Coping style	R^2= .151	R^2= .376**	R^2= .093	R^2= .456**	R^2= .561**
	$F(9,79)$=	$F(9,46)$=	$F(9,87)$=	$F(9,37)$=	$F(9,27)$=
	1.563	3.084	.995	3.451	3.826
Control coping	β = .309	β = .451***	β = .233	β = .491**	β = .577***
Escape coping	β = -.135	β = -.128	β = -.131	β = -.475**	β = .229
Step 3: Cultural conformity	R^2= .205	R^2= .496**	R^2= .128	R^2= .503*	R^2= .586*
	$F(13,75)$=	$F(13,42)$=	$F(13,83)$=	$F(13,33)$=	$F(13,23)$=
	1.488	3.179	.936	2.568	2.500
Power distance	β = .186	β = -.158	β = .046	β = .156	β = .072
Uncertainty avoidance	β = .058	β = -.018	β = .075	β = .089	β = -.131
Individualism	β = .124	β = .131	β = .177	β = .169	β = .070
Career success	β = .114	β = .264*	β = -.074	β = .078	β = .121

$+p < 0.06$; $*p < 0.05$; $**p < 0.01$; $***p < 0.001$.

$$EE = \downarrow \text{control coping}$$

For depersonalization (DP), both lower control coping and higher escape coping combine with a higher-than-cultural-average subscription to career success (CS deviation) to predict alienation and loss of empathy (see Table 13.4).

$$DP = \downarrow \text{control coping} + \uparrow \text{escape coping} + \uparrow \text{CS deviation}$$

Finally, for personal accomplishment (PA), higher control coping alone was related to higher levels of perceived achievement at work (see Table 13.5).

$$PA = \uparrow \text{control coping}$$

Taken together it seems that Australian child and youth care workers find individual coping styles more potent than work environment or individual deviations from cultural norms. Increased problem-focused coping and decreased emotion-focused coping helped buffer the impact of work stressors. To some degree, the strength of coping styles in explaining burnout in Australia may stem from the way in which service provision was organized. Most workers were not employed by large agencies with well-established bureaucratic procedures. The impact of the work environment was probably quite diverse, and therefore its effects may have cancelled each other out.

United States

For the United States, coping styles did not show significance for any burnout subscale. For emotional exhaustion (EE), high work pressure (WP) combined with low task orientation (TO) to set the stage for feelings of emotional wear and tear (see Table 13.3).

$$EE = \uparrow WP + \downarrow TO$$

For depersonalization (DP) only the cultural conformity variables of higher-than-average individualism (IND deviation) in an already high individualist culture and lower-than-average career success (CS deviation) were related to depersonalization. No significant results appeared for personal accomplishment.

$$DP = \uparrow \text{IND deviation} + \downarrow \text{CS deviation}$$

Taken together, U.S. child and youth care workers suffered emotional fatigue when their work was pressing and chaotic at the same time. Those workers who valued individual action and at the same time valued lesser career involvement showed greater detachment from clients.

Detailed discussions of the contributors to burnout of England and Scotland can be found in Chapter 9, and a similar discussion concerning Canada-English can be found in Chapter 11.

As a summary of the contributors to burnout for all five English-speaking cultures, Tables 13.3, 13.4, and 13.5 indicate that coping styles showed the most explanatory power when considering the burnout subscales. Of the fifteen separate analyses (three burnout subscales for five different cultures), nine indicated significant contributions from coping styles. On the other hand, only four of fifteen analyses found significant relationships between burnout and either work environment or cultural conformity. Work environment was seen as important in understanding emotional exhaustion, but not as important for depersonalization and not important at all for personal accomplishment. There may be something in the English language that fosters internal rationales for explaining strategies for dealing with stress. The construal of the "self" as separate rather than connected with others may heighten the sense of individual responsibility for outcomes. (Matsumoto, 1996). Coping styles are more clearly the province of the individual than of an external source.

Culture as a Catalyst

An interesting phenomenon occurred when all cultural work values together were related to burnout across the five English-speaking cultures. Individualism by itself did not show a significant relationship with emotional exhaustion. As previously reported, both individualism–collectivism and emotional exhaustion showed significant differences when English-speaking cultures were compared, so it might be expected that these variables were related. However, when all cultural work values were considered together, the combination of individualism and career success did significantly predict emotional exhaustion. That is, career success served as if it were a catalyst to activate the impact of individualism. High individualist cultures such as Canada-English showed low emotional exhaustion when they also showed lower career success. High individualist cultures such as the United States showed high emotional exhaustion when they also showed higher career success. It appears that the two cultural work values operate in concert. When career advancement and identity are important in a culture, then a culture that also advocates individual action and responsibility is more likely to spawn emotional fatigue. This result is consistent with the cognitive-mediation model of stress (Lazarus, 1999) which states that important goals (e.g., success at work) have the power to alter perceptions of stress. The framing of individual blame for important work distresses is felt more intensely when work is the major source of self-esteem.

ENGLISH SPEAKERS IN RELATION TO
ALL OTHER CULTURES

Finally, despite the differences between the five English-speaking cultures, they do share some commonalties when compared to the other eight non-English-speaking cultures in the present sample. For example, on the two cultural work value dimensions that showed no difference between the English-speaking cultures (uncertainty avoidance and career success–quality of life), English-speaking cultures differed significantly from the grouping of all other

Figure 13.3
Comparison of All Cultures on Uncertainty Avoidance and Career Success–
Quality of Life

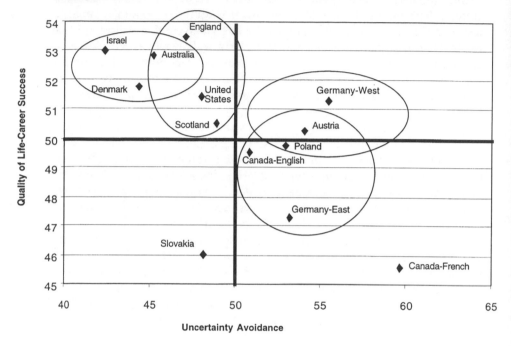

cultures. Figure 13.3 shows that the cluster of England, the United States, Scotland, and Australia hold a firm position in the career success–low uncertainty avoidance quadrant of this two-dimensional comparison. Canada-English was the only English-speaking culture not in this cluster. In general, with the exception of Denmark and Israel, English-speaking cultures show a stronger value for the combination of career success and low uncertainty avoidance.

When English-speaking cultures were compared to the grouping of all others on the burnout subscales, significantly higher scores were noted for all burnout subscales. That is, English-speaking cultures showed higher levels of the unpleasant aspects of burnout (emotional exhaustion and depersonalization), while at the same time showing higher levels of personal accomplishment. English-speaking cultures indicated a greater intensity of reaction to work stressors. Workers claimed more of the blame for problematic situations and more of the credit for achievements. To some degree, this intensity relates back to the combined values of career and individual responsibility.

CONCLUSION

Clear similarities and differences existed between the five English-speaking cultures. The cultures have evolved in unique ways throughout their separate histories. Territorial and political differences have overcome the shared language. Obvious, external similarities of these strong, Western economies mask deep-seated value differences. The five cultures differed on cultural dimensions, burnout levels, and contributors to burnout. Discussion about these cultures must acknowledge differences in how they perceive hierarchy and how they view individual versus group action.

However, these cultures also share important features. Shared is the potential influence of the interaction of career success and individualism to intensify reactions to work situations. Also shared is a trend to mediate burnout through application of coping styles rather than to perceive burnout as completely driven by the environment. This trend may indicate a preference for an internal locus of control, and may also indicate that such a preference may be related to language.

There is some evidence that language can have an effect on perceptions of stress. Research on explanatory style (Abramson, Seligman, & Teasdale, 1978) indicates that the language we use to describe events can influence our mood. The English language, the language in which most of the research on explanatory style has taken place, is particularly susceptible to trait as opposed to situational explanations of events (Matsumoto, 1996; Sanford & Mischel, 1985).

In comparison, other languages commonly avoid trait language expressions. For example, in the German language there are customary ways for a person to express that he or she is anxious or fearful: "Ich habe Angst," or "Ich fühle mich nervös." Literally translated these sentences mean, "I have anxiety" and "I make myself feel nervous." In the first sentence, "anxiety" is treated as an object or event that the person may or may not possess; for example, "I have red socks." In the second sentence the person owns responsibility for the feeling of "nervousness"; it is not thrust upon him or her by some unseen hand. In both cases the feelings are separable from the person; and the expressions imply a time-limited condition. In the English language expression, "I am anxious," the feeling of anxiety is equated with the person. The two are inseparable, and the condition has no implied end point. It can be perceived as a stable condition. Such a belief can lead to problematic personal outcomes. In fact, two therapeutic approaches popular in the English-speaking cultures have addressed this issue: Narrative therapy is aimed at disconnecting the person from the feeling (Freedman & Combs, 1996), while Gestalt therapy encourages ownership of process of creating or enhancing the feeling (Perls, 1969). Clearly, in German one can say he or she is anxious: "Ich bin ängstlich." In English one can say, "I make myself feel nervous."

However, these phrasings are not as typical. Common language usage may have an effect on how we perceive our relation with stress.

In relation to the current emphasis on coping for English speakers, trait explanations are more likely to locate the responsibility for both good and bad outcomes internally. That is, people attribute the cause of the outcome to their own actions rather than to the influence of external events. Thus, English speakers are more likely to assume both more blame and more credit, to some extent, because their language more easily construes events in this fashion. Maybe the common language of the five English-speaking cultures exerts its power in spite of the differences between the cultures.

THEMES AND RECOMMENDATIONS

Part V attempts to pull together the information from the previous parts into themes, conclusions, and recommendations concerning burnout and culture.

Chapter 14, "Emerging Themes in Culture and Burnout," acknowledges both the pan-cultural analyses and the cross-cultural analyses to pull together the threads of this research. Ten different themes are identified. Their consistency with previous research and theory are evaluated to give them some contextual support. The themes do not originate entirely from the current research, but have shown some consistency within the body of knowledge relating to burnout and culture. However, the description of cultural impact adds a new dimension.

Chapter 15, "Burnout Prevention, Remediation, and Recovery," offers a list of suggestions to support prevention of, remediation for, and recovery from burnout. Following tenets of the positive psychology movement (Seligman & Csikszentmihalyi, 2000), an effort is made to craft recommendations that not only decrease the problematic conditions that may create burnout, but also to highlight those that may increase conditions which enhance engagement with work. Building on the work of Maslach and Leiter (1997), a model is offered that integrates both personal and environmental factors in a general strategy that may be taken by either individuals or organizations to address the roots of burnout.

Finally, Chapter 16, "Implications for the Twenty-First Century," takes the themes and recommendations of the previous chapters to the next level of abstraction. Child and youth care work specifically and human service professions generally can benefit from the findings from the current study and other burnout research. However, benefits can only be accrued if the lessons learned are applied. Several suggestions are made to help set the stage for more effective responses to burnout.

CHAPTER 14

Emerging Themes
in Culture and Burnout

It is time to pull together the results of various analyses in an effort to articulate themes that will help to understand burnout from a cross-cultural perspective. Clearly, the pan-cultural analyses of Chapters 7 and 8 present the possibility that some generalizations can be made about burnout across the span of cultures included in this study. On the other hand, the cross-cultural comparisons of Chapters 9 through 13 suggest unique adjustments of cultures to the demands of child and youth care work. Work environments, coping styles, and various demographic and work variables have played stronger or weaker roles in relation to burnout, depending on the cultural work value patterns evident in the different cultures.

The field of cross-cultural psychology has struggled with the question of which findings might be broadly generalizable and thus useful to all cultures; and which might be findings unique to individual cultures and thus not applicable elsewhere (Matsumoto, 1996). The current study is no different. Since burnout across cultures has not been widely studied, the themes suggested here must be tested by future research. Some may stand the test of time, while others may need to be modified. Thus, the following themes and the discourse that attends them are not meant to pronounce the final Truth, but rather to promote further discussion.

In the early chapters of this book, several points of reference were mentioned as guides for understanding burnout: the cognitive-mediational approach to stress and coping (Lazarus, 1999), the discussion of chronic stressors at work (Gottlieb, 1997), and a meta-analysis of contributors to burnout (Lee & Ashforth, 1996). We will touch upon these guides in an effort to find theoretical and research support for the larger themes identified in this section. Findings consistent with the theories and previous research suggest themes that that may be robust. Inconsistent findings or those not predicted by theories and previous research need to be viewed with more caution.

Finally, much of the discussion of the themes will center on not only the features that may increase burnout, but also on features that will make individuals and organizations less likely to burn out. We agree with Maslach and Leiter who say, "It is not simply a matter of reducing the negatives in the workplace; it is also an attempt to increase the positives. Strategies for developing engagement with work are those that enhance energy, involvement, and efficacy" (1997, p. 77). Such a view is consistent with the emerging perspective of "positive psychology" (Seligman & Csikszentmihalyi, 2000).

OVERALL THEMES FROM PAN-CULTURAL ANALYSES

The first set of themes derive from the pan-cultural analyses both for each separate burnout scale (emotional exhaustion, depersonalization, and personal accomplishment) and for burnout configurations. The themes will follow the categorization of variables used in these analyses: situational factors, coping, cultural conformity, and general cultural values.

Situational Factors

In the cognitive-mediational model of stress and coping (Lazarus, 1999), situational factors exist side by side with specific acute stressors. These situational factors may either exacerbate or buffer the intensity of the acute stressors. Additionally, they may deplete or add to the resources an individual requires in order to cope (Riolli-Saltzman & Savicki, 2001c). Such situational demands, constraints, and resources form a more enduring strata of stress-related environment that has been shown to be associated with burnout and other affective responses to work (Lee & Ashforth, 1996; Lazarus, 1999). The first set of themes evolve from the analyses of these proximal environmental conditions.

Social Support

A strong finding in both pan-cultural analyses was the relationship of lowered social support to higher burnout, especially the effects of lowered supervisor support on emotional exhaustion and depersonalization. Conversely, higher levels of social support were related to lower levels of burnout. Such findings echo the research results reviewed by Lee and Ashforth (1996). Likewise, a resource-erosion view of how burnout develops supports the notion that depleted social support places more pressure on the resources of the individual to cope with both acute and chronic stressors (Hepburn, Loughlin, & Barling, 1997; Hobfoll, 1989; Lazarus, 1999). In contrast, the addition of resources in the area of social support may not only expand the range of coping strategies available, but may also provide an emotional buffer to absorb the pressures of the job. In addition, it may be that both support from supervisors and peers can encourage workers to develop new skills and knowledge that allow them to move beyond merely sloughing off the effects of stressors to actually using such events to add to their store of personal resources available in future stressful situations (Carver, 1998). For example, formal and informal mentoring may address both the task and the socioemotional levels of work behavior.

Work Structure

Characteristics of work structure also show strong relationships to burnout. Both the intensity of the workload and its organization were related to higher burnout; higher work pressure especially was related to emotional exhaustion, and both work pressure and chaotic organization were related to depersonalization. Work overload has been a prime explanatory construct for burnout both in research findings and in theory (Maslach & Leiter, 1997). The cognitive-mediational theory suggests having too much to do and not enough time or resources to do it can overwhelm a worker's resources and lead to the experience of threat (Lazarus, 1999). Work that is inefficiently organized or inherently unpredictable only exacerbates the stress already present from a high workload. On the other hand, some research suggests that successful achievement in the presence of high workload is related to a feeling of personal accomplishment (Riolli-Saltzman & Savicki, 2001c). The key seems to be not only the level of perceived pressure to work, but also the extent to which workers feel that they have the resources necessary to accomplish the work. Adequate resources may allow workers to perceive the workload as a challenge rather than a threat. In addition, work pressure may compress time available for workers to consolidate whatever gains in skill and knowledge they might have achieved during a stressful period (Carver, 1998). Thus, work structures may both erode worker resources and prevent them from developing new resources.

Job Enhancement

Increases in the opportunity for workers to take control of their work and to learn and apply new ideas at work seem to be related to lower levels of burnout. This theme was related to theories of job design (Hackman & Oldham, 1980) and of burnout development and prevention (Maslach & Leiter, 1997). In both theories, a lack of worker autonomy led to lowered satisfaction with work and decreased performance. Likewise, the support for learning and applying new ideas was a key feature of how workers in a ten-year follow-up study reported that they overcame burnout (Cherniss, 1993). Autonomy and innovation show clear relationships to the ability for workers to thrive and grow in their careers (Carver, 1998). However, such independent activity requires boundaries. Workers, when faced with unlimited possibilities, can only take advantage of those possibilities when they have guidance either in the form of supervision and feedback or in the form of clear work structures and parameters (Riolli-Saltzman & Savicki, 2000). Without such guidance, workers may lack appropriate resources and become overwhelmed, thus only exacerbating the impact of stressors (Lazarus, 1999). The psychological literature on control (Skinner, 1995; Steptoe & Appels, 1989) and self-efficacy (Bandura, 1986) corresponds to these results.

When examining the impact of situational demands, constraints, and resources, it seems evident that a resource-erosion model of burnout is consistent with the findings of the present study (Hobfoll & Freedy, 1993). Work pressure and inefficient work structure place demands on the resources of the workers. Social support from supervisors and peers can buffer, restore, and even add to individual resource levels. Job enhancements may provide an opportunity for further resource development. When all these factors fall in the wrong direction, worker resources are threatened, and their abilities to restore or add to their resources are blocked or removed. Over time, such a condition accumulates in a downward spiral in which continued impaired survival may reach the threshold at which the individual abandons efforts at coping and gives up (Carver, 1998). On the other hand, when the situational factors all line up correctly, workers at least have opportunities to restore rather than only deplete their resources to deal with stress. In most cases, there is probably a mixture in the direction of situational variables, and they also may change over time. It is probably fair to say that no one situational variable by itself guarantees burnout if it is in the wrong direction. Rather, work situations present a mix and mismatch condition that interacts with the appraisal and coping abilities of individual workers.

Coping

Coping styles form an enduring approach to appraising and dealing with stressors (Lazarus, 1999). They are of course related to specific coping strategies that workers may employ in a given situation, but coping styles tend to be more pervasive and characteristic of the individual rather than the specific situation (Latack, 1986). The next set of themes evolved from findings in the current study concerning coping styles.

Escape or Emotion-Focused Coping

The style of coping that focuses on escaping from the unpleasant feelings associated with a stressful situation has been strongly linked to high levels of burnout, especially higher emotional exhaustion and depersonalization. This coping style seems to provide some immediate, short-term relief while specifically avoiding taking steps to change the source of stress. The immediate alleviation of stress-related affect is seductive, since tension is reduced instantaneously. However, in the long term, the source of stress is left unchanged. Even easily altered stressors go unchallenged. The individual is then driven to depend more and more on the escape processes since the source of the unpleasant feelings continues. An undue pressure is placed on personal resources to cope in the face of continued stress. Exclusive use of the escape style may lead to a negative self-evaluation with regard to self-efficacy or ability to impact one's working life. In the manner of a self-fulfilling prophecy, it becomes easier to give up in attempts at actual problem solving; workers are less likely to persist in the face of negative affect, so they have fewer successes at working through the difficulties to a more satisfactory conclusion. Their sense of optimism may suffer (Sheier & Carver, 1985). Overuse of escape coping may be related to reactive depression (Hallsten, 1993). Several authors have proposed that burnout and depression are synonymous (Cordes & Dougherty, 1993). If short-term relief is used as a form of respite to gather one's resources for a later attack on the source of stress, then emotion-focused coping can be beneficial. It is the employment of the escape style long term, and to the exclusion of the problem-focused approach, that leads to difficulties.

Control or Problem-Focused Coping

The style of coping that focuses on changing the sources of stressful situations has been strongly linked to low levels of burnout, especially to higher levels of personal accomplishment. Successful problem-focused coping strategies have the benefit of removing or reducing stress over the long term. It is not just immediate reduction, but rather a change in one's perception or in the stressful situation itself that results from successful control coping. Adequate problem-solving skills seem to be a requisite resource for successful control coping. Furthermore, as workers continue to employ this style, they also learn additional methods of coping which expand the resources that they can draw upon in future situations. A personal sense of efficacy and optimism develops with repetition of successful problem-focused coping. In addition, workers employing this strategy are more likely to find meaningful stress-reduction solutions since they are more likely to persist rather than give up. In the terms of the cognitive-mediational approach, problem-focused coping may allow workers to transform threats into challenges. The ability to find aspects of a stressful situation that are amenable to change may alter the equation between stressors and resources. What was once overwhelming may be transformed into difficult but attainable. Of course, not all problems are solvable. However, control coping has been positively correlated with disposition of optimism (Riolli-Saltzman & Savicki, in press), indicating that even in the face of persistent stress, workers employing problem-focused coping may be better able to maintain their ability to view the situation as less terrible. They are less likely to give up and lapse into a sense of helplessness (Carver, 1998).

The two themes regarding coping styles tend to confirm Lazarus's (1999) model which links personal and environmental factors in the stress and coping process. Workers are quite sensitive to the loss, or threat of loss, of workplace resources (Hobfoll & Freedy, 1993). There is some evidence that when situational factors meet the conditions supporting lower burnout, then coping styles do not add to the understanding of burnout. However, when situational factors related to burnout exist, then coping styles moderate the relationship between situations and burnout (Riolli-Saltzman & Savicki, 2001c). In other words, the personal factor of coping style has a significant impact in stress-related conditions. The key reasons for the differential impact of escape versus control coping seem to stem from the short- versus long-term reduction of stress and from the optimistic versus pessimistic world view that accompanies them. This impact may result in observed levels of depression in individual workers.

Cultural Conformity

Not everyone in a culture subscribes to the general values of their culture with the same level of intensity (Trompenaars & Hampden-Turner, 1998). Individual variation in this regard may reflect differences in socialization or in the match between personality characteristics and the demands of cultural norms. In any event, conformity to or deviation from cultural norms reflect an individual difference that has been linked to burnout in the current research. The following themes address those linkages.

Higher-than-Average Uncertainty Avoidance

Individuals who subscribe to the cultural work value of uncertainty avoidance to a degree higher than the average of their culture show higher levels of burnout, especially higher emotional exhaustion and depersonalization. In other words, individuals suffered from higher levels of burnout when they showed a higher-than-average preference for formality and comprehensive rules and procedures aimed at ameliorating ambiguity and uncertainty at work. A problem in interpretation ensues when a variable originally assigned to describe variations in general culture is used to describe variations of individuals. However, the reader probably knows people in his or her own life that like to follow the rules and go "by the book," as well as people who freely deviate from the usual norms and "go with the flow." It is this range of responses that is represented by the deviation from the cultural norm of uncertainty avoidance. Some research indicates that individuals with higher levels of neuroticism or anxiety are more likely to experience higher levels of stress which persist longer than those with lower levels (McFarlane, 1988). It may be that this susceptibility to intensify stress is represented by higher-than-average levels of uncertainty avoidance. In any event, both the propensity to experience stress more intensely and the preference to avoid stress through rules and rituals may lead the individual to disengage from the situation and seek immediate resolution through the rules and rituals rather than persisting in the service of finding unique aspects of the situation that may be harnessed to deal with the stress. In the long run, rules and rituals can become sources of stress in and of themselves, demanding compliance even under benign circumstances.

Higher-than-Average Individualism

Individuals who subscribe to the cultural work value of individualism to a degree higher than the average of their culture show lower levels of burnout, especially higher personal accomplishment. In other words, workers who value individual action and responsibility more than the average of their culture were more likely to experience a greater sense of achievement at work. This is true in both individualist and collectivist cultures. A deviation to higher individualism may or may not reflect differences in ability or differences in actual action to reduce stress. It may more reflect a level of egocentrism (Triandis, 1995) that allows the worker to take more individual credit for work outcomes. Matsumoto (1996) discusses the tendency in Western cultures for individuals to take more credit for successes and shift blame for failures. The current result has some similarity. It would be interesting to determine if the deviation from the norm of individualism has the same effect in Asian and Latin American cultures as it had in the current research sample. Nevertheless, the ability to take credit for successes while avoiding responsibility for failures has been linked to greater levels of mental health (Alloy & Abramson, 1979). A little bit of self-delusion may be helpful to prevent burnout.

Individual variations from the cultural norm of uncertainty avoidance and individualism represent an interesting source of study. In any workplace, workers will show variation on these and other cultural dimensions. It is useful to note that such variations may have consequences with regard to burnout.

Cultural Work Values

The general values of cultures provided a broad environmental context within which practitioners delivered service to children and youth. This context was the furthest distant from the day-to-day activities of the workers, yet was indivisible from it in the sense that the norms of thought and behavior of the general culture formed the backdrop against which workers and their charges played out their interactions. Two themes emerged with regard to these broad influences.

Higher Career Success Value

The degree to which the culture emphasized the value of work and career as an integral part of its citizens' identities was related to higher levels of burnout, especially with regard to emotional exhaustion and depersonalization. It seems logical that workplace stress and its attendant reactions would play a more central part in cultures that emphasized career and career performance or status than in cultures with a more balanced view of career and other aspects of life. Hofstede (1980) lists "stronger achievement motivation," "greater work centrality," and "higher job stress" as connotations of a high career success work value (p. 200). To the degree that workers felt that their self-worth in the culture was related to their success at work, they might experience greater pressure; that value itself might place more stress on an individual to define success only in regard to work performance. In contrast, in a culture with a different evaluation of work, an individual might be able to see themselves as successful or a valuable person through activities in other parts of their lives (e.g., family, community) even though work experiences were not going well. It is interesting to note that the cultural work value of career success was linked only to the unpleasant aspects of burnout (emotional exhaustion and depersonalization) and not to the more positively toned aspect (personal accomplishment). These results lend credence to the notion that cultural pressure to succeed may place higher demands on individual worker resources on the job, while actual success might only be expected and therefore not of special note.

Lower Power Distance Value

Cultures that valued approachable leaders who exerted their influence via consultation were more likely to show lower burnout, especially higher levels of personal accomplishment. To some degree, workers who depend on someone else to tell them what to do may find it difficult to attribute their work outcomes to themselves as much as workers who take a more active role in influencing how the work should be done. Hofstede (1980) lists "high value on independence," "stronger perceived work ethic," and a negative evaluation of close supervision as connotations of low power distance (p. 92). Certainly theories of work motivation attribute higher levels of intrinsic motivation to conditions in which workers experience autonomy (Hackman & Oldham, 1980). A greater sense of accomplishment in low power distance cultures may arise not so much from actual differences in achievement at work, but rather to whom the workers believe acknowledgement should be given. A more equal-status hierarchy allows the credit to be shared more than does a steeply differentiated hierarchy.

In the current study the general cultural work values were tested with regard to burnout only after personal and more proximal environmental factors had already had their impact. The resulting emergence of career success and power distance findings indicates that culture is indeed a powerful force. It provides not only an overall description of the context in which work takes place, but also reaches down to the level of its individual members' adjustment to work stress.

In summary, there seem to be some themes concerning burnout that may be applied across cultures. Even though these generalizations capture issues that may be relevant for many cultures on average, there will of course be some variations on the themes mentioned previously. The following section attempts to give some perspective by weaving together further cross-cultural analyses.

CULTURE-ORGANIZATIONAL FIT IN RELATION TO BURNOUT

In contrast to identifying generalizations across cultures, this section will focus on themes that may help in understanding how specific cultures may use their cultural values and work-related factors to deal with burnout. The general theme identified in this section may be called "culture-organizational fit." The structure of the organization and various work-related practices may coincide with cultural values in ways that either advance or hinder burnout in its employees. The topic of "organizational resilience" (Horne & Orr, 1998; Mallak, 1998) speaks to the issue of how organizations may adapt themselves to survive and thrive in times of stress. Riolli-Saltzman and Savicki (2001a) emphasize the parallel development of resilience at both the organizational and individual level, suggesting that although resilient workers may not guarantee resilient organizations, the lack of resiliency at the individual level prevents resiliency at the organizational level. Thus, culture-organizational fit is one level of analysis that may set the context for burnout.

Unique Cultural Adaptations to Burnout

In an attempt to draw some conclusions about how different cultures respond to burnout, the high and low burnout cultures identified from the pancultural analyses done previously will be compared. Figure 14.1 shows a three-dimensional model placing some of the high and low burnout cultures in a three-dimensional space. The dimensions represent high versus low uncertainty avoidance, individualism versus collectivism, and career success versus quality of life.

Upper Right–Lower Left: Low Burnout

The first comparison is between the section of the cube representing low uncertainty avoidance, individualism, and career success (upper right) with

Figure 14.1
Cultures with High and Low Burnout in Relation to Uncertainty Avoidance, Individualism–Collectivism, and Career Success–Quality of Life Cultural Work Value Dimensions

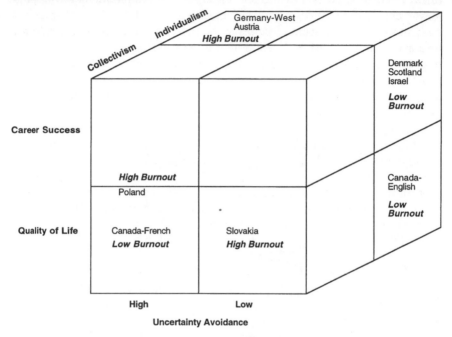

the section representing high uncertainty avoidance, collectivism, and quality of life (lower left). These two sections are exact opposites, yet they contain most of the cultures who showed low burnout overall. In Denmark, Scotland, and Israel, individualism and low uncertainty avoidance make it possible for individual workers to take more independent action within a context that does not hinder them through excessive rules and regulations. With a cultural value focused on achievement at work, this combination has allowed the cultures to provide different kinds of support for child and youth care workers that may help them maintain lower burnout. By and large, work structures are malleable, not written in stone; recognition is available for satisfactory individual performance; and the development of the individual as a resource for the organization is accepted.

In total contrast is Canada-French in the lower left portion of the cube. High uncertainty avoidance is combined with collectivism and quality of life. Even though the position of Canada-French contrasts completely with that of Denmark, Scotland, and Israel, the outcome is also low burnout. One interpretation of this result stems from the nature in which the Canada-French culture deals with stress under high uncertainty avoidance conditions. Rather than relying on universally applied rules or regulations to guide them, the

Canada-French culture emphasizes collective discussion and exploration. That is, they talk through the issues extensively with relevant others. Even though rules may exist, discussion may, and often does, justify exceptions to the rules. Evaluative criteria evoked during these discussions include not only how to deal with the stressors, but also how to balance the impact of solutions on both work and nonwork circumstances. Individuals are more likely to see themselves as a part of and responsible to a larger collective entity. Therefore, decisions are typically not made quickly, but they are made in a way that satisfies the range of needs within a larger group. Whenever a conclusion is reached, it has broad acceptance. The individual feels supported by the group. Thus, burnout is less likely to accumulate.

Two polar opposites in the three-dimensional cube have developed work adaptations that both lead to lower burnout. Switching the mechanisms of one to the other would not function well. Individualists would grumble at the Canada-French solutions; high uncertainty-avoidance people seeking universal solutions would flounder without some unvarying structure or rule to apply in stressful situations. The solutions seem to have been developed for the unique set of cultural values of the cultures.

Upper Left–Lower Right: High Burnout

The next comparison is between the section of the cube representing high uncertainty avoidance, individualism, and career success (upper left) with the section representing low uncertainty avoidance, collectivism, and quality of life (lower right). These two sections are exact opposites, yet they contain most of the cultures who showed high burnout overall. In Germany-West and Austria, individualism combines with high uncertainty avoidance in the context of emphasis on career achievement. In this portion of the cube, a cultural value of avoiding ambiguity and uncertainty at work takes the form of formality and a plethora of rules and regulations that attempt to anticipate all variations. These rules, once in place, are often not reevaluated as circumstances change, but rather are seen as having importance in and of themselves. Sometimes outdated or even conflicting regulations contribute more stress to the situation rather than avoiding it. Workers who value individual responsibility can get caught in this tangle of regulations. They may deem it more important to satisfy the rules than to respond to the uniqueness of the situation. Not following the rules can increase anxiety, and following the rules may lead to unsatisfactory outcomes: a real double bind.

In complete contrast is Slovakia in the lower-right portion of the cube. Low uncertainty avoidance is combined with collectivism and quality of life. Even though the position of Slovakia contrasts totally with that of Germany-West and Austria, the outcome is also high burnout. In this case, however, burnout is heavily loaded with low personal accomplishment. That is, Slovak child and youth care workers generally showed a very low sense of achievement at work (lowest of all thirteen cultures). Low salaries, centralized management structures, and lack of career options combined to make many Slovak child and youth care workers feel trapped in their positions. The absence of individualism as a cultural value also made it more difficult for workers to press for better circumstances or to seek other jobs.

The upper-left–lower-right contrast illustrates how circumstances in the culture may either exacerbate an expectable level of stress or serve to hinder the development of achievement at work. In either case, burnout levels rose.

Historical and Political Influences

As the former East Bloc countries move into decentralized, market-driven economies, we might expect some movement toward individualism (Hofstede, 1997). Cultural work values adjust to the demands on the individuals within the culture. However, it is unlikely that there will ever be a homogeneous, universal culture. In fact, differences are sometimes accentuated in circumstances that draw attention to cultural variations, for example, the existence of a diverse workforce (Adler, 1997).

More relevant to child and youth care practice is the fact that there is already a move in former East Bloc countries to adopt the smaller, decentralized agency service delivery format applied commonly in the West. Deinstitutionalization and mainstreaming, trends in mental health and educational service delivery well established in the West, will become more possible in the former East. To some extent, the collectivist orientation of most former East Bloc cultures should make such adaptations easier, while the value of higher power distance may make it more difficult.

In Europe, the European Union may have some influence on consistency of child and youth care practice. Even if there are no regulations that span the different cultures, cross-fertilization of ideas have already led to promising collaborations (EUROARRCC, 1998).

Culture-organizational fit seems to be an important factor in how the general themes identified earlier in this chapter need to be applied. There continue to be unique adjustments within unique cultures and historical moments. The presence of general themes does not obviate the necessity for sensitivity to unique conditions.

Therefore, the results found in this study should be considered a snapshot in time rather than a description for the ages. Culture and burnout mutually influence each other. We need to continue to study these influences.

CURRENT THEMES IN COMPARISON WITH MASLACH AND LEITER AND CHERNISS

Maslach and Leiter (1997) identified six themes that relate to burnout, and Cherniss (1995) described a broad range of themes related to burnout. The following is a side-by-side comparison of the themes identified in the current study in relation to the Cherniss and Maslach and Leiter themes:

Savicki	Maslach and Leiter, 1997	Cherniss, 1995
Social support	Community	Lack of collegiality
Work structure	Workload	Crisis of competence, difficulties with clients
Job enhancement	Control	Professional autonomy, meaningful work
Escape coping		Self-efficacy
Control coping		Self-efficacy
Cultural conformity: higher uncertainty avoidance	Values	Professional versus the system
Cultural conformity: higher individualism	Values	
Cultural values: career success		Striking a balance between work, family, and leisure
Cultural values: power distance		Professional versus the low system
Culture-organizational fit		
	Reward	Organizational negotiation skill
	Fairness	Quest for meaning

Some of the themes show a relatively strong similarity, and some have been pulled and tugged a bit to attain their overlap. At the bottom of the list are themes identified by the other writers that did not appear directly in the current research. The purpose of this exercise is to demonstrate that the themes emerging from the current research are robust. That is, others have found such themes in relation to burnout. Therefore, current themes reveal real burnout-related processes, not just chance outcomes.

Strong similarities in themes exist in relation to the situational factors that may be present in the work environment: social support, work structure, and job enhancement. Such similarity is not surprising considering the emphasis on environmental conditions found in much of the burnout research (Maslach & Schaufeli, 1993). The different language used by the different authors represents their attempt at capturing important features of the work situation and to some degree the differences in methodology used. Maslach and Leiter based their theorizing on quantitative studies, while Cherniss developed his understandings through qualitative approaches. All authors propose that organizational factors should be viewed as causal of burnout rather than shifting blame for burnout to the individual workers who suffer from it.

The relationship of escape and control coping with self-efficacy focuses on personal variables not found in the Maslach and Leiter approach. Their view is that burnout should be controlled at the organizational level. Cherniss on the other hand spends a great deal of time probing the personal cognitions and behaviors of individuals for keys to burnout. Cherniss finds that the experience of self-efficacy is key to recovering from or preventing burnout. Some examples that he gives illustrate effectiveness of a preference for problem-focused coping and a shift away from emotion-focused coping (Cherniss, 1993).

The values theme that Maslach and Leiter raise focuses primarily on the corrosive effect of a mismatch between individual and organizational values. To some extent Cherniss echoes this theme when he discusses the conflicts between the professional and the system. Deviations from cultural conformity fit with these concerns since individuals with higher-than-average uncertainty avoidance and higher-than-average individualism seem to experience burnout-related consequences. The mismatch in terms of cultural conformity is between the individual and the general culture, not necessarily between the individual and the organization. Nevertheless, it seems clear that such mismatches, whether with an organization or with a culture, can pose problems for the individuals who deviate.

Although neither Cherniss nor Maslach and Leiter discuss cross-cultural concerns, Cherniss does discuss issues within the U.S. culture that may have influence on burnout. His theme, "Striking a balance between work, family, and leisure," links directly with the high career success theme found at the general cultural level in the current study. He found that those workers who recovered from or prevented burnout were able to find the appropriate balance in their lives. Also, in Cherniss's description of the professional versus the system, he suggests that worker involvement, as in a lower power distance culture, may also buffer against burnout. His conclusions related specifically to the United States, but the themes identified in the current study imply that they may also have some relevance across cultures.

The culture-organizational fit theme from the current research is not clearly found in either Maslach and Leiter or Cherniss, since their efforts presumed a single, uniform culture. Of course, the addition of culture into the mix of variables used to understand burnout was the major rationale for the current research.

Finally, several themes suggested by Cherniss and Maslach and Leiter do not register in the current study. Maslach and Leiter identify reward and fairness as important antidotes to burnout. That is, if workers receive adequate pay and recognition, and if decisions made about them and their work by management are perceived as fair, then workers are less likely to burn out. The current study did not address these issues specifically, although they may relate to some degree to higher individualism and lower power distance. Since these two cultural values are consistent with the U.S. culture, it may be that fairness and reward need to be interpreted differently in different cultures. Cherniss's emphasis on the quest for meaning strikes an existential chord that is similar to that of Pines (1993). The approach used by many workers who recover from burnout is to "settle for less" and come to grips with the "limits of personal virtue" (Cherniss, 1995). Cherniss bemoans the fact that, ironically, workers in the helping professions may abandon many of the ideals that initially led them into the field in order to avoid leaving the field. Cherniss also identified organizational negotiation as an important skill that new workers lack and older, nonburned-out workers have gained. This skill is quite consistent with the approach that Maslach and Leiter suggest to change one's organization to achieve lower burnout.

With the exception of culture-organizational fit, all of the themes identified in the current research have been discovered and described in some form by other key burnout researchers. Although it may be inviting to pronounce these themes as completely relevant for all cultures, the variations shown by separate cultures lead us to advise caution before believing that such generalizations are always valid. Although the themes may be present in all cultures, how they play out will be affected by unique cultural and historical circumstances.

CHAPTER 15

Burnout Prevention, Remediation, and Recovery

Several approaches to dealing with burnout are possible, depending on the severity of burnout experienced. When an individual is experiencing end-stage burnout, issues of recovery emerge, since harm and loss have already occurred. When an individual is struggling with burnout as it is progressing, but prior to the phase of giving up, remediation is called for. Most people experiencing the effects of burnout fall into this category. They exhibit some of the symptoms, but probably fall into the mixed category of burnout configuration with some aspects of burnout high while others are low. They experience several stressors as threats and expend personal resources in continuing efforts to deal with them. Finally, prior to or in the very early stages of burnout, prevention is called for. Prevention heads off burnout or catches it very early so that its toxic effects do not damage the individual. Prevention, remediation, and recovery in this context follow the classic categories of primary, secondary, and tertiary prevention that describe mental health service delivery options (Caplan, 1964; Caplan & Caplan, 2000).

The emphasis on recovery clearly focuses on the individual, since both physical and psychological damage may have occurred. However, both remediation and prevention can be applied to both individuals and organizations. Organizational interventions may be more powerful because they influence many workers, rather than one at a time. A public health perspective suggests that eradicating the environmental incubators of stress may have widespread beneficial effects. The analogy from public health is that treating stagnant ponds that breed mosquitoes may be more functional for preventing the spread of infection than only slapping the insects that attempt to bite.

In its clearest sense, the term "prevention" "is reserved for those interventions targeted to a population before the initial onset of a problem or diagnosable disorder" (Mrazek, 1998, p. 7). Interventions aimed at prevention may take the form of universal preventive interventions in which a whole population is exposed to some sort of information or practice. In the case of burnout, an example might be a course or seminar in preservice training or job orientation concerning what burnout is and how to prevent it. Such training would be delivered to all child and youth care workers regardless of personal or environmental vulnerabilities. Selective preventive interventions target at-risk individuals or subgroups. Some assessment or observation of coping skills, for example, might reveal deficits in problem-focused coping abilities of individual workers. It is also possible that unavoidable environmental conditions of a specific type of job may make stressors more difficult to deal with. In either case, the individuals with the skill deficits or environmental exposure would be at higher risk for burnout and therefore in need of intervention to moderate those risks. The themes identified in this book suggest a framework for identifying high-risk conditions.

Finally, indicated prevention (early intervention) to deter progression of a disorder may be indicated at early signs of burnout, prior to full-blown, diagnosable levels of this phenomenon. In current practice, early intervention is the most likely level of intervention. Workers begin to show signs of burnout, and peers, supervisors, or managers notice and attempt to head off its progression. Such interventions tend to be haphazard and inconsistently applied. More systematic screening and approaches to intervention are called for at this level of burnout prevention.

Beyond attempting to remediate or remove problematic situations, the positive psychology perspective also suggests developing both personal and environmental factors that enhance thriving rather than succumbing to stress. As Maslach and Leiter (1997) say, "Greater success in coping with burnout will come from focusing on promoting engagement with work rather than from just focusing on reducing burnout" (p. 22). They also say, "It is not simply a matter of reducing the negatives in the workplace; it is also an attempt to increase the positives. Strategies for developing engagement with work are those that enhance energy, involvement, and efficacy" (p. 77).

Although the suggestions to follow can be applied to prevention, remediation, and recovery, a major emphasis will be placed on prevention and early intervention. I agree with Maslach and Leiter (1997) that "it is far better to invest in avoiding burnout than to pick up the costs in its wake" (p. 102).

The suggestions that follow for prevention, remediation, and recovery are classified into individual and organizational focus. Following a model of organizational resilience (Riolli-Saltzman & Savicki, 2001a), individual and organizational factors are interdependent. Although interventions may be proposed to deal with issues at each of the levels, individuals and organizations are inextricably intertwined. Therefore, each of the suggestions should not be taken in isolation, but rather multiple approaches should be used.

None of the suggestions is proposed in great detail. Such detailed intervention plans are beyond the scope of this book. Rather, each suggestion derives from aspects of the current research or related studies. The resulting list of ideas may form a set of alternatives for people seeking ideas concerning burnout.

INDIVIDUAL FOCUS

The interventions suggested at the individual level attempt to increase important skills, knowledge, and abilities that may increase the personal resources that each worker brings to the helping enterprise. The goal is individual resilience or thriving; or at least resistance to the erosion of personal resources.

The Organism

Goal: To develop personal strength and resistance to erosion of personal energy

In order to resist the erosion of personal resources, one important step to take involves caring for personal physical and psychological health. The ability to resist the impact of stressors and to bounce back from setbacks requires that one's organism be strong and in reasonable physical condition. That implies staying healthy by eating sensibly, sleeping enough, and maintaining at least a modest exercise regimen. On the flip side, avoid depletion of physical health by drug use, smoking, or extensive reliance on alcohol. Above and beyond caring for physical needs, each individual would benefit from learning physically oriented stress-reducing techniques such as relaxation, meditation, and yoga. These physical and mentally soothing activities can help to build one's confidence in being able to withstand the unpleasant feelings associated with stress. Finally, other diversions from stress such as hobbies that require enough concentration to interrupt preoccupations with stress can provide some respite. It is the ability to modulate stress levels by using some of these methods that gains the individual some sense of mastery and decreases the probability of prematurely foreclosing problem-focused efforts at coping.

Coping

Goal: To practice coping styles leading to successful reduction of stressors

The major suggestion with regard to coping is to practice problem-focused coping. Each of us has learned some degree of problem-solving skills, but the level of learning and practice can vary widely. Individuals can take time to learn specific techniques of problem solving. Organizations can support training to teach their employees such skills. Preservice training programs can integrate such skills into their curriculum (Heppner & Hillerbrand, 1991).

The key is to use problem-solving strategies to stay engaged with one's work. Even in overwhelming situations, people can find something that is amenable to systematic problem solving (Riolli-Salztman & Savicki, in press).

Persist in the situation until find something can be found that can be changed from a threat to a challenge. Avoid becoming fixated on only one aspect of the stressful situation. If one approach doesn't work, try something else. Using social support and group-oriented practices helps dramatically, even in highly individualistic cultures.

Finally, rely on only short term use of emotion-focused coping. Finding some respite from stress may allow time and energy to return with a more problem-focused coping strategy in mind. Extensive reliance on escape coping is a dead end with regard to dealing with burnout.

Frame of Reference

Goal: To use an appraisal of stress which is more likely to produce positive outcomes

Much literature indicates that taking an optimistic view yields lower levels of distress (Carver, 1998; Scheier & Carver, 1985) and burnout (Riolli-Saltzman & Savicki, 2001b, 2001c). This does not mean ignoring stress, but rather viewing it as less threatening and more amenable to change. The old adage, "If God gives you lemons, learn to make lemonade," applies here. A key tactic in this regard is to break down the stressful situation and find something amenable to influence. The old African saying says, "The only way to eat the elephant in your path is to cut it into little pieces." Lower burnout is related to the ability to persist and be flexible while staying engaged in the stressful situation (Riskind, Sarampote, & Mercier, 1996; Seligman, 1991).

A corollary to this is to avoid a pessimistic view. Avoid fatalism, and continue to look for opportunities. Optimistic people are not necessarily smarter; they just persist longer and thus are more likely to happen upon a successful solution. Don't give up too soon.

Finally, look for allies. Even the most individualistic person can achieve more with the help of others.

Balance between Career and Other Aspects of Life

Goal: To avoid a narrow focus which forecloses access to other resources or at least respite from work-related stress

The straightforward advice embodied in this suggestion is to plan for a balance between work and other aspects of life. This suggestion recognizes that career success is only one source of identity for workers. Time with family, attention to other relationships in life, and attention to one's community responsibilities all allow workers to expand the manner in which they describe themselves. A greater number of meaningful aspects of life create the possibility of more resources for the individual to use in order to combat stress that may develop at work. There is always a dynamic tension between focus and specialization on the one hand and balance and range of action on the other. Burnout research seems to suggest the benefit of balance.

Cherniss (1995) also indicates that avocational ways of finding meaning in life (e.g., religion, volunteer activities, social contacts) may also help to create balance. The quest for meaning beyond the workplace may help to create a quality of life that makes the individual a more resilient worker in the workplace.

Organizational Awareness and Negotiation

Goal: To develop an awareness of and facility at changing the organizational situational factors that may perpetuate the severity stress

In its simplest form, this suggestion advocates that workers gain an understanding of the organization they work for. Try to develop a sense of the organizational dynamics, structures, and processes without getting overly caught up in them. This requires the ability to step back with some detachment in order to view the organization as a whole. Usually workers have their heads down, focusing on the details of their everyday lives at work. While such concentration may be admirable, it does not allow the individual to understand where his or her work fits into the mission of the organization as a whole. Workers can lose sight of the significance of their work and the sense of their contribution to the organization by a "nose to the grindstone" approach. On the other hand, a worker may get caught up in the politics of the job in a way that develops more stress. Both understanding and detachment are necessary.

Beyond understanding and detachment comes problem solving aimed at the organizational level. Organizations change because individuals and groups within the organizations raise issues and create alternatives to the ways in which the organization has previously gone about its business. Individual workers can have innovative ideas, but the follow through to implementation requires group alliances and action. Unfortunately, preservice education for child and youth care workers, as well as other helping professionals, does not usually include organizational awareness and negotiation training. See Maslach and Leiter (1997) for a pattern that may be employed to develop organizational change.

Job Ownership

Goal: To develop joy and personal meaning in one's job

The final suggestion at the individual level is to find fun things to do on the job and make time for them. People who are burning out generally are working more and enjoying it less. Typically, at work there are a range activities that are called forth in a working day. Some of these activities may be fun in their own right (e.g., playing with the children) or could be made fun with a little bit of creativity (e.g., making lining up for activities into a game). Laughter and smiles are the enemy of burnout. Take control of your own work environment and accent the fun.

Along the same lines, develop tasks and assignments that you are interested in and challenged by. Cherniss (1995), for example, found that workers who had recovered from burnout had found some unique, personally appealing job-related task that they could make their own. Such an approach is consistent with the idea of job enlargement (Herzberg, 1966). It may seem contradictory to suggest that workers take on additional tasks when they are feeling overwhelmed by the tasks that they already are required to perform, but it is often not the absolute level of work but rather its lack of meaningfulness that makes work stressful. Working hard at something one enjoys or finds fulfilling may indeed be exhilarating rather than depleting.

In general, workers can benefit by taking control of their work rather than letting their work control them.

ORGANIZATIONAL FOCUS

There is general agreement that organizational factors are primary contributors to burnout (Maslach & Schaufeli, 1993). As Maslach and Leiter say, "The moral of the story is that although it is the person who experiences burnout, it is the job situation that is the primary cause" (1997, p. 37). In their six-factor scheme to explain and change burnout through organizational means, Maslach and Leiter (1997) emphasize the need for match between the job and the worker. As guideposts to the match which lead to worker engagement rather than burnout, they list the following characteristics:

1. Sustainable workload
2. Feelings of choice and control
3. Recognition and reward
4. A sense of community
5. Fairness, respect, and justice
6. Meaningful and valued work

The following section integrates their ideas with those found in the current study in order to suggest organizational patterns that promote burnout prevention, remediation, and recovery.

Social Support (Community)

Goal: To maximize the emotional and technical support available from others in the workplace so that stressors can be buffered and burnout reduced

Organizations would do well to train their workers in the basic skills of teamwork and group process. Often we take for granted that people can work together well in group situations. However, we cannot make that assumption if we want to avoid burnout. Both in individualist and collectivist cultures, some of the basic tenets of successful group activity may be missing. Individualists may believe that group activity only dilutes individual expertise, while collectivists may overlook important deviations from the group norm while searching for successful group action. As more and more activity takes place in a group context, specific training for group action is necessary. Social support in groups can nurture both the socioemotional level and the task level of group behavior. Leaving effective group practices to chance may set the stage for reduced social support and increased burnout. There needs to be a balance between individualist and collectivist approaches.

Another aspect of social support is the effective use of supervision. Supervision is a two-handed enterprise. Supervisors need to be trained to be effective; supervisees need to learn how to use the supervision process to their benefit. There is no guarantee that successful child and youth care workers who are promoted to supervisory positions will be successful supervisors. In many industries, the talented worker in terms of technical expertise is unprepared to deal with the interpersonal and social demands required of a supervisor. Supervisors should be trained rather than cast into their role in a "sink or swim" fashion.

From the supervisee's position, learning how to use supervision is important. Simple suggestions such as learning the supervisor's orientation and discussing events using the supervisor's vocabulary may make this relationship more productive. Clearly, supervisees need to process and use the feedback they are given rather than off-handedly rejecting it. Change is one goal of the supervision relationship. Utilizing the supervisor's advice may facilitate more effective performance. Finally, the supervisee is not a passive participant in the relationship. Supervisees should ask for what they want. If you find one type of feedback more useful than others, ask. Take some control over the interaction rather than feeling victimized by it.

Work Demands and Organization (Workload)

Goal: To modulate the work flow and structure so that worker resources are not overwhelmed or threatened but rather challenged to produce lower burnout and higher performance

In much of the burnout literature, overwhelming workload sets the stage for burnout. Therefore, adjusting the flow and intensity of work becomes very important. Objective versus subjective perceptions of workload may vary. Some workers with a great deal to accomplish view the workload as challenging because they find personal investment or meaning in the work. Others with boring or routine work of not especially demanding character may experience burnout not so much because of the level of work demanded, but rather the kind of work and the lack of personal investment required. Organizations must seek to define work as meaningful, personally engaging, and relevant to its overall mission. Obviously, an objective threshold may be crossed beyond which reappraisal of the workload is not possible. However, this threshold seems quite high.

Another feature of workload that may make it more tolerable is the efficiency of its organization. Generally, work structures that avoid chaos and provide adequate but not rigid structure will modulate the effects of workload. Workers can indeed get more done in less time if the work structure supports it.

Implicit in the results of the current study is the paradox of providing enough work structure (task orientation) without falling into the bureaucratic trap to too may rules and regulations (high uncertainty avoidance). The concept of "empowerment" may provide a solution (Conger & Kanungo, 1988; Randolph, 1995). The key to arranging an environment that empowers workers is for management to draw explicit parameters concerning the outcomes and general methods to be used to complete a task and then grant autonomy to workers to produce the specified outcomes. This balance between providing structure and allowing autonomy explains several of the findings in the current study. Too much autonomy without structure (e.g., in Slovakia and England) may lead to burnout, just as too little autonomy and innovation and inefficient work structure may lead to burnout (e.g., in the United States and Germany-West). It is the balance of structure and autonomy that must be sought. In the language of the current study, organizations need to provide sufficient resources so that organizational requirements or organizational needs are perceived as challenging rather than threatening.

Facilitate Involvement (Control)

Goal: To engage workers actively both in daily control over their work activities and in developing innovations to enhance the performance of the organization

In general, increasing autonomy of workers, given the comfort of clear guidelines and outcome definitions, seems to decrease burnout. Clearly, autonomy means different things in individualist versus collectivist cultures. In individualist cultures, exerting individual action and assuming individual credit for desired outcomes is consistent with this work value. In collectivist cultures, autonomy might be expressed as the individual expressing the norms of the group while the group is not present, or by engaging in actions beneficial to the group independent of group instruction. Nevertheless, making room for individual workers to express themselves in the service of the specific cultural values seems to have value.

In high uncertainty avoidance or high power distance settings, managers need to set structure within which workers can function autonomously (Riolli-Saltzman & Savicki, 2001a). Such structure harkens back to the suggestion made previously to enhance empowerment.

One way to support innovation and creative ways of working is to install an organization level mechanism to regularly evaluate "rules and procedures" (i.e., keep them up to date and meaningful rather than having them dictate the work). The goal is to avoid a situation in which "the workplace has been polarized. Dedicated professionals see themselves as doing good work in spite of management rather than with its assistance" (Maslach & Leiter, 1997, p. 48).

Values

Goal: To align personal and organizational goals so that they support rather than conflict with one another

As a part of the socialization to work process described in Chapter 2, workers identify and adjust to the values of the organization. Ideally, a worker and the organization have made an overt evaluation of each other's values during the hiring processes. However, even under the best of circumstances, neither individuals nor organizations always act consistently with their stated values. A sustained values conflict adds to the situational factors that may erode personal resources and set the stage for burnout. Therefore, several steps can be taken at the organizational level that may minimize extended values conflicts. First, the organization should have a written statement of its mission and values that prospective employees can review to determine how they might fit into the values climate of the job they are applying for. Second, this mission and values statement should be reviewed as a component of the orientation of the new employee to the organization. Third, management needs to be alert and responsive to questions about the consistency between values and action. They need to be ready to discuss as opposed to ignoring such employee concerns. Finally, the mission and values position of the organization should be reviewed regularly.

In the context of culture, these suggested steps would probably be carried out somewhat differently in individualist as compared to collectivist cultures. Even the phrasing of the values would likely be different, emphasizing personal versus group goals. Also, who is involved in the various steps might also be influenced by the power distance stance of the culture. In any event, to capture the most energy and involvement from their workers, organizations need to work to align individual and organizational values. Such alignment helps individuals by reducing a potential source of stress. Enhancing meaningfulness of work also helps the organization become more resilient when the organization as a whole experiences difficult times (Riolli-Saltzman & Savicki, 2001a).

Fairness

Goal: To convey trust, openness, and respect to workers who then can feel some security in their jobs rather than experiencing the organization as an untrustworthy, sometimes malevolent entity

When workers are not sure how they will be treated by the organization, a substrata of anxiety and dread can add to other stressors to exacerbate burnout. The perceptions of management as capricious, careless, and unpredictable undermine loyalty to the organization and may even provoke retaliation by workers. Consistent communication with workers by management is key to gaining trust. In high uncertainty avoidance cultures, specific structures or procedures for appeal of grievances would be helpful. Also, communication between management and workers may take different forms in low versus high power distance cultures. The expressions of respect by management for individual workers probably would be somewhat different between individualist cultures in which individual merit is valued versus collectivist cultures in which shared action and responsibility are valued.

The concept of procedural justice (Allegro & Kruidenier, 1991) may capture a method of gaining and sustaining the perception of fairness during difficult times. The major point of procedural justice is to establish a procedure that involves and informs all workers prior to taking action. Successful methods of this sort can make the traumatic process of downsizing and laying off employees, if not pleasant, at least understandable and justifiable to both those workers who leave and those who stay. Obviously, the exact procedures for procedural justice would need to take into account the culture in which the organization resides.

Reward

Goal: To establish conditions in the organization so that workers feel that they are receiving both intrinsic and extrinsic rewards commensurate with their activities or position

The easiest point of focus when discussing reward is salary and benefits. Child and youth care work salaries have generally been lower than they should be. However, once a specific threshold of salary has been attained, other incentives to work can actually exceed salary and benefits in their power to reward. The extrinsic reward of recognition and status by management has great power. Even more motivating can be intrinsic motivators of challenge, achievement, and the satisfaction of being a good team member and performing good work.

Management can influence rewards, both extrinsic and intrinsic, so that workers feel that they have been acknowledged. Extrinsic rewards are easiest to arrange. However, such rewards must be consistent with culture. Individualist cultures will value reward for individual performance, while collectivist cultures will value reward for shared action and effective team membership. Likewise, the bestowing of status as a reward must be sensitive to the levels of power distance in the culture.

Intrinsic rewards are obviously not bestowed by management. Rather, individual workers experience them as they perform under conditions that allow them to be internally motivated by their jobs. Job design theory (Hackman & Oldham, 1980) and other work motivation approaches give many suggestions for creating working conditions that enhance the likelihood that workers will respond with intrinsic motivators (Steers & Porter, 1991).

Culture-Organizational Fit

Goal: To design organizational structures and processes that are both responsive to the home culture of the organization and at the same time ameliorative of conditions that create burnout

Finally, as has been indicated in the discussion of all of the organizationally based suggestions, it is important to acknowledge the values of the culture in which the organization resides. Organizational structures and processes that conflict with broader cultural values will introduce another form of values conflict for workers. Even when workers wish to subscribe to the values of the organization, an underlying dissonance will heighten the situational stress level in the workplace. Workers will view as alien organizational procedures that they perceive to violate general cultural norms.

Organizations, however, are not locked into a limited set of structures and procedures. A wide variety of changes and adjustments can be made as long as they are couched in the language of the culture and justified in relationship to its values. For example, asking workers in a high power distance culture to perform more autonomously flies in the face of their dependence on leadership from management. Therefore, workers need to have the safety of explicit management limits on their autonomous behavior and the blessing of those with high status who can legitimize this seemingly unacceptable form of behavior.

Although the current study is based on a cross-cultural approach developed in a mostly international context, most of the recommendations can also be applied to a cross-cultural situation within a single organization. That is, in situations of "diversity" of culture within an organization, many of the same concerns must be addressed. In all the nations where data were collected for this study, there are a growing number of minority cultures that require attention. Organizations cannot assume that their workers originate from a homogeneous culture. The notion of culture-organizational fit can be extended to issues of cultural diversity within a single organization.

In the current study the cultural work value dimensions of Hofstede (1980) have been used to articulate key distinctions in describing culture. Other authors have also elaborated both distinct and similar dimensions (Triandis, 1995; Tompenaars & Hampden-Turner, 1998). All these authors provide language and concepts that may be useful in understanding an organization's home culture and how to be sensitive to the values embodied in it.

STRATEGIES FOR TREATMENT, PREVENTION, AND RECOVERY

The identification of specific strategies for carrying out the individual and organizational burnout prevention suggestions made is beyond the scope of this book. Instead, I refer the reader to organizational change literature (Keys, 1986) and to the approach proposed by Maslach and Leiter (1997) which is

Figure 15.1
Integration of Personal, Organizational, and Cultural Level Approaches to Prevent and Remediate Burnout

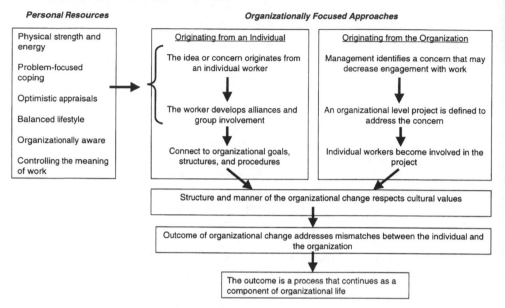

Source: C. Maslach and M. P. Leiter, *The Truth about Burnout: How Organizations Cause Personal Stress and What To Do about It* (San Francisco: Jossey-Bass, 1997).

specifically aimed at burnout. Maslach and Leiter provide a template for changing situations that breed burnout. Their emphasis is on organizational change; however, individual concerns can be accommodated. The organizationally focused approach side of Figure 15.1 shows Maslach and Leiter's formulation. In the origination from the individual column, they describe the sequence of events when an individual is the initiator of change. In the originating from the organization column, the organization through its management is the initiator of change. In either case, the process addresses the mismatches between the individual and the job that may develop burnout.

Figure 15.1 also shows two significant additions to the Maslach and Leiter model. First, personal resources are listed as contributors to change originated by the individual. In order to take the steps suggested by Maslach and Leiter's model, individuals need to have accumulated enough personal resources so that they can both believe that they can effect change and mobilize the action necessary to initiate the change process. A worker in the end-state burnout condition is unlikely to view themselves as a viable change agent.

The second addition to the model is the inclusion of the necessity for cultural sensitivity in organizational change. This sensitivity applies both to the final outcome of the change process as well as to the manner in which that process is planned and implemented. Many good ideas have been undermined by the manner in which they are proposed or carried out. Awareness of and responsiveness to cultural values will make planned changes more acceptable.

In general terms, the recommended approach is based on the general systems theory of organizational change (Nadler & Tushman, 1988). Individuals and organizations are not separate from one another, but rather are engaged in interdependent interaction in which a change in one part of the organization ripples through the whole. Therefore, it is useful to think in systemic terms of establishing a long-term process rather than a short-term fix. Healthy, resilient organizations set the stage for healthy, resilient workers. Taking the larger view has beneficial effects at all levels.

CHAPTER 16

Implications for the Twenty-First Century

The results of the cross-cultural study reported here have implications both for human services practice and for future research on burnout. Although the current study suffers from limitations, I will take the liberty of drawing somewhat broad conclusions in an effort to highlight what I think are important issues. Some of these implications have been described before, and some are new. Each draws on both the current study and the research and theory that has gone before. These thoughts are meant to be both summative and a bit provocative.

PREVALENCE OF BURNOUT

Although the current study did not use systematic, random sampling procedures, it still gives some inkling of what the prevalence of high burnout might be in the field of child and youth care work specifically, and possibly in human service occupations in general. Roughly 20 percent of workers in the current study were categorized as experiencing high burnout using the configural procedure identified in Chapter 8. This does not mean that all of them were necessarily at the end stage of burnout in which physical and psychological harm is severe. However, it does suggest that those 20 percent are, at a minimum, moving toward that end-stage condition. They are probably functioning at a lower level both physically and psychologically, and their work performance is probably suffering.

The implication for human service professions is that burnout needs to be recognized as a significant problem. The well-being of individual workers as well as the effectiveness of service-providing organizations are impacted by burnout. The identification of themes and suggestions for prevention should be taken seriously. When one fifth of employees in an organization are suffering a condition that will reduce their performance and increase their intentions of leaving, the organization would be negligent to ignore it.

EMOTIONALITY AS A JOB SKILL

A basic mode of interaction in the human service professions is the ability to connect with clients at the emotional level. Empathy, warmth, respect, and genuineness have all been recognized as necessary conditions for effective helping (Carkhuff & Anthony, 1984; Rogers, 1992). Modern economies are moving even more strongly toward a service economy in which the ability to make emotional contact with clients is a vital part of daily job expectations. Where emotionality as a job skill is required, burnout poses a threat to job performance. In the approximately thirty years since the concept of burnout emerged, the number of jobs that may be affected by it has grown dramatically. Rather than being confined to helping professionals such as child and youth care workers, teachers, psychologists, social workers, doctors, and nurses, the concept of burnout has been extended to other professions where human interaction is the medium through which work is accomplished. The concept of burnout has become more important as the number of workers employed in such jobs has increased. It is vital that the threat of burnout be recognized beyond the helping professions. In the middle ages, prior to the increase in medical knowledge, people would tolerate open, running wounds as a matter of course. They saw nothing amiss. I believe we are in somewhat the same position today regarding burnout. Clearly much has been done to identify burnout and its precursors; but the move to treat and prevent it has been slow in developing. We need to do more.

WORK ETHICS AND WORK AESTHETICS

In the United States, workers' expectations about work have changed over the past thirty years. I believe similar concerns may exist in other cultures as well. Earlier, workers would present their bodies at the job and collect their paycheck at the end of the week. The exchange was simple: time for money. More recently, workers want more from work. Their motivation and performance relate to the aesthetics of work as well as the paycheck. They want to be respected, to exert some autonomy, to receive some emotional support, and to perform meaningful work. Clearly, the ways in which this happens may differ from culture to culture. However, the emerging theme is that engagement and involvement at work depends to a great degree on the work organization. Organizations that continue with demeaning and uncaring processes will have workers that disengage and perform poorly. In recent years, there has been a reaffirmation of the work ethic. People still work hard. There has been, however, a change in the aesthetics of work (Katzell, Yankelovich, Fein, Ornati, & Nash, 1975). Workers now demand more from their employers in return. It is my belief that this shift in values concerning work was an important context supporting the popularity of and interest expressed in burnout as a concept. When workers are unaware of the options available to them to change burnout-producing conditions, they may actually make a virtue out of persistence in toxic conditions. A variation of the "wounded healer" concept (Miller & Baldwin, 1987) implies that burnout could be seen as a badge of honor since it indicates heroism above and beyond the call of duty. While this notion still holds sway in some places, the shift to an appreciation of work aesthetics has led to its decline. Workers in human service professions who had merely adjusted to burnout-producing conditions in the past have now begun to object. This type of objection has begun to spread to jobs and professions beyond the helping professions.

TRAINING AND SUPPORT

Workers need training in the skills and knowledge that may make them more resistant to burnout. Much of what both preservice and in-service training focuses on is skills and knowledge related to effective therapeutic or care delivery tasks. These are indeed important. Sorely lacking, however, is training in skills and knowledge concerning personal factors identified in this research which may resist burnout: relaxation and self-care, group processes, effective use of supervision, problem-focused coping, optimism, personal balance, organizational awareness, and meaning making on the job. We know enough now from research and theorizing to have some confidence that skills such as these would help individuals thwart burnout. Unfortunately, many of these categories of training seem to fall outside of the "officially" defined characteristics of the job or the curriculum of preservice education training programs. Over the years burnout has been seen as inevitable and the responsibility of the individual who is experiencing it. Such a view seems to discharge employment and educational organizations from responsibility. Many workers who had the potential to give years of effective service have had their working lives cut short because they were not aware of ways to bolster their resources in the face of added stressors. Training in effective burnout-resisting skills could make a dramatic difference to both individuals and organizations. Both educational programs and organizations need to incorporate such training as part of their standard package of skills.

ORGANIZATIONAL SENSITIVITY

Even organizations that view their primary mission as being sensitive and responsive to their clients are not necessarily sensitive and responsive to their employees. Clearly, organizations have limits and must accomplish their tasks within the monetary and physical means assigned to them. However, organizations can overemphasize the performance of their work-related tasks to the neglect of the employees who accomplish those tasks. In order to keep employees engaged with the work and to encourage them to be innovative and loyal, organizations need to be sensitive to Maslach and Leiter's (1997) six factors:

1. Sustainable workload
2. Feelings of choice and control
3. Recognition and reward
4. A sense of community
5. Fairness, respect, and justice
6. Meaningful and valued work

In addition, they need to install regular, easily accessible methods for employees to raise issues that they believe might threaten any of those six factors. Workers laboring in the trenches often first become aware of these issues while managers whose jobs focus elsewhere may miss them. The key to sensitivity is to view the issue of continued employee engagement and burnout prevention as a basic mission of the organization.

ROLE SPECIALIZATION, ROLE GENERALIZATION

In general, there is a trend away from large, centrally controlled child and youth care service facilities. More and more of the agencies that deliver care to children, youth, and their families are based in communities close to their clientele. In most cultures, this decentralization of service has been accompanied by role specialization within the field. Clearly, the largest proportion of workers in the field of child and youth care are those that care for and treat children and youth in the daily-living context of day or residential facilities. However, a decentralized distribution of service provision requires access to specialized services within local communities. Therefore, many cultures show a trend toward differentiated staffing in which teachers, family workers, community-contact workers, and various levels of supervisors and managers are affiliated with the child and youth care agency. This trend seems to represent both a philosophy of care and a recognition of the diverse needs of clientele. Different job roles focus on differing aspects of service delivery. Another way to accomplish the same result for each child and youth care worker is to expand the range of skills he or she is trained to perform. Only a few cultures have chosen employ this solution.

An important implication of role differentiation within the field of child and youth care has been the ability of workers to stay within the field over long periods of their working careers. In most cultures, entry level positions do not pay well enough to support workers and their families in comfort. In order to stay in the field, workers find it necessary to seek higher-paying positions. When those positions exist within the same agency or similar agencies, the worker can make a commitment to child and youth care work as a profession. Otherwise, many workers feel compelled to leave the work that they enjoy and understand in order to fulfill responsibilities to their families. In cultures in which the basic threshold of financial support exists, and in which opportunities for advancement or differentiated skill performance exist, longevity in the field and continued high levels of performance might also be expected to exist. One exception to the goal of longevity in the field comes when workers feel trapped in their positions over long periods of time without the opportunity to innovate or find meaning in their work. Under these conditions, the long-term worker may emotionally withdraw from work and merely put in their time.

CULTURE AS CONTEXT—CULTURE AS COGNITION

Culture can be viewed as context, that is, a type of broad, environmental influence equally pressing on all members of the culture. Viewed in this fashion, culture does indeed affect burnout. Career success and power distance values have shown relationships with burnout above and beyond the impact of work environment and personal factors. Given this restrictive test of culture's impact, it is clear that culture has a good deal of power for clarifying which work and personal factors in which combinations are related to burnout. The implication of this result is that findings concerning factors related to burnout and its prevention need to be evaluated within each culture prior to being accepted as appropriate to the culture.

Culture can also be viewed as cognition; that is, each individual within a culture carries their own interpretation of the culture within themselves. There can be a good deal of individual variation within any single culture concerning the degree to which individual members of the culture subscribe to its values. This individual variation of conformity to cultural norms has also been found to be related to burnout. Individual variations in uncertainty avoidance and individualism showed relations to burnout. These findings also emerged above and beyond the impact of work environment and personal factors. Such individual conformity to or deviance from cultural norms implies that care must be taken within a single culture not to overgeneralize. Organizations planning burnout-prevention efforts must be sensitive to variations within their own employees. The aspects of the work environment that some workers hate, others might find comforting. Time and care should be taken explore these variations before installing an organizational change.

IMPLICATIONS FOR BURNOUT RESEARCH

As with many other psychological concepts, burnout should be considered within the context of culture. Although there seem to be some themes that transcend specific cultures, the ways in which those themes play out show some cultural variation; there is both consistency and variation. The current research examined only a fraction of the possible contributors to burnout. Much more needs to be done to examine a fuller range of both environmental and personal factors. Theoretically, the cognitive-mediational approach seems to be robust enough to give guidance to this research. Both environmental and individual expressions of culture can be incorporated into the model. However, the emphasis needs to be shifted slightly to focus on chronic job-related conditions as well as specific, acute stressors. Because burnout develops over a long period of time, the resource-erosion model begins to capture the burnout process more closely. In addition, a shift to a more positive view is also beneficial. Finding the situational factors that increase engagement with work that may not only prevent burnout but also engender thriving is imperative. As research is conducted, it would be helpful to identify which culture is sampled in order to understand how broadly to generalize the findings. Of course, future cross-cultural research is necessary. There is much more to discover about the variations of burnout across cultures.

IMPLICATIONS OF CULTURE FOR THE BURNOUT CONCEPT

Although there is good evidence that the measurement of burnout is relatively consistent across cultures, the sources and expressions of burnout seem to be different in different cultures. Cultures quite low in burnout generally, like Denmark, still have some individuals experiencing high burnout; conversely, a culture with high average levels of burnout, like Germany-West, still has low burnout individuals. One issue not addressed in the current study is, "How high a score on the burnout scales passes the threshold for experienced burnout in an individual?" Some workers may be able to function quite adequately with relatively high levels of measured burnout, while others are incapacitated by relatively low levels of measured burnout. Humans adapt to stress levels. Workers appraise differing levels of stress as threats or challenges. The threshold-level question has been unanswered in general. It would be interesting to determine if culture affects the perception of the burnout threshold. How much burnout is too much probably varies by culture. Also, configurations of burnout scales may affect the perception of experienced burnout. For example, sources and definitions of personal accomplishment may vary with individualism–collectivism. Much remains to be clarified regarding culturally unique definitions of burnout.

FINAL THOUGHTS

Finally, I wish to express my gratitude to all the workers across the thirteen cultures who contributed to this study. I believe that the findings contained in this book make a meaningful contribution to understanding burnout in the field of child and youth care work in an international context. The book could not have been written without the cooperation of the people who actually do the work. Real responses from real people doing real work marks a strong advantage of burnout research. In spite of limitations of sampling, I believe that the findings are quite generalizable, since they are derived from participants who are identical to the people to whom they are to be applied. Future research will test this assumption.

References

Abramson, L. Y., Seligman, M.E.P., & Teasdale, J. (1978). Learned helplessness in humans: Critique and reformulation. *Journal of Abnormal Psychology, 87,* 32–48.

Adler, N. L. (1997). *International dimensions of organizational behavior.* Cincinnati, OH: South-Western College Publishing.

Allegro, J., & Kruidenier, H. (1991). Aspects of distributive and procedural justice in quality of working life. In R. Vermunt & H. Steensma (Eds.), *Societal and psychological consequences of justice and injustice: Critical issues in social justice.* New York: Plenum.

Alloy, L. B., & Abramson, L. Y. (1979). Judgment of contingency in depressed and nondepressed students: Sadder but wiser? *Journal of Experimental Psychology: General, 108,* 441–485.

Arieli, M., Beker, J., & Kashti, Y. (1990). Residential group care as a socializing environment: Toward a broader perspective. In J. P. Anglin, C. J. Denholm, R. V. Ferguson, & A. R. Pence (Eds.), *Perspectives in professional child and youth care.* Binghamton, NY: Haworth.

Armstrong-Stassen, M., Al-Ma'Aitah, R., Cameron, S., & Horsburgh, M. (1994). Determinants and consequences of burnout: A cross-cultural comparison of Canadian and Jordanian nurses. *Health Care for Women International, 15,* 413–421.

Baer, D. E., & Curtis, J. E. (1984). French Canadian–English Canadian differences in values: National survey findings. *Canadian Journal of Sociology, 9,* 405–428.

Bandura, A. (1986). *Social foundations of thought and action: A social-cognitive view.* Englewood Cliffs, NJ: Prentice Hall.

Barnes, F. H., & Bourdon, L. (1990). Cross-cultural perspectives in residential youthwork: The French educateur and the American child care worker. In J. P. Anglin, C. J. Denholm, R. V. Ferguson, & A. R. Pence (Eds.), *Perspectives in professional child and youth care.* Binghamton, NY: Haworth.

Bartz, C., & Maloney, J. P. (1986). Burnout among intensive care nurses. *Research in Nursing & Health, 3,* 147–153.

Belcastro, P. A., Gold, R. S., & Hays, L. C. (1983). Maslach Burnout Inventory factor structure for samples of teachers. *Psychological Reports, 53*, 364–366.

Bettelheim, B. (1967). *The empty fortress: Infantile autism and the birth of the self.* New York: Free Press.

Boyd, B. J., & Pasley, B. K. (1989). Role stress as a contributor to burnout in child care professionals. *Child and Youth Care Quarterly, 18*, 243–258.

Brendtro, L. K., & Ness, A. E. (1983). *Re-educating troubled youth: Environments for teaching and treatment.* New York: Aldine.

Büssing, A., & Perrar, K. M. (1992). Die Messung von Burnout. Untersuchung einer deutschen Fassung des Maslach Burnout Inventory (MBI-D) [The measurement of burnout: Investigation of a German version of the Maslach Burnout Inventory]. *Diagnostica, 38*, 328–353.

Buunk, B. P., & Schaufeli, W. B. (1993). Burnout: A perspective from social comparison theory. In W. B. Schaufeli, C. Maslach, & T. Marek (Eds.), *Professional burnout: Recent developments in theory and research.* Washington, DC: Taylor & Francis.

Caplan, G. (1964). *Principles of preventive psychiatry.* New York: Basic Books.

Caplan, G., & Caplan, R. B. (2000). The future of primary prevention. *Journal of Primary Prevention, 21*, 131–136.

Caplan, R. D., Cobb, S., French, J.R.P., Jr., Harrison, R. V., & Pinneau, S. R., Jr. (1975). *Job demands and worker health.* Washington, DC: HEW Publ. No. (NIOSH) 75-160.

Carkhuff, R. R., & Anthony, W. A. (1984). *The skills of helping: An introduction to counseling skills.* Amherst, MA: Human Resource Development Press.

Carver, C. S. (1998). Resilience and thriving: Issues, models, and linkages. *Journal of Social Issues, 54*, 245–266.

Cherniss, C. (1980). *Staff burnout: Job stress in the human services.* Beverly Hills, CA: Sage.

Cherniss, C. (1993). Role of professional self-efficacy in the etiology and amelioration of burnout. In W. B. Schaufeli, C. Maslach, & T. Marek (Eds.), *Professional burnout: Recent developments in theory and research.* Washington, DC: Taylor & Francis.

Cherniss, C. (1995). *Beyond burnout: Helping teachers, nurses, therapists and lawyers recover from stress and disillusionment.* New York: Routledge.

Conger, J. A., & Kanungo, R. N. (1988). The empowerment process: Integrating theory and practice. *Academy of Management Review, 13*, 471–482.

Cordes, C. L., & Dougherty, T. W. (1993). A review and an integration of research on job burnout. *Academy of Management Review, 18*, 621–656.

Cramer, P. (2000). Defense mechanisms in psychology today: Further processes for adaptation. *American Psychologist, 55*, 637–646.

Curbow, B. (1990). Job stress in child care workers: A framework for research. *Child and Youth Care Quarterly, 19*, 215–231.

Daley, M. R. (1979). Burnout: Smoldering problem in protective services. *Social Work, 24*, 375–379.

Denholm, C. J. (1990). 2000 and beyond: Future career directions for child and youth care professionals. In J. P. Anglin, C. J. Denholm, R. V. Ferguson, & A. R. Pence (Eds.), *Perspectives in professional child and youth care.* Binghamton, NY: Haworth.

Dolan, N. (1987). The relationship between burnout and job satisfaction in nurses. *Journal of Advanced Nursing, 12,* 3–12.

Duncan, R. (1979). What is the right organizational structure? *Organizational Dynamics, 7,* 59–80.

Edelwich, J., & Brodsky, A. (1980). *Burn-out: Stages of disillusionment in the helping professions.* New York: Human Sciences Press.

Etzion, D., & Pines, A. (1986). Sex and culture in burnout and coping among human service professionals: A social psychological perspective. *Journal of Cross-Cultural Psychology, 17,* 191–209.

EUROARRCC. (1998). *Care to Listen? Haluakto Kuunnella? Nos esforzamos por escuchar?* Glasgow, Scotland: European Association for Research into Residential Child Care.

Feldman, D. C. (1976). A contingency theory of socialization. *Administrative Science, 21,* 433–452.

Fernandez, D. R., Carlson, D. S., Stepina, L. P., & Nicholson, J. D. (1997). Hofstede's country classification 25 years later. *Journal of Social Psychology, 137,* 43–54.

Fleischer, B. M. (1985). Identification of strategies to reduce turnover among child care workers. *Child Care Quarterly, 14,* 130–139.

Folkman, S., & Moskowitz, J. T. (2000). Positive affect and the other side of coping. *American Psychologist, 55,* 647–654.

Freedman, J., & Combs, G. (1996). *Narrative therapy: The social construction of preferred realities.* New York: Norton.

Freudenberger, H. J. (1974). The staff burnout syndrome in alternative institutions. *Psychotherapy: Theory, Research and Practice, 12,* 73–82.

Freudenberger, H. J. (1977). Burn-out: Occupational hazard of the child care worker. *Child and Youth Care Quarterly, 6,* 90–99.

Freudenberger, H. J., & Richelson, G. (1980). *Burnout: The high cost of high achievement.* Garden City, NJ: Anchor.

Fujigaki, Y., & Mori, K. (1997). Longitudinal study of work stress among information system professionals. *International Journal of Human-Computer Interaction, 9,* 369–381.

Fuqua, R., & Couture, K. (1986). Burnout and locus of control in child day care staff. *Child Care Quarterly, 15,* 98–109.

Garigue, P. (1973). The French-Canadian family. In B. R. Blishen, R. E. Jones, K. D. Naegeli, & J. Porter (Eds.), *Canadian society: Sociological perspectives.* Toronto: Macmillan of Canada.

Gold, Y. (1984). Factorial validity of the Maslach Burnout Inventory in a sample of California elementary and junior high school classroom teachers. *Educational and Psychological Measurement, 44,* 1009–1010.

Golembiewski, R. T., & Munzenrider, R. F. (1983). Testing three phases model of burnout: Mapping of worksite descriptors. *Journal of Health and Human Resources Administration, 5,* 374–393.

Golembiewski, R. T., & Munzenrider, R. F. (1988). *Phases of burnout: Development in concepts and applications.* New York: Praeger.

Golembiewski, R. T., Scherb, K., & Boudreau, R. A. (1993). Burnout in cross-national settings: Generic and model-specific perspectives. In W. B. Schaufeli, C. Maslach, & T. Marek (Eds.), *Professional burnout: Recent developments in theory and research.* Washington, DC: Taylor & Francis.

Gottlieb, B. H. (1997). Conceptual and measurement issues in the sutdy of coping with chronic stress. In B. H. Gottlieb (Ed.), *Coping with chronic stress*. New York: Plenum.

Green, D. E., Walkey, F. H., & Taylor, A. J. (1991). The three-factor structure of the Maslach Burnout Inventory: A multicultural, multinational confirmatory study. *Journal of Social Behavior & Personality, 6,* 453–472.

Hackman, J. R., & Oldham, G. R. (1980). *Work redesign.* Reading, MA: Addison-Wesley.

Hallsten, L. (1993). Burning out: A framework. In W. B. Schaufeli, C. Maslach, & T. Marek (Eds.), *Professional burnout: Recent developments in theory and research*. Washington, DC: Taylor & Francis.

Hepburn, C. G., Loughlin, C. A., & Barling, J. (1997). Coping with chronic work stress. In B. H. Gottlieb (Ed.), *Coping with chronic stress*. New York: Plenum.

Heppner, P. P., & Hillerbrand, E. T. (1991). Problem-solving training: Implications for remedial and preventive training. In C. R. Snyder & D. R. Forsyth (Eds.), *Handbook of social and clinical psychology: The health perspective. Pergamon general psychology series, 162*. New York: Pergamon.

Herzberg, F. (1966). *Work and the nature of man.* Cleveland, OH: World.

Hobfoll, S. E. (1989). Conservation of resources: A new attempt at conceptualizing stress. *American Psychologist, 44,* 513–544.

Hobfoll, S. E., & Freedy, J. (1993). Conservation of resources: A general stress theory applied to burnout. In W. B. Schaufeli, C. Maslach, & T. Marek (Eds.), *Professional burnout: Recent developments in theory and research*. Washington, DC: Taylor & Francis.

Hofstede, G. (1980). *Culture's consequences: International differences in work related values.* Beverly Hills, CA: Sage.

Hofstede, G. (1997). *Cultures and organizations: Software of the mind.* New York: McGraw-Hill.

Hofstede, G. (1998). *Masculinity and femininity: The taboo dimension of national cultures.* Thousand Oaks, CA: Sage.

Horne, J. F., & Orr, J. E. (1998). Assessing behaviors that create resilient organizations. *Employment Relations Today, 24,* 29–39.

Iwanicki, E. F., & Schwab, R. L. (1981). A cross validation study of the Maslach Burnout Inventory. *Educational and Psychological Measurement, 41,* 1167–1174.

Jamal, M. (1999). Job stress and employee well-being: A cross-cultural empirical study. *Stress Medicine, 15,* 153–158.

Jayaratne, S., & Chess, W. A. (1984). Job satisfaction, burnout, and turnover: A national study. *Social Work, 24,* 448–453.

Kahill, S. (1988). Symptoms of professional burnout: A review of the empirical evidence. *Canadian Psychology, 29,* 284–297.

Kanner, A. D., Coyne, J. C., Schaefer, C., & Lazarus, R. S. (1981). Comparison of two modes of stress measurement: Daily hassles and uplifts versus major life events. *Journal of Behavioral Medicine, 4,* 1–39.

Katzell, R. A., Yankelovich, D., Fein, M., Ornati, O. A., & Nash, A. (1975). *Work, productivity, and job satisfaction: An evaluation of policy-related research.* New York: Psychological Corporation.

Kelly, C. S. (1990). Professionalizing child and youth care: An overview. In J. P. Anglin, C. J. Denholm, R. V. Ferguson, & A. R. Pence (Eds.), *Perspectives in professional child and youth care*. Binghamton, NY: Haworth.

Keys, C. B. (1986). Organization development: An approach to mental health consultation. In F. V. Mannino & E. J. Trickett (Eds.), *Handbook of mental health consultation*. Rockville, MD: National Institute of Mental Health.

Kingsley, R., & Cook-Hatala, C. (1988). A survey of child care workers: Implications for administrators regarding job stress and satisfaction. *Child and Youth Care Quarterly, 17*, 281–287.

Koeske, G. F., Kirk, S. A., & Koeske, R. D. (1993). Coping with job stress: Which strategies work best? *Journal of Occupational and Organizational Psychology, 66*, 319–335.

Krueger, M., & Drees, M. (1995). Generic teamwork: An alternative approach to residential treatment. *Residential Treatment for Children and Youth, 12*, 57–69.

Krueger, M. A., Laurerman, R., Beker, J., Savicki, V., Parry, P., & Powell, N. W. (1987). Professional child and youth care work in the United States and Canada: A report of the NOCCWA research and study committee. *Journal of Child and Youth Care Work, 3*, 17–31.

Langelier, R. (1983). French Canadian families. In M. McGoldrick, J. K. Pearce, & J. Giordano (Eds.), *Ethnicity in family therapy*. New York: Guilford.

Latack, J. C. (1986). Coping with job stress: Measures and future directions for scale development. *Journal of Applied Psychology, 71*, 377–385.

Lazarus, R. S. (1999). *Stress and emotion: A new synthesis*. New York: Springer.

Lazarus, R. S., & Folkman, S. (1984). *Stress, appraisal, and coping*. New York: Springer.

Lee, R. T., & Ashforth, B. E. (1990). On the meaning of Maslach's three dimensions of burnout. *Journal of Applied Psychology, 75*, 743–747.

Lee, R. T., & Ashforth, B. E. (1993). A longitudinal study of burnout among supervisors and managers: Comparisons between the Leiter and Maslach (1988) and Golembiewski et al. (1986) models. *Organizational Behavior and Human Decision Processes, 54*, 369–398.

Lee, R. T., & Ashforth, B. E. (1996). A meta-analytic examination of the correlates of the three dimensions of job burnout, *Journal of Applied Psychology, 81*, 123–133.

Leiter, M. P. (1991). Coping patterns as predictors of burnout: The function of control and escapist coping patterns. *Journal of Organizational Behavior, 12*, 123–144.

Leiter, M. P. (1993). Burnout as a developmental process: consideration of models. In W. B. Schaufeli, C. Maslach, & T. Marek (Eds.), *Professional burnout: Recent developments in theory and research*. Washington, DC: Taylor & Francis.

Leiter, M. P., & Maslach, C. (1988). The impact of interpersonal environment on burnout and organizational commitment. *Journal of Organizational Behavior, 9*, 297–308.

Leung, K., & Bond, M. H. (1989). On the empirical identification of dimensions for cross-cultural comparisons. *Journal of Cross-Cultural Psychology, 20*, 133–151.

Lewin, K. (1935). *A dynamic theory of personality*. New York: McGraw-Hill.

Lindsay, M. (2000, May). *Aspects of professionalism*. Presented at the International Federation of Child Educative Communities Congress, Maastricht, The Netherlands.

Linklater, E. (1965). *The prince in the heather*. New York: Harcourt, Brace & World.

Luthans, F., Marsnik, P. A., & Luthans, K. W. (1997). A contingency matrix approach to IHRM. *Human Resource Management, 36*, 183–199.

Maier, H. W. (1969). *Three theories of child development: The contributions of Erik H. Erikson, Jean Piaget, and Robert R. Sears, and their applications*. New York: Harper & Row.

Mallak, L. (1998). Putting organizational resilience to work. *Industrial Management, 40,* 8–14.

Maslach, C. (1993). Burnout: A multidimensional perspective. In W. B. Schaufeli, C. Maslach, & T. Marek (Eds.), *Professional burnout: Recent developments in theory and research.* Washington, DC: Taylor & Francis.

Maslach, C., & Jackson, S. E. (1981). *The Maslach Burnout Inventory* (Research ed.). Palo Alto, CA: Consulting Psychologists Press.

Maslach, C., Jackson, S. E., & Leiter, M. P. (1996). *The Maslach Burnout Inventory* (3d ed.). Palo Alto, CA: Consulting Psychologists Press.

Maslach, C., & Leiter, M. P. (1997). *The truth about burnout: How organizations cause personal stress and what to do about it.* San Francisco: Jossey-Bass.

Maslach, C., & Schaufeli, W. B. (1993). Historical and conceptual development of burnout. In W. B. Schaufeli, C. Maslach, & T. Marek (Eds.), *Professional burnout: Recent developments in theory and research.* Washington, DC: Taylor & Francis.

Matsumoto, D. (1996). *Culture and psychology.* Pacific Grove, CA: Brooks/Cole.

Mattingly, M. A. (1977). Sources of stress and burn-out in professional child care work. *Child and Youth Care Quarterly, 6,* 127–137.

McFarlane, A. C. (1988). The longitudinal course of posttraumatic morbidity: The range of outcomes and their predictors. *Journal of Nervous and Mental Diseases, 176,* 30–39.

McMullen, M. B., & Krantz, M. (1988). Burnout in day care workers: The effects of learned helplessness and self-esteem. *Child and Youth Care Quarterly, 17,* 275–280.

Miller, G. D., & Baldwin, D. C. (1987). Implications of the wounded healer paradigm for the use of the self in therapy. *Journal of Psychotherapy and the Family, 3,* 139–151.

Miller, J. G. (1997). Theoretical issues in cultural psychology. In J. W. Berry, Y. H. Poortinga, & J. Pandey (Eds.), *Handbook of cross-cultural psychology: Theory and method* (2d ed.). Boston: Allyn and Bacon.

Moos, R. H. (1981). *Work environment scale manual.* Palo Alto, CA: Consulting Psychologists Press.

Mrazek, P. J. (1998). *Preventing mental health and substance abuse problems in managed health care settings.* Alexandria, VA: National Mental Health Association.

Nadler, D. A., & Tushman, M. L. (1988). A model for diagnosing organizational behavior. In M. L. Tushman & W. L. Moore (Eds.), *Readings in the management of innovation* (2d ed.). Cambridge, MA: Ballinger/Harper & Row.

Perls, F. S. (1969). *Gestalt therapy verbatim.* Lafayette, CA: Real People Press.

Pines, A. M. (1993). Burnout: An existential perspective. In W. B. Schaufeli, C. Maslach, & T. Marek (Eds.), *Professional burnout: Recent developments in theory and research.* Washington, DC: Taylor & Francis.

Pines, A., Aronson, E., & Kafry, D. (1981). *Burnout: From tedium to personal growth.* New York: Free Press.

Podsakoff, P. M., MacKenzie, S. B., & Bommer, W. H. (1996). Meta-analysis of the relationships between Kerr and Jermier's substitutes for leadership and employee job attitudes, role perceptions, and performance. *Journal of Applied Psychology, 81,* 380–399.

Powell, D. R. (1990). Professionalism and the child care field: What model? In J. P. Anglin, C. J. Denholm, R. V. Ferguson, & A. R. Pence (Eds.), *Perspectives in professional child and youth care.* Binghamton, NY: Haworth.

Raider, M. C. (1989). Burnout in children's agencies: A clinician's perspective. *Residential Treatment for Children and Youth, 6*, 43–51.

Randolph, W. A. (1995). Navigating the journey to empowerment. *Organizational Dynamics, 23*, 19–33.

Redl, F., & Wineman, D. (1951). *Children who hate: The disorganization and breakdown of behavior controls.* New York: Free Press.

Riolli-Saltzman, L., & Savicki, V. (2000). *Millennial stress: Coping, optimism and burnout.* Waikoloa, HI: Western Academy of Management.

Riolli-Saltzman, L., & Savicki, V. (2001a). *The impact of culture on human resource management approaches for creating resilient organizations.* Manuscript submitted for publication.

Riolli-Saltzman, L., & Savicki, V. (2001b). *Optimism and coping as moderators of the relationship between chronic stress and burnout and performance.* Manuscript submitted for publication.

Riolli-Saltzman, L., & Savicki, V. (2001c). *Optimism and coping as moderators of the relationship between work environment and burnout and performance.* Manuscript submitted for publication.

Riolli-Saltzman, L., & Savicki, V. (in press). Resilience in the face of catastrophe: Optimism, personality and coping in the Kosovo crisis. *Journal of Applied Social Psychology.*

Riskind, J. H., Sarampote, C. S., & Mercier, M. A. (1996). For every malady a sovereign cure: Optimism training. *Journal of Cognitive Psychotherapy, 10*, 105–117.

Rogers, C. R. (1992). The necessary and sufficient conditions of therapeutic personality change. *Journal of Consulting and Clinical Psychology, 60*, 827–832.

Ronen, S., & Shenkar, O. (1985). Clustering countries on attitudinal dimensions: A review and synthesis. *Academy of Management Review, 10*, 435–454.

Sanford, N., & Mischel, W. (1985). Personality. In S. Koch & D. E. Leary (Eds.), *A century of psychology as science.* Washington, DC: American Psychological Association.

Sargent, L. T. (1996). *Contemporary political ideologies: A comparative analysis* (10th ed.). Belmont, CA: Wadsworth.

Savicki, V. (1990). Modern times: Trends in the context of work suggesting future roles for child and youth workers. In J. P. Anglin, C. J. Denholm, R. V. Ferguson, & A. R. Pence (Eds.), *Perspectives in professional child and youth care.* Binghamton, NY: Haworth.

Savicki, V. (1993). Clarification of child and youth care identity through an analysis of work environment and burnout. *Child and Youth Care Forum, 22* (6), 441–457.

Savicki, V. (1999a). Cultural work values for supervisors and managers: A cross-cultural look at child and youth care agencies. *Child and Youth Care Forum, 28*, 239–255.

Savicki, V. (1999b). Stress, Burnout und Bewältigungsstrategien in der Jugendhilfe: Ein interkultureller Vergleich [Stress, burnout and coping strategies in youth work: An intercultural comparison]. *Forum Erziehungshilfen, 5*, 232–238.

Savicki, V. (1999c). Udbrændthed inden for børneforsogen i Danmark [Burnout in child care work in Denmark]. *Tidsskrift for Socialpaedagogik, 4*, 37–43.

Savicki, V., & Brown, R. (1981). *Working with troubled children.* New York: Human Sciences Press.

Savicki, V., & Cooley, E. J. (1983). Theoretical and research considerations of burnout. *Children and Youth Services Review, 5* (3), 227–238.

Savicki, V., & Cooley, E. J. (1987). The relationship of work environment and client contact to burnout in mental health professionals. *Journal of Counseling and Development, 1*, 249–252.

Savicki, V., & Cooley, E. J. (1994). Burnout in child protective service workers: A longitudinal study. *Journal of Organizational Behavior, 15*, 655–666.

Savicki, V., Cooley, E. J., & Gjesvold, J. (in press). Harassment as a predictor of job burnout in correctional officers. *Criminal Justice and Behavior*.

Savicki, V., Kelley, M., & Oesterreich, E. (1998). Effects of instructions computer-mediated communication in single- or mixed-gender small task groups. *Computers in Human Behavior, 14*, 163–180.

Schaufeli, W., & Janczur, B. (1994). Burnout among nurses: A Polish–Dutch comparison. *Journal of Cross-Cultural Psychology, 25*, 95–113.

Schaufeli, W. B., & Van Dierendonck, D. (1995). A cautionary note about the cross-national and clinical validity of cut-off points for the Maslach Burnout Inventory. *Psychological Reports, 76*, 1083–1090.

Scheck, C. L., Kinicki, A. J., & Day, J. A. (1995). A longitudinal study of a multivariate model of the stress process using structural equations modeling. *Human Relations, 48*, 1481–1510.

Scheier, M. F., & Carver, C. S. (1985). Optimism, coping, and health: Assessment and implications of generalized outcome expectancies. *Health Psychology, 4*, 219–247.

Schutte, N., Toppinen, S., Kalimo, R., & Schaufeli, W. (2000). The factorial validity of the Maslach Burnout Inventory—General Survey (MBI—GS) across occupational groups and nations. *Journal of Occupational and Organizational Psychology, 73*, 53–66.

Schwab, R. L., & Iwanicki, E. F. (1982). Perceived role conflict, role ambiguity and teacher burnout. *Educational Administration Quarterly, 18*, 60–74.

Seligman, M.E.P. (1991). *Learned optimism*. New York: Knopf.

Seligman, M.E.P., & Csikszentmihalyi, M. (2000). Positive psychology: An introduction. *American Psychologist, 55*, 5–14.

Shay, R. (2000). Comparative values of political ideologies. Unpublished manuscript.

Shealy, C. N. (1996). The "therapeutic parent": A model for the child and youth care profession. *Child and Youth Care Forum, 25*, 211–271.

Shirom, A. (1989). Burnout in work organizations. In C. L. Cooper & I. Robertson (Eds.), *International review of industrial and organizational psychology*. New York: John Wiley & Sons.

Shirom, A., & Mazeh, T. (1988). Periodicity in seniority–job satisfaction relationship. *Journal of Vocational Behavior, 33*, 38–49.

Simon, H. A. (1957). *Models of man: Social and rational*. New York: John Wiley & Sons.

Skinner, E. A. (1995). *Perceived control, motivation and coping*. Thousand Oaks, CA: Sage.

Steers, R. M., & Porter, L. W. (1991). *Motivation and work behavior*. New York: McGraw-Hill.

Steptoe, A., & Appels, A. (Eds.). (1989). *Stress, personal control and health*. New York: John Wiley & Sons.

Thong, J.Y.L., & Yap, C. (2000). Information systems and occupational stress: A theoretical framework. *Omega, 28*, 681–692.

Triandis, H. C. (1995). *Individualism and collectivism*. Boulder, Colo.: Westview.

Triandis, H. C. (1996). The psychological measurement of cultural syndromes. *American Psychologist, 51*, 407–415.

Triandis, H. C., Bontempo, R., Leung, K., & Hui, C. H. (1990). A method for determining cultural, demographic, and personal constructs. *Journal of Cross-Cultural Psychology, 21*, 302–318.

Trieschman, A. E., Whittaker, J. K., & Brendtro, L. K. (1969). *The other 23 hours: Child-care work with emotionally disturbed children in a therapeutic milieu*. Chicago: Aldine.

Trompenaars, F., & Hampden-Turner, C. (1998). *Riding the waves of culture: Understanding cultural diversity in global business* (2d ed.). New York: McGraw-Hill.

Vander Ven, K. (1981). Patterns of career development in group care. In F. Ainsworth & L. C. Fulcher (Eds.), *Group care for children*. London: Tavistock.

Vander Ven, K. (1990). From two years to two generations: Expanded career options in direct child and youth care practice. In J. P. Anglin, C. J. Denholm, R. V. Ferguson, & A. R. Pence (Eds.), *Perspectives in professional child and youth care*. Binghamton, NY: Haworth.

Van de Vijver, F., & Leung, K. (1997). Methods and data analysis of comparative research. In J. W. Berry, Y. H. Poortinga, & J. Pandey (Eds.), *Handbook of cross-cultural psychology* (2d ed.). Boston: Allyn and Bacon.

Vorrath, H. H., & Brendtro, L. K. (1974). *Positive peer culture*. Chicago: Aldine.

Wade, D. C., Cooley, E., & Savicki, V. (1986). A longitudinal study of burnout. *Children and Youth Services Review, 8*, 161–173.

Wright, T. A., & Bonett, D. (1997). The contribution of burnout to work performance. *Journal of Organizational Behavior, 18*, 491–499.

Index

ABOUT THE AUTHOR

Victor Savicki is a professor of psychology at Western Oregon University. He has spent 30 years involved in child and youth care work, as a family therapist, private practitioner, consultant, trainer, educator, and researcher.